THE DAY THAT SHOOK THE WORLD

UNDERSTANDING SEPTEMBER 11th

Edited by
Jenny Baxter and Malcolm Downing

BBC Worldwide Limited will give all the net profits arising
from the sale of this book to the Disasters Emergency
Committee and a designated American charity equally, to
help families affected by the September 11th terrorist attacks
and to contribute aid to the Afghan crisis.

BBC NEWS

First published 2001
© BBC Worldwide Ltd 2001

ISBN 0 563 48802 6

Published by BBC Worldwide Limited, Woodlands,
80 Wood Lane, London W12 0TT

Commissioning Editor: Sally Potter
Project Editors: Diana Goodman and Martin Redfern
Designer: Linda Blakemore
Cartographer: Olive Pearson

Printed and bound in Great Britain by Mackays of Chatham
Cover printed by Belmont Press Limited, Northampton

CONTENTS

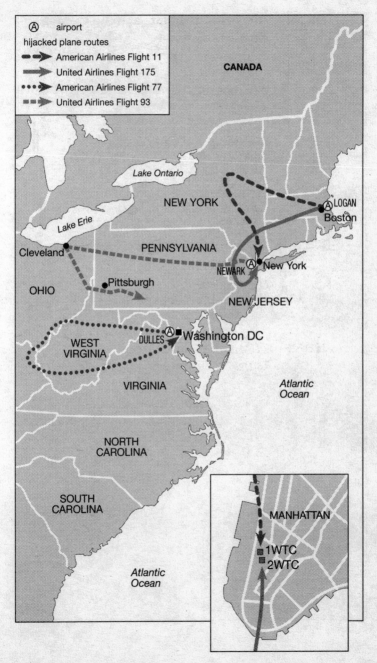

airport

hijacked plane routes

American Airlines Flight 11
United Airlines Flight 175
American Airlines Flight 77
United Airlines Flight 93

CANADA

Lake Ontario

NEW YORK

Lake Erie

LOGAN
Boston

Cleveland

PENNSYLVANIA

OHIO

Pittsburgh

NEWARK
New York

NEW JERSEY

DULLES
Washington DC

WEST
VIRGINIA

VIRGINIA

Atlantic
Ocean

NORTH
CAROLINA

SOUTH
CAROLINA

MANHATTAN

1WTC
2WTC

Atlantic
Ocean

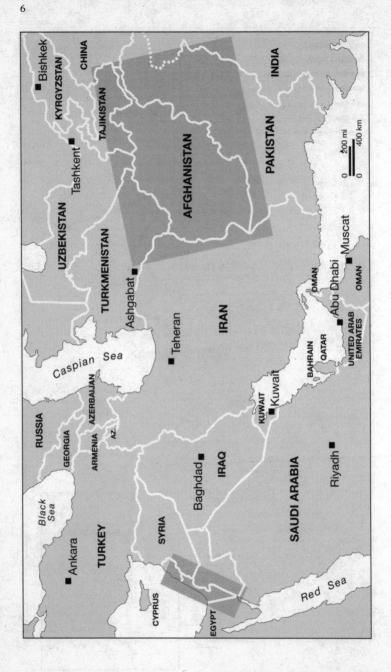

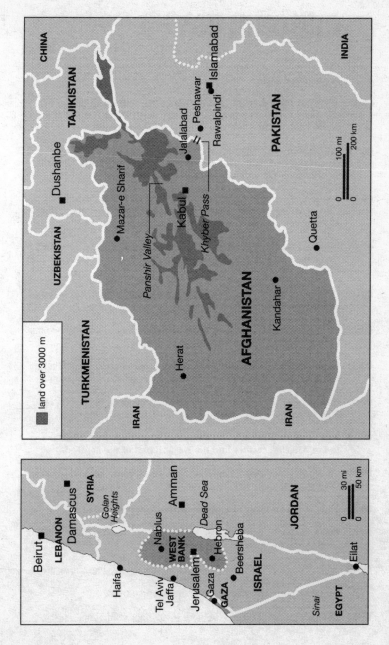

CHRONOLOGY

September 11th

08:47 American Airlines Flight 11, a Boeing 767 en route from Boston to Los Angeles, crashes into the 110-storey north tower (1WTC) of the World Trade Center, between the 95th and 103rd floors.

08:57 One of a torrent of frantic calls logged by emergency service operators says: 'People screaming in background. Caller states cannot breathe. Smoke coming through door. Floor 103. Trapped.'

09:03 A second Boeing 767, United Airlines Flight 175, also flying from Boston to Los Angeles, hits the south tower (2WTC) at about the 80th floor.

09:05 President Bush is informed of the second attack while visiting an elementary school in Sarasota, Florida. (He had been told about the first as he went into the school.)

09:09 Emergency log: '2WTC, male caller states people are jumping out of a large hole. Possible no one catching them.'

09:12 Emergency log: 'Male caller states on 106th floor about 100 people in room. Need directions on how to stay alive.'

09:31 President Bush calls the crashes an 'apparent terrorist attack on our country', and pledges 'terrorism against our nation will not stand'.

09:36 Emergency log: 'Female caller states they are stuck in the elevator. States they are dying.'

09:38 American Airlines Flight 77, a Boeing 757 en route from Washington to Los Angeles, crashes into the western part of the Pentagon.

09:39 Emergency log: 'Female caller states floor very hot, no door – states she's going to die... still on phone... wants to call mother.'

09:43 The Capitol building and the White House are evacuated.

09:47 Emergency log: 'Female caller 2WTC – Flr 105 – states floor underneath her – collapse.'

09:49 Emergency log: '1WTC... 20 people on the top waving... they are alive please send help.'
All US airports are closed – an unprecedented move.

09:55 Emergency log: '2WTC – 106 floor – 105 floor crumbling.'

09:59 2WTC, the south tower, collapses. At 34 seconds after 10:00, all calls from that building to the fire department suddenly end. Calls for help continue to come in from the north tower.

10:04 United Airlines Flight 93, a Boeing 757 flying from Newark to San Francisco, crashes 80 miles south-east of Pittsburgh, killing all 45 people on board. For more than 20 minutes before the crash passengers had made calls saying they'd been hijacked; they planned to try to do something about it.

10:28 1WTC, the north tower, collapses.

11:40 President Bush arrives from Florida at the Barksdale Air Force Base, Louisiana, where he says that the US military at home and around the world is on 'high-alert status'. On security advice, he later travels to the US Strategic Command at Offutt Air Force Base, Nebraska.

13:10 The European Union condemns the 'cowardly attack on innocent civilians'. NATO Secretary-General Lord Robertson calls the attacks 'an intolerable aggression against democracy'.

13:44 The Pentagon redeploys five battleships and two aircraft carriers along the east coast of the US to provide upgraded air defence for the New York and Washington areas.

15:09 Tony Blair announces that Britain stands 'shoulder to shoulder' with America.

19:00 President Bush arrives in Washington from Nebraska.
Shortly after 20:30, he addresses the nation: 'These acts of mass murder were intended to frighten our nation into chaos and retreat. But they have failed… We will make no distinction between the terrorists who committed these acts and those who harbour them… America and our friends and allies…stand together to win the war again terrorism.'

September 12th
President Bush describes the attacks as 'acts of war' and asks Congress for an emergency $20 billion 'to provide resources to address the terrorist attacks…and the consequences'. Congressional leaders double it to $40 billion two days later.

September 13th
Secretary of State Colin Powell confirms that Osama bin Laden, believed to be in Afghanistan, is a suspect.
President Bush promises that America will 'lead the world to victory' over terrorism and describes the conflict as the first war of the twenty-first century.

September 14th
Day of prayer and remembrance for the victims of the attacks.
President Bush visits the ruins of the World Trade Center.

September 17th
Taliban leaders call on Muslims to wage a 'holy war' on America if it
attacks Afghanistan.
The New York Stock Exchange reopens after the longest shutdown
since the Great Depression.

September 20th
Afghan clerics recommend that bin Laden should be persuaded
to leave the country. Washington demands that the Taliban hand
him over.

September 22nd
President Bush lifts US sanctions on Pakistan and India, imposed on
the two countries in 1998 after their nuclear tests.

September 23rd
The Taliban say they don't know the whereabouts of their 'guest',
bin Laden.

October 2nd
For the first time, NATO formally invokes its mutual defence clause,
whereby an attack on any member state is considered to be an attack
on all.

October 4th
The World Medical Association warns world governments to take
seriously the risk of biological and chemical weapons attacks by
terrorist groups. A case of anthrax is discovered in a patient in
Florida, raising fears of a possible biological attack, although
the FBI later says it thinks the source is probably domestic.

October 7th
The United States and Britain begin air and missile strikes against
the Taliban and Al-Qaida in Afghanistan.

November 2nd
New York firefighters stage a demonstration at Ground Zero, which
is still smouldering, to protest against an order that the search-and-
rescue operation is to be scaled down.
The official presumed death toll from the September 11th attacks
stands at 4,799. Three weeks later, that figure is lowered to 3,915,
and New York Mayor Rudolph Giuliani comments: 'This is as close to
accurate as we are going to get'.

November 13th
Northern Alliance fighters enter the Afghan capital Kabul after
taking control of other major cities in the north of the country.

FOREWORD

For the BBC staff who were on duty, September 11th was a day that will stay with them for the rest of their lives. Some were experienced frontline journalists who have reported from war-zones and scenes of human disaster, others were used to the 'in house' business of news – getting breaking stories on air, putting out the sound and pictures that illustrate what is happening, providing analysis and context to explain complex news stories. But few were prepared for what unfolded before us as news came in from America.

Speaking since that day to colleagues and competitors in other newsrooms around the world, I realize that they too had shared the same experience – the sense that, as we watched the Twin Towers burn on our television screens, some of the rhythms and certainties that had governed our professional and personal lives were shifting.

For all of these organizations, what came first was getting the news out, helping the public to grasp what was happening. Providing the BBC's first eyewitness reports from the scene was our correspondent Stephen Evans, who had been inside the World Trade Center when the first plane struck. Halfway through one of his early reports the phone went dead and we waited anxiously for over an hour before we heard from him again. Communications with the USA were extremely difficult but staff in New York and Washington battled to report the emerging crisis as a second plane hit the World Trade Center, another struck the Pentagon and yet another crashed near Pittsburgh.

At the BBC we serve both a domestic and an international audience through TV, Radio and Online. Correspondents in the USA were passed back and forth from one network to another to explain each new development. Many of our correspondents are based abroad or travel regularly from our World Affairs Unit. They became the backbone of our immediate coverage, providing much-needed background and analysis. World Affairs

Editor John Simpson had just come out of Afghanistan. From neighbouring Pakistan, together with our Kabul correspondent Kate Clark who had been expelled by the Taliban in March 2001, he quickly assessed the possibility of a connection to Osama bin Laden and the likely ramifications for Al-Qaida's Taliban hosts. In the Middle East, correspondents like Orla Guerin reported on the likely consequences for the peace process. And throughout it all, our diplomatic, political and business staff worked round the clock to help the audience to understand the unfolding crisis.

The attacks on America and the aftermath are arguably the biggest news events that journalists of my generation have had to cover. The BBC's long-standing commitment to covering foreign news has proved to be a very worthwhile investment. Contacts and experience, built up by our journalists over many years, enabled us to position three correspondents in Kabul, when the city was still under Taliban control, and five more to walk in ahead of the Northern Alliance troops.

We are constantly receiving messages from viewers, listeners and online users. In particular, since September 11th, e-mails have flooded in, including moving accounts from survivors and, early on, poignant appeals from people looking for missing family members or friends. The size and range of our audience ensure that the feedback comprises very diverse views, some questioning and criticizing our coverage. But it's clear that many who phone and write want to learn more about the current situation.

That need for explanation and understanding is one of the reasons we've chosen to publish this book. It can't by any means provide a complete picture of the extent to which our world has changed since September 11th. We can't yet judge with certainty what has shifted temporarily and what has changed irrevocably. What this book can do, I hope, is to help readers to examine different aspects of the crisis through the eyes of some of the BBC's most experienced correspondents, to understand what has happened and to interpret some of the consequences.

Richard Sambrook, Director, BBC News, November 26th 2001

PROLOGUE

The instant that details started to emerge of the events in New York, messages from all over the world began tumbling into BBC News Online. In the 48 hours after the first plane crashed into the World Trade Center, the forum received 20,000 e-mails; by the end of the week it was 75,000. Some came from people directly involved in the tragedy. These are a few of their stories.

SURVIVORS

ADAM MAYBLUM was in his office on the 87th floor of the north tower, joking with colleagues at May Davis, a financial services firm, and checking e-mails, when the first plane hit a few storeys above.

The building lurched violently and shook as if it were an earthquake. People screamed. I watched out my window as the building seemed to move 10 to 20 feet in each direction. Light fixtures and parts of the ceiling collapsed. The kitchen was destroyed. We were certain that it was a bomb.

We did not panic. The building was standing and we were shaken but alive. The smoke was thick and white. I grabbed my laptop, took off my t-shirt and ripped it into three pieces, soaked it in water and gave two pieces to my friends. Tied my piece around my face to act as an air filter. And we all started moving to the staircase.

In the halls there were tiny fires and sparks. The ceiling had collapsed in the men's bathroom. It was gone, along with anyone who may have been in there. We did not go in to look. We missed the staircase on the first run and had to double back. Once in the staircase we picked up fire extinguishers just in case.

A brave man was fighting a fire with the emergency hose. I stopped with two friends to make sure that every-one from our office was accounted for... In retrospect,

I recall seeing Harry Ramos, my head trader, doing the same several yards behind me. We were moving down very slowly and orderly, no panic. At least not overt panic. My legs could not stop shaking. My heart was pounding.

We checked our cell phones. Surprisingly, there was a very good signal. I knew I could not reach my wife so I called my parents. I told them what happened and that we were all okay and on the way down. We kept making way for the wounded to go down ahead of us. No one seemed seriously wounded. Just some cuts and scrapes.

On the 53rd floor we came across Victor, a heavyset man sitting on the stairs. He needed help. I knew I would have trouble carrying him because I have a very bad back. But my friend and I offered anyway. He chose to wait for help.

On the 44th floor my phone rang. It was my parents. They were hysterical. I said relax, I'm fine. My father said get out, there is a third plane coming. I still did not understand.

Firemen, policemen, WTC K-9 units without the dogs, anyone with a badge, started coming up as we were heading down. I stopped a lot of them and told them about the man on 53 and my friend on 87. I later felt terrible about this. They headed up to find those people and met death instead.

On the third floor the lights went out and we heard and felt this rumbling coming towards us from above. I thought the staircase was collapsing upon itself. It was Tower 2 collapsing next door.

Someone had a flashlight. We passed it forward and left the stairwell and headed down a dark and cramped corridor to an exit. We could not see at all. I recommended that everyone place a hand on the shoulder of the person in front of them and call out if they hit an obstacle so others would know to avoid it. They did. It worked perfectly.

We were ushered out into the courtyard, the one where the fountain used to be. I could not understand where all of the debris had come from. There was at least five inches of this grey, pasty, dusty drywall soot on the ground as well as a thickness of it in the air. Twisted steel and wires.

A girl on a bike offered us some water. Just as she took the cap off her bottle we heard a rumble. Tower 1 collapsed. We had been out less than 15 minutes.

Adam Mayblum's friend Harry Ramos, the head trader at May Davis, was last seen trying to help Victor down the stairs from the 36th floor.

* * * * * *

ERIC LEVINE worked for Morgan Stanley on the 64th floor of the south tower and was being evacuated from the building when the second plane struck.

We heard a huge explosion, which shook the building like crazy! I grabbed hold of the stairwell to steady myself when a women who had fallen from a flight up hit me in the back and sent me down a flight of stairs with her on my back.

I tried to stand up but the building was still shaking and the lights were flickering on and off... Then the building began to sink, that's the only way I can describe it. The floor began to lower under your feet and all I could think about was that it would crack open and I would fall hundreds of feet to my death.

People began screaming and crying and praying out loud for God to help them. I remember that I began to pray once the floor gave out. Asking God to just let the building stop shaking long enough for me to get out.

After what seemed like an eternity the building settled and the evacuation began in earnest. People were panicking and a stampede started. Myself and a few people that I remember from my floor pushed up against the wall and waited for the initial surge of people to subside and then we began to move out again.

After this things began to speed up somewhere along

the route and between the 44th and 34th floors. I lost sight of the little Philippina woman who had been hanging on to my arm for dear life. She was there one moment and gone the next... This really bothers me a lot.

Somewhere around the 25th floor we began to smell jet fuel and a lot of it. I have asthma and it began to become a little difficult to breathe, but by the 15th it became unbearable due to the amount of smoke that was now entering the stairwell. I took off my shirt and wrapped it around my head to help me breathe and it worked, but my eyes were stinging real bad. After what seemed like an eternity, but actually took about 40 minutes, we saw our first glimpse of the outside world.

People were screaming and running everywhere. Emergency vehicles everywhere you looked and I was about to take my first look at the two towers. I could not believe what I was seeing... Both buildings were on fire with flames shooting out of them about 100ft high. Huge plumes of thick black smoke were billowing out of them and when I looked at Tower 2 you could still see the tail end of the jet hanging out of the building.

I ran 15 blocks to my apartment where I sat in shock watching the replay of the buildings falling.

I can't believe that I made it out alive. I have still been unable to locate a few associates of mine who worked on the floor with me and I pray that they made it out alive. My prayers are with all the survivors and families of those lost in this cowardly act of violence.

* * * * * *

SUSAN FREDERICK had walked down dozens of flights from the 80th floor of the north tower and was nearing safety when the lights went out.

I remember thinking: there is no way I am going to die three floors from safety. We climbed back up to [level] four where a firefighter punched a hole in the wall to get us out. We made a human chain, hanging on to the person in front and the person in back of us as we made our way out into the fourth floor rotunda in the dark.

We got our first glimpse of what looked like a war zone. We walked through ankle-deep dust and out through a doorway to the outside plaza.

We climbed over girders and moved around office furniture and layers of office papers, twisted metal, broken glass and other debris. By now we were wet and covered in this ash. People all looked like their hair had turned prematurely grey. We were told to walk quickly up the street.

Within minutes (we now know it was no more than four) we heard a rumble, and turned to see our tower begin to collapse and a large cloud of black moving up the street. We ran.

It is by God's miracle alone that I am convinced I got out. I'm not sure what is next. But for now smelling the flowers is just fine with me.

* * * * * *

WITNESSES
PATRICIA FARRELL works on Broadway, a block from the World Trade Center.

People on the upper floors began jumping out of the windows right before my eyes. We all started screaming but we could not help them. Someone told me that a plane had hit the center. Just then I noticed the tail and wing of another plane flying very low. I lost sight of it as it went around building two. There was a loud explosion and the sound of breaking glass that shook us.

I then heard a massive, loud, rumbling, crunching sound. People started screaming 'run! run!' I saw this huge cloud of smoke or dust racing towards us. I turned and ran down a side street looking to run into a building, but all the stores were shuttered. Then I saw a building whose side entrance was recessed into the wall. About 15 of us had made it there.

The cloud had enveloped us and now it was so black that you could not see your hand in front of you. My eyes were burning and I was choking. We were all banging on the door screaming 'please open up'. Finally the building manager opened it and we rushed inside. Some of us just hugged one another despite being perfect strangers.

There was no panicking as I can recall. We were all covered with a light-brown yellowish dust. My eyes were burning and the dust was all down my throat. After 10–15 minutes we were told to make a run for it as the air was clearing. I couldn't believe what I saw when I got outdoors.

The dust had obliterated the sky. As far as I could see, up and down Broadway, was covered with what looked like light volcanic ash. There was broken glass and pieces of debris covering the ground. It looked as if an atomic bomb had hit. I still didn't know what had happened. The ambulance attendants directed us down a block to a city bus which was taking the survivors on board to the nearest hospital. Everyone was just numb.

* * * * * *

RICHARD WAJDA was late for work that day and walking towards the Twin Towers when he heard an explosion. He believes he would certainly have been killed if he had been on time.

I looked up and saw flames. I immediately thought it was a bomb. Debris was falling everywhere as if it were the ticker tape parade for the Yankees. Suddenly I was hit in the head, and, as I was on the phone, I saw a body fall from the building. Tears were running down my face.

Seconds later the second plane hit the second tower and exploded. All I saw was the burst of flames. Everyone started running. I was knocked over and someone else ran right over me. Fortunately someone helped me up. I was so scared to look back because I thought the building was going to fall on me. I ran and ran all the way to the FDR Drive, which is on the east side near the South Street Seaport. I looked back then, and the smoke was following us.

I kept on running, this time I was running along the riverside uptown to get as far from the fire as possible. I was running with several strangers. A few of us then stopped in a nearby park to rest. It was far from the towers, but we were still able to see them, when the first one fell. The sound sent chills up my spine. I told the people to run, so we continued.

The streets were a mess, and believe it or not, the city held itself together. Locals handed out water, volunteers helped the injured. I was OK and kept on going. I made it to the 59th Street bridge to walk across to Queens and ran across with thousands more. The fear of the bridge being hit was scary.

Now I am finally home and I am still in shock and in pain, I can barely walk. I fell and was trampled. My legs are cut up, and my back is in severe pain, and my feet are ripped up. But I am home and safe.

* * * * * *

A RESCUER
JESSICA McGEARY, a Red Cross worker, helped the rescuers searching for survivors in the rubble of the World Trade Center.

The place looks like a scene from a movie where someone is trying to show that human civilization has had its day and has been and gone. It looks like 500 years of archaeology happened in a single incident. Everything's covered in grey-white ash, and papers, and bits of people's lives. It's the kind of thing that makes you pray that nobody else you know comes down there, because you don't want them ever to have to know what it smells like, or looks like, or any of it...

We spent our time in the city feeding and watering and otherwise assisting the emergency workers – firefighters, police, soldiers, Transit Authority workers, whoever. We answered a lot of questions from people who wanted to help, too. I don't think I've ever seen so many people who've wanted to help their fellow citizens – their fellow human beings – with anything.

There will never be a 'normal' day again, I don't think. Well, maybe there will, who knows... But thank you all. Thank you for being good people... thank you.

* * * * * *

A PRIEST

REVEREND BRIAN CARROLL watched his friend Father Mychal Judge rush to the aid of his firefighter colleagues.

I was walking down 6th Avenue at 31st Street right around the corner from our Church of St Francis of Assisi as the first jet crashed into the World Trade Center. I gasped and yelled to people on the sidewalk but they looked at me as if I were a madman. I was in shock; it was not real. I rushed back to the friary and went to the room of Fr Mychal Judge (a fire department chaplain) and alerted him to what I thought was an accident. He got into his fire gear and was off before his pager sounded.

Fr Mychal died in the collapse... He came back home ...wrapped in sheets, and was placed in the 31st Street firehouse. The friars gathered around and we prayed over Mychal late in the afternoon. His brother firefighters, soot-covered, were at his side in tears.

I will say my prayers for all who have died and, as I prepare for bed, I ask God to bless Fr Mychal. He died among those whom he loved and served so well.

CHAPTER ONE

GROUND ZERO

Stephen Evans

Stephen Evans is the BBC's North America Business Correspondent. Before that, he reported on industry and the economy in the UK for the BBC as well as a number of British newspapers. He was posted to New York in April 2001 and was in the World Trade Center on September 11th when the first plane struck.

There was no bigger symbol of America. The twin tower-blocks of the World Trade Center dominated New York and way beyond. 1WTC and 2WTC, slightly to its south, were immense global icons of the American way: an assertion to the world of can-do confidence and defiant grandeur. They were high profile in all senses.

On a crystalline blue morning in late summer, the air was fresh and life felt good. People having breakfast in the Windows on the World restaurant on the 107th floor of the north tower could see for 40 miles. Likewise, the pilots of two airliners flying high towards the two symbolic blocks which dwarfed Manhattan, would have seen the buildings from perhaps 20 minutes out.

What the hijackers in the cockpits wouldn't have seen, but might have imagined, were the tens of thousands of people performing ordinary tasks at the start of another business day in what was surely the busiest office complex in the world.

In those two 110-storey blocks, there were individuals of every background, from 86 different countries. Countless lives ended – some instantly with a crashing violence, some slowly with unimaginable pain and terror – when American Airlines Flight 11 slammed into the top floors of the north tower at 8.47

in the morning and United Airlines Flight 175 hit the south tower a third of the way down at 9.03.

Of the thousands in the towers, I was among those best placed to escape. I had arrived at about half-past-eight to interview an economist, a particularly gloomy practitioner of the 'dismal science', who thought a recession was inevitable. The morning of September 11th, though, was stunningly beautiful – warm but with a hint of autumn in the air as I emerged from the darkness of the Cortland Street subway station onto the piazza between the towers. The sky was flawless over the Hudson and the sun made the buildings shine.

I was a little early so I was sitting languidly in the vast lobby, passing the time reading the *New York Times*, when there was a loud thud, something like a huge iron door slamming shut or a large container full of concrete crashing from high above me. The walls shuddered. I had to tell myself: 'Those walls really did shake. I felt it.' I thought: 'Earthquake? No, that's San Francisco. This is New York.'

A film of smoke descended on the piazza. People streamed past me through the lobby. I turned my mini-disc recorder on to capture the sound of what was happening, scrabbling with the machine's tangle of cables on the marble floor before joining the exodus. Strangely, no one was screaming at this point, no one was panicking – there was just a determined movement away from trouble.

As I left, I stopped and stared at the flames and smoke pouring from the top of the tower. People were telling each other that a plane had crashed into the building and I assumed there must have been some sort of accident with a light aircraft. Whatever the cause, I knew that the World Trade Center on fire was a story and I had to call London. At the bottom of the tower there was a clutch of shops and offices so I went from one to the next seeking a phone that worked until I reached a newsagent who let me use his. He turned down my offer of a credit card, saying 'just use it'.

The broadcaster's equivalent of 'Hold the front page' is 'Just put me on the air'. I rang the editor on duty in London and was soon broadcasting. I was switched quickly from programme to programme to describe what I had seen. As I was talking, the second plane hit 2WTC. The newsagent took his phone back, pulled down the shutters, and the two of us rushed away.

The whole situation seemed completely unreal but I had to find another phone urgently, so I hired a room at the nearby Embassy Suites Hotel. From the window of Room 620, I could see along Vesey Street, where an orderly line of ambulances was forming, waiting to move up to the foot of the north tower. People on the ground still assumed they were in no danger, even as the Twin Towers burned above them – a false and fatal assumption. I was again on the air, trying to convey the scene unfolding around me, when suddenly there was a huge explosion of dust and debris; 2WTC was collapsing. The phone line went dead.

Alarms blared in the hotel. A voice on the tannoy instructed people to leave. With other guests, I filed down the inner stairwell. One elderly woman couldn't move quickly so she stood aside to let others pass, but her offer was refused and people insisted on filing down slowly behind her. By now, the scene outside had become more chaotic. Police were trying to usher people away. With no phone, my task was to get a cameraman so I rushed from crew to crew, trying to buy their services, and failed. In the end, I did a deal with a local television company: I gave them my eyewitness account in return for their doing some filming for me and giving me the tape to take away. As we recorded, the north tower collapsed behind me. The danger suddenly became very real. I remember thinking: 'That cloud is coming at me faster than I can run', so I ran and, luckily, the cloud stopped short of me.

* * * * * *

I've thought a lot since then about the terror felt by those on board the two Boeing 767s, seized after leaving Boston. The tactics of the hijackers emerged from transcripts of conversations within the aircraft but overheard by air traffic controllers and other planes in the area. The ploy was to dupe the passengers into thinking that their lives weren't in danger and then to terrorize them if they resisted. Twenty-four minutes into Flight 11, a hijacker is overhead saying, 'We have some planes. Just stay quiet and you will be OK. We are returning to the airport. Nobody move, everything will be OK. If you try to make moves, you'll endanger yourself and the aeroplane. Just stay quiet.' Twenty-three minutes later, Flight 11 crashed into the north tower of the World Trade Center. It had 11 crew and 81 passengers.

The second aircraft had 9 crew and 56 passengers, including 4 hijackers bent on suicide. A half-hour into the flight, radio contact was lost and the air traffic controller in Boston said, 'We may have a hijack.' The plane was last seen on the radar at an altitude of 18,000 feet, flying at 550 miles an hour. Three minutes later it smashed into the south tower.

Next it was Washington's turn, as American Airlines Flight 77 hit the Pentagon. The US military headquarters were built of reinforced concrete in the depths of a more conventional war in 1943 to withstand a bomb attack – but not the impact of a Boeing 757 hitting at 450 miles an hour.

The airliner sheared the top off street lights on its skewed trajectory into the south-western side of the building. The Pentagon consists of five 'rings' of offices, one inside the other, and the plane struck three of these rings on one side – the opposite side of the building, as it happened, from where the Secretary of Defense Donald Rumsfeld was working at the time.

Those immediately near the impact described a roar from deep within the building. As in New York, the inferno of aviation fuel did much of the damage. Within the pandemonium of heat and choking smoke, firefighters dragged some people clear and guided others out with their flashlights.

Despite their efforts, 189 people died, including 64 on the plane. Many perished as the airliner continued to explode after impact, sending sheets of flame down the corridors.

Twenty-six minutes after the attack on the Pentagon, United Airlines Flight 93 crashed into a field near the town of Shanksville in Pennsylvania, having failed to reach a prominent target, possibly even the White House. That was thanks to passengers who learned of the earlier attacks on the World Trade Center and realized they were probably doomed if they didn't tackle the hijackers. Mobile phones meant this life-or-death drama, which Hollywood might have deemed incredible, was followed with horror from afar.

Herded by the hijackers into the back of the plane, some of those on board made final, desperate calls. Flight attendant CeeCee Ross-Lyles phoned her husband at home in Fort Myers, Florida, to tell him how much she loved him and their sons; Jeremy Glick, a 31-year-old internet company sales manager, called his wife, Lyz, who confirmed that other planes had been hijacked; Mark Bingham, a 31-year-old publicist, spoke to his mother; Thomas Burnett, a 38-year-old executive and father of three, phoned his wife and told her: 'I know we're all going to die… If they're going to run this into the ground, we have to do something', ending with, 'I love you, honey'.

Todd Beamer, a 32-year-old accounts manager with the Oracle software company, spoke to an in-flight telephone operator. He told her that one passenger was dead and that one hijacker claimed to have a bomb. And he gave the operator his home phone number to pass on the message that he loved his wife and sons. His last words heard by the operator were: 'Are you ready, guys? Let's roll.'

It's thought that these four unarmed passengers, plus 42-year-old Lou Nacke, a weight-lifter with a Superman tattoo on his shoulder, then took on the hijackers. In the ensuing fight in the cockpit, the jet went out of control and crashed. Asked to look for the crash site, the pilot of another plane reported that he could see 'a dark cloud, like a puff of black smoke'.

* * * * * *

Heroism and tragedy went hand in hand that day. Many acts of courage were quiet and undocumented; others occurred very publicly at the World Trade Center – in the full glare of a bright Manhattan sun, on television screens the world over.

In the Twin Towers, people in the immediate area of the impacts probably died instantly, or at least quickly. Those above the impact, particularly in the south tower, were not so 'lucky' (a strange use of the word, I know). To them, the heat and thick smoke from burning aviation fuel were so painful and made death so utterly certain that jumping from windows they'd smashed open was preferable. Some jumped holding hands. Many clung to the outside of the building up to a quarter of a mile high in the air, torn between the unbearable heat inside and the sheer drop below. Does the word 'terror' begin to convey the anguish?

Shortly after nine o'clock, the fire trucks started to arrive. Nine o'clock is a change of shift, so firefighters from both night and day shifts went straight to the inferno.

One group that suffered particularly harshly for its bravery was the fire department's 'special operations command', the specialist rescuers who go into burning, tottering buildings first. They're the ones who rush in and up when everyone else is rushing down and out. On the morning of September 11th, this group lost 75 of the more than 300 firefighters who died.

Other tales of great fortitude emerge. The men of Squad Company 1 (motto: Squad Company 1 – the One and Only Squad) sped to the scene from their base on Union Street in Brooklyn. Twelve of them didn't return, leaving 11 widows and 22 father-less children, 5 of them the children of one man, firefighter Steve Siller. In the days that followed, the 15 survivors of Squad Company 1 kept coming back to work, returning to their fire station to shower and attend the funerals of their comrades – men whose jackets still hung on the walls around them.

Amongst the heart-breaking stories of death and injury there were also some incidents of good fortune. Five members of Ladder Company 6 survived when if they had moved more slowly, or more quickly, they would surely have died. Their fire station in Lower Manhattan was close enough for them to hear the impact of the first plane. Within minutes, their truck was parked in front of the burning north tower, in time to see the second plane hit its twin.

The company captain, John Jonas, calculated that the fire in the north tower had probably consumed the top 30 floors, leaving 80 to climb. They went in and, resting every ten floors to pace themselves, they had reached the 27th floor when the north tower they were in shook with the vibration from the collapsing south tower. Captain Jonas said, 'If that building can go, so can this. It's time to head down.'

He and his men turned and descended but met a middle-aged woman who couldn't move very quickly so one of the men supported her and helped her move slowly forward, all with a clock ticking in the mind of Captain Jonas.

On the fourth floor, the woman collapsed with exhaustion and the men scoured the offices for a chair on which to carry her. That delay saved them. They had paused in a stairwell which protected them as the north tower collapsed around them. Some of them were thrown down two flights in the swirling debris of the 106 storeys above them. They radioed for help from what might have been their tomb. Eventually, the dust cleared and they saw open air – light where the north tower of the World Trade Center had once stood.

Others also survived through luck and ingenuity. At 8.47 a.m. window cleaner Jan Demczur got into an express lift that wasn't supposed to stop until it reached the 67th floor of 1WTC. Moments later, as the lift ascended, there was a jolt and the lift stopped dead. After ten minutes, a voice on the intercom said there had been an explosion, and smoke started seeping into the lift cage.

Demczur and his fellow captives prised open the door to face a solid wall on which was marked the number 50 – it was the fiftieth floor and one with no door since the lift was never meant to stop there. The window cleaner used the metal edge of his window-cleaning squeegee to carve a way through until he reached the tiles on the other side.

Mr Demczur took 95 minutes to escape from the building. The time between the impact and the collapse of the tower was 100 minutes. Window cleaners in high-rise buildings tend to know people on all floors, the people with whom they share all the small civilities of daily life from having coffee to talking about a ball game. Long after the horror of the day, Mr Demczur continued to see faces in the darkness of his mind: the security guard who never escaped from the 93rd floor; the executives who were kind to him on the 92nd.

Apart from live television and radio conveying personal pain and death to every part of the world, modern electronics guaranteed the tragedy struck chords harder and longer; like some passengers on the planes, many of those trapped above the flames in the World Trade Center left their last words with an immediacy unavailable to previous generations.

Thirty-nine-year-old Daniel Lopez, who worked on the 96th floor of 1WTC as a financial analyst at Carr Futures, left this message to his wife on their answering-machine: 'Liz. It's me, Dan. My building has been hit. I made it to the 78th floor. I'm OK but will remain here to help evacuate people. See you soon.'

Or this e-mail from a trapped man to a friend: 'I don't think I'm going to get out. You've been a really good friend.'

Sean Harrington-Hughes found an answer-phone message from his wife, Melissa: 'Sean, it's me. I just wanted to let you know I love you and I am stuck in this building in New York. A plane hit or a bomb went off – we don't know, but there's a lot of smoke and I just wanted you to know I loved you.'

Cantor Fitzgerald bond broker Kenneth Van Auken, who worked on the 102nd floor of the north tower, left this on his home answering machine to his wife Lorie: 'I love you. I'm in the World Trade Center and the building was hit by something. I don't know if I'm going to get out. But I love you very much. I hope I'll see you later. Bye.'

* * * * * *

September 11th also produced one political hero. In the months before the attacks, Mayor Rudolph Giuliani had become something of a figure of fun in New York. He was widely credited with curbing both street and organized crime, but all that was way in the city's past. More recently, he had dominated the newspapers with his highly public split from his wife, which led to a spat over whether the new woman in his life should be barred from the official mayoral home, Gracie Mansion. Spin doctors and lawyers were signed up, journalists had a field day, the public was endlessly entertained.

On the morning of September 11th, the Mayor was in Midtown, Manhattan on Fifth Avenue on his way downtown to City Hall when he took a call saying a plane had crashed into the World Trade Center. He went straight there, later describing it as 'the most horrific scene I've ever seen in my whole life'. On site, he met the fire chief Peter Ganci, moments before the fireman walked away to his death.

New York's emergency command centre was actually inside the World Trade Center and unusable, so Mayor Giuliani went instead to a suite of offices at 75 Barclay Street, a block away and in the shadow of the towers. When they collapsed, he had to run for his life.

For the rest of the day, he gave a series of impromptu press conferences, often in streets strewn with debris. Of course there was nothing unusual about that – it's what politicians do at disasters – but many fail to connect with the public, missing the moment, their presence seeming like an intrusion.

By contrast, Giuliani created leadership in chaos. He shared the city's grief, but also instilled determination and resolution. The term 'City Father' has become moribund, one of those phrases used by officialdom, but rarely by the public. On that day, Mayor Giuliani gave the term meaning.

He caught the mood of his citizens, articulating their thoughts, shaping feelings barely formed in the public mind. He exhorted New Yorkers to partake of the good things of life. It was the kind of instruction that might have seemed insensitive if the Mayor hadn't known the true spirit of his city. His leadership, and his support for Britons bereaved by the tragedy, earned him an honorary knighthood from the Queen.

One of his big concerns was getting the city back to as normal as it could be, for good economic reasons as much as anything else. New York was traumatized emotionally but also hit by a series of economic blows. Airports, tunnels and bridges were closed and the travel industry shut for a profitless week. It then faced what threatened to be months of financial hardship as tourists stayed away.

And there was the problem of ten-million square feet of office space in the towers turned to dust, with the closure and relocation of many of the firms at the heart of the world's financial system. The New York Stock Exchange closed for four working days, at a time when the North American economy had anyway been teetering on the edge of recession.

There were longer-term questions about how to replace the Twin Towers. It was not a matter of engineering but of psychology. Many people hadn't liked working in them anyway. They swayed in the wind, which made office workers feel vulnerable. Would people want to work again in buildings so high? Would rebuilding them simply be an invitation to the next generation of people with a fanatical grievance to destroy them?

Both of the towers were designed to withstand the impact of a Boeing 707 (the biggest passenger plane flying when the World Trade Center was designed). They were basically steel tubes, with a central steel core, a spine up the middle plus the steel outer supporting walls.

The flexibility that the occupants found so unsettling, meant, for example, that the bomb on February 26th 1993 failed. Then, a device was placed in a van in the basement garage of 2WTC by the forerunners of the suicide pilots. The intention was to blow out one of the supporting walls at the base, causing the whole tower to topple into the other one. Even though the blast shook the tower, it didn't knock it off its centre of gravity.

But it wasn't the impact that brought the towers down on September 11th. It was the fire. The heat from burning aviation fuel was far greater than that needed to melt the steel. As the steel on the top floors buckled, they fell on the ones below producing a downward cascade. Under normal circumstances, engineers would describe it as a 'perfect demolition', one in which the building fell largely within its own base rather than toppling sideways, causing even greater damage.

Actually, it wasn't quite as tidy as that. Shortly before 10 a.m. the top 35 or so floors of 2WTC, above where the aircraft hit, simply twisted and fell away onto 4WTC, the Marriott Hotel at its base. The rest of the tower then disintegrated, falling on the Bankers Trust and American Express buildings. At 10.28 a.m. the other tower went, with burning material falling on 7WTC, causing it to catch fire. Some debris also crushed the Customs House. It seems the antenna on top of 1WTC speared this building, piercing through to the basement.

The result was a mess of steel and dust and detritus from which rescuing survivors would be virtually impossible, and the recovery of human remains would be as grim a task as one could imagine.

* * * * * *

The psychological repercussions were also profound. In the days and weeks after September 11th, the mood changes in New York were extraordinary. The city grieved like a huge extended family. Taxi horns became noticeably silent. If strangers went into bars in that first week, the barman might look them straight in the eye and shake them by the hand, using both of his, and ask if they were all right. Initially, there was no raucous laughter to be heard. Countless small acts of kindness took place on buses or in launderettes or shops, or wherever people brushed against each other.

After two days, on the Thursday, the noise level began to rise after the stunned silence. In Lower Manhattan, on the West Side Highway which leads to the World Trade Center, New Yorkers of every description came to cheer trucks and their crews going into the site of devastation. People told me: 'Now we need our heroes.' And heroes they found.

The flag started to appear everywhere. People who would have run a mile from obvious gestures of patriotism before September 11th now displayed the Stars and Stripes with unselfconscious pride. It was, they said, a demonstration of solidarity against an attempt by a small number of people to terrorize them into relinquishing their values of liberty and equality and freedom of belief.

As the week wore on, mourning became more public. Posters appeared: 'Missing: Scott Saber; 37 years old; 5 ft 6; heavyset, balding; blue eyes. Was on the 106th floor of One WTC. Call Bruce Saber on the following number...' And there he was in the photograph, relaxing in an armchair. Or there was firefighter David DeRubbio, smiling and confident in his helmet and tunic as his face shone from the fence in Union Square where a shrine grew, with thousands of candles illuminating the silent mourners each night. Or the photograph on the wall of an underground station, of Milton Bustilli, 'last seen September 11th, 102nd floor'. Underneath, someone had written, 'We love you', and then 'Please find him'. Earlier in the year Mr Bustilli had become the proud father of a baby girl. His body was found by rescuers – identified by his wedding ring.

There were thousands of posters, each putting a human face to anonymous tragedy. Some of them were carried by relatives wandering the streets. Daphne Bowers held a picture of her daughter, 28-year-old Veronique, the mother of a young child with muscular dystrophy. 'She called me when the building was on fire,' Mrs Bowers said. 'She told me "Mommy, there's smoke coming through the walls. I can't breathe." Then she said "I love you, Mommy, goodbye".'

Many of the people who were searching appeared composed, probably knowing in their hearts that their loved ones were dead, but hoping against all real hope that they had somehow gone to work that morning and got lost or detained and would reappear.

The reverberations of emotion continued to shake New York. Poems that resonated with the moment sold out quickly in bookshops. Musical tastes changed; one country music disc-jockey told me that many of her audience requests were for Louis Armstrong singing 'What a Wonderful World'. In particular listeners wanted to hear a version he recorded in 1970, when the Vietnam War was at its height, in which Armstrong prefaced the performance with a declaration that, even with bombs and poverty, the song was an assertion of the positive. The music played in clubs like the 'Knitting Factory', which was so near the World Trade Center that it was closed for a time, became less aggressive; 'comfort music' was the order of the evening. And then tastes changed again, with people seeking joyful music; some of the musicians in the New York Philharmonic ('the Town Band') went to Lower Manhattan and played 'Teddy Bears' Picnic' to much acclaim.

Just as the flag had appeared, so patriotic songs were played everywhere. The Director of Music at Stuyvesant High School, where pupils and staff had fled from the collapsing towers which literally overshadowed them, told me he found new meaning in 'The Star-Spangled Banner'. After the Vietnam War, it became associated with the jingoism of a particular politics; after September 11th, he said, it was reclaimed by all the people as a symbol of unity.

There were dark sides. For example, some looting occurred. But the overwhelming impression was of people acting with dignity and thinking big thoughts about big questions. I remember interviewing a black woman for BBC News 24. The conversation turned to revenge and she said that was for 'the Lord'. After the cameras stopped filming, we – two strangers – just looked at each other and embraced.

Over the weeks, changes also occur in the personal psyche. There are all the symptoms of shock, of course: a frisson of fear when a bus clanks over a steel sheet, or when a group of people suddenly start rushing in the street, or when thick smoke appears. For a while I couldn't go near big windows inside high-rise buildings – I kept imagining the nose of an airliner suddenly shattering the plate-glass.

More personal questions occur when you have been close to such a big, terrible event, questions to yourself about who it is that you really love; about what you should have said to repair a friendship; how you are pleased you said this or that to your father; who you would have wanted to sort out your affairs.

But one of the great privileges of being in New York after September 11th is to have witnessed the solidarity of a whole people uniting in grief and dignity. A big, hard-nosed city became quiet and thoughtful. It seemed gentler. It seemed human, in the best sense of the word – unlike the explosive destruction that shattered the world we thought we had known before.

CHAPTER TWO

SHAKING THE FOUNDATIONS

George Alagiah

George Alagiah was Africa Editor of South *magazine before joining the BBC as Developing World Correspondent. In that role, and subsequently as Africa Correspondent, he reported on the human cost of war, disease and natural disaster in many countries. He now presents, and reports for, BBC Television's main news bulletins, and was sent to New York in the wake of the September 11th attacks. He reflects here on his impressions of a traumatized America.*

'I'll be back as soon as I can.' Reassuring words. The same ones I had used on countless occasions before. Easy words. They hide the uncertainty, they get over the awkward business of separation. But this time was different. I knew it the minute I settled into the cab taking me to Stansted Airport, just north of London. The uneasiness, the sense of foreboding had set in a couple of hours earlier when, like so many millions of others, I watched real-time terror on TV. It was the collapse of the first tower – eerily reminiscent of the destruction of an ageing high-rise apartment block to make way for new housing – that I found especially unnerving.

When the phone rang, and the news editor at Television Centre told me to head for the airport, I felt unusually nervous. There had been many other phone calls over the years, terse and rushed conversations that had sent me headlong into harm's way: to Sierra Leone, Liberia, Afghanistan, Somalia – a register of places where man had shown his capacity for violence.

It takes a couple of hours from my home to the airport. Halfway through the journey I had worked it out. I knew what was bothering me. My concern was less about what I was heading towards than about what I was leaving behind; I didn't want my children – boys, Adam aged 14 and Matt, 11 – to see the explicit TV footage unsupervised. I rang home. My wife, Fran, answered. Quickly, we agreed that she would record the coverage and then replay some of it later, when she'd had a chance to talk to the children and provide some context. This was not something we had ever done before. We had never felt the need to protect either of them from my film reports over a decade of war reporting. There is a gross, tangible reality about conventional warfare: pain and suffering, death and bodies. Even the young can cope with that – it is within the bounds of what they know to be a less than perfect world.

But Tuesday September 11th, with its clean, efficient exercise of malice, was outside any accepted notion of modern-day conflict. Aircraft and skyscrapers – so familiar and reassuring in our version of civilization – had been transmuted into symbols of death and destruction. The ordinary had become dangerous – that was the subliminal caption those TV pictures conveyed. And that is why, like many parents, we feared for our children.

As it turned out, it would be another three days before I (and about a hundred other British journalists) got to New York. North American airspace was closed shortly after the World Trade Center attacks. Canada began lifting its restrictions on Thursday night. Our chartered Boeing 747 flew into Montreal, from where we picked up cars for the seven-hour drive down to New York.

During the long wait at Stansted I went, as usual when I'm at an airport, to the bookshop. Normally I pick up something to help me get into the mood and history of whichever place I'm heading for. Even as I scoured the shelves I began to understand that no book could do the job now. America's *Zeitgeist* had changed, perhaps for ever. What use would Bill Bryson be now, with his tales from the blissfully ignorant idyll of small-town America? This time I bought a copy of Antony Beevor's *Stalingrad*. Somehow this epic story of despair and heroism in the winter wasteland of Russia 60 years ago seemed the most appropriate reading.

At Stansted we were in the news world's equivalent of no-man's-land. We were stranded, unable to begin the assignment that we had set out on. On the TV screens in the departure hall we could see the aftermath of the terrorist attacks. Every time you looked up there seemed to be yet another angle from which the suicide planes had been filmed – a testament to the video age. I wondered whether the terrorists had predicted this when they planned the deadly sequence of hijackings. If they had, then the constant replaying of their 'moment of glory' was more eloquent than any suicide note they might have written.

As these wasted airport hours ticked away and turned day into night and day again, I had time to think back to all the other airports I had passed through, the stepping stones to disaster and conflict. I began to see that even in death the rich and poor worlds are divided.

On the dust-devilled plains of Somalia in the early 1990s, when war and famine had stalked the land, death came in the tens of thousands. It dragged on for months, even years. The vast majority were silent deaths, unheralded and soon forgotten. No leader stood up to protest. There were no speeches of defiance, no singing of a patriotic anthem. All that belongs to the world of nation states, governments and politicians. Somalia was different – a dog-eat-dog world of competing warlords hell-bent on power. Sometimes a tired and broken mother watched a child slip silently into oblivion; occasionally a father would be present to ease the passage from a state of diseased half-life into death itself. But mostly these were lonely, ignominious deaths. The Red Crescent barrow boys would cart away the corpses like so much garbage. Fodder for unmarked graves.

Later came the genocide in Rwanda. A hundred days of slaughter in which 800,000 people were killed. A hundred days in which the world could have done something. It didn't; at least not until it was too late. In New York, at the United Nations, delegates debated this way and that. They even found it difficult to call the killings in Rwanda by the correct name – genocide. The Clinton White House, that repository of the power of the free world, was no different. A spokeswoman for the President found weasel words to distinguish between 'acts of genocide' and genocide itself. It was a distinction that seemed difficult to fathom unless you understood the real purpose of all this – to prevaricate and delay. To have admitted that genocide had taken place would have committed America and her allies to action. But none wanted to accept that obligation; at least not when the killing was going on in far-away Rwanda.

I had covered both those crises. The deaths had gone on for weeks and months. How different it was on September 11th, when the attacks happened so quickly and when virtually everything was witnessed live on television around the world. In Somalia and Rwanda the question of whether we would see the suffering of millions hung on the decisions of news editors – to send TV crews or not. The deaths in Africa took place hidden in the shadows, behind the convenient sanctity of national borders; in America they happened under the full and penetrating gaze of the TV cameras. Even so, many of the most telling images of the attack and its aftermath were taken by members of the public – so-called amateurs. The term seemed irrelevant now. Everybody was an eyewitness that day. Who will forget the running commentary of a young doctor, trying to get into Ground Zero to provide medical help, then crouching behind a car as a curtain of dust rolled ever closer?

Quite soon, the TV networks had access to taped telephone messages left by passengers on the doomed aircraft. In their last frightened and frantic minutes they had spoken final words for their loved ones. Again, in my enforced reverie at the airport, I couldn't help but compare these self-proclaimed notices of death – voiced in private, heard in public – with the thousands of quiet, almost acquiescent victims of terror that had peopled my reports from far-flung corners of the world. From Afghanistan to Zaire, I had seen people teeter on the edge of life, as if unsure whether their death would matter much one way or the other. Who cares? Who will listen? Those were the unspoken questions I sensed in their vacant eyes. Some even seemed to welcome the onset of death's emptiness, as a deliverance from the tribulations of being alive in a troubled and unfair world. Not so for the passengers on the hijacked planes. They left their messages certain that they would be heard, sure that they would be missed.

And their voices *were* heard – not just by the families to whom they were addressed but by men who had the power to act. That day of mass murder in New York galvanized politicians into action. Like millions of people around the world, they felt that the outrage could not go unanswered. And in fact they went even further – likening the attacks on the Twin Towers to an assault on civilization itself. People began to say that these deaths had changed everything, that the world could never be the same again. What they meant, of course, was that life in the wealthy Western world would never be the same. This easy conflation of the fate of the rich world with the fate of all mankind is part of the arrogance that so many in the poor world railed against, and still do. In the majority world, among the wretched billions, life had not changed much at all. It was as precarious and cruel as it had always been.

Finally, a full two days after I'd got into the taxi at home, our charter flight was given permission to take off. The journey from Montreal to New York became an education, a study in what it was that the September 11th terrorist Mohammed Atta and his deadly accomplices had tried to annihilate. Tragedy or no tragedy, the branded emblems of American power slipped past our smoked-glass car windows, standing proud and undiminished: the John Dere farm equipment depot, symbol of America's ability to feed itself; the golden arches of McDonald's, symbols of America's ambition to feed the world outside. America may not have gone in for the business of colonization, but it nevertheless found a far more effective way to leave its stamp on the far reaches of the world.

From gas station staff, from truck drivers taking a break, and from the ubiquitous radio talk show hosts – those silver-tongued arbiters of American small-town morality – I began to understand how its people were coping with the aftermath of disaster.

There is perhaps no country on earth that is so ready to

seek solace and fortitude in the symbols of nationhood. Flying the flag is something Americans do in the best of times; now it had become an obsession. Stuck to bedroom windows, tied to car aerials, displayed in shop fronts, and hanging at half-mast from municipal buildings, the Star-Spangled Banner became a visual shorthand for the way America was feeling. It became a kind of national comfort cloth, a version of the tatty flannel my son would insist on holding whenever we left home, whenever he felt a little insecure.

It was as if, by clutching on to 'Old Glory', Americans were trying to preserve the myth of impregnability. In times to come, September 11th will be remembered not only for the thousands who perished, or the buildings that no longer grace New York's skyline, but also for the loss of America's lofty self-assurance. For a nation reared on the luxury of moral certainty, this was the biggest blow of all and may end up becoming the most enduring legacy of the suicide attacks. Americans had got used to living on an 'island' of their own making. In the modern age they had taken sides in many foreign wars and fuelled several others but only once before – at Pearl Harbour – had any of the consequences been truly felt at home. Now the war had come to them.

So the Stars and Stripes served another purpose too, one that was more important as a shocked and disoriented people tried to work out what to do next. It was a symbol, something to rally round. This was a time to stand up and be counted; to say 'I am an American' after September 11th was much more than a statement of identity, it was a promise of commitment.

But a commitment to what? There were two ideas vying for the heart and soul of America – justice and revenge. 'Nuke them', said one caller on the car radio, without really being able to say who or what the target would be. 'We have to show we're better than they are,' said another, rarer, voice of reason. This was an appeal to America's best instincts, to the values that have made this country a magnet for 'huddled masses yearning to breathe free'. That was the America I drove through that

Friday morning; a country caught between doing the right thing and the easy thing, justice and revenge.

Very soon after the collapse of the towers people began to post pictures and names of missing relatives in public places. As striking as the faces were the names printed underneath. They were a tribute to America's melting pot of cultures and peoples. Old-established names, Jewish in origin, jostled with more recent entrants into the American way of life – Hispanics and Africans. There were Hindus and Muslims, Catholics and Protestants. In their home countries they might have been sworn enemies; here they were brought together, all of them searching for the American Dream.

For many Americans this was a matter of pride, proof that their country deserved its place at the head of the free world. But out west, in the land of Bible-thumpers and isolationists, there were people who saw in the World Trade Center's polyglot occupants the seeds of the destruction that had been visited on their country. Muslims in particular, and dark-skinned foreigners in general, were seen as a fifth column.

When I visited a friend on New York's Upper East Side, virtually the first thing she said after we greeted each other was 'Are you okay?' I didn't understand the question; she had to explain. I am Sri Lankan-born but I could be mistaken for an Arab. That's what she feared. She thought I might have had some trouble. My friend is a Japanese–American and her parents had been interned after Pearl Harbour. She was more acutely aware than most about what happens when you look too much like the enemy.

To be fair, no one of any consequence was talking about internment, but the danger of a backlash against immigrants was apparent for all to see. By September 17th a poll published in the popular newspaper *US Today* showed that 58 per cent of respondents wanted to see special security for Arabs travelling by plane. Just under 50 per cent thought Arab–Americans should be issued with special ID cards. There were many other suggestions, all of which involved what one TV pundit called 'racial profiling'.

Within a couple of days of the terrorist attacks, reports were coming through of mosques being attacked. Ignorance and prejudice came together. In New York and Florida, even Sikhs were attacked. Osama bin Laden wears a turban, went the thinking; Sikhs wear turbans – ergo Sikhs must be linked to terrorism.

I spent an evening in Jackson Heights, a part of Queens now virtually colonized by immigrants from Asia. In every shop, in every restaurant, there seemed to be someone who knew someone who had been abused or worse. Muslim women who normally wore a burka either stayed indoors or decided not to wear it when they ventured out of the area. In the suburb of Richmond, I found 66-year-old Addar Singh, who had been attacked as he walked home from the temple. Four or five youths – he wasn't sure exactly how many there were – shot him at close range with paint-pellets and then laid into him with a baseball bat. They left him bleeding and bruised on the ground.

At the Eat Again Deli on Ninth Avenue, a favoured haunt for the Indian and Pakistani drivers who operate a large proportion of New York's yellow cab fleet, Surinder Singh spoke of a climate of fear. All his colleagues had been shouted at and some people had refused to get into his car.

Afghan immigrants were in the most invidious position of all. Most of them are refugees from the Taliban regime which harboured Osama bin Laden, but they were tarred with the same brush. In College Point, Flushing, another suburb of Queens, the windows of a grocery store owned by Afghans were smashed.

Most, though not all, of the people I spoke to were long-time American citizens. Yet they felt they had to prove their worth all over again. 'We have to be more American than the Americans,' one of them said to me.

Recognizing the dangers of racial tension, and no doubt mindful of the Muslim support he would need to mount any retaliation, George Bush made a point of being seen with Islamic community leaders. The director of the FBI spoke of his determination to hunt down those guilty of what he called 'hate crime'. By the end of the first week after the terrorist attacks there were 49 such cases under investigation. The administration's tough line seemed to work. There were other incidents but they never coalesced into the kind of national hysteria some had feared.

Thus America came through its first, and most important, test. The country resisted the temptation to take the easy options. The political establishment wobbled a bit at first but soon found its bearings. Had George Bush acted instantly, had he fired off his missiles in anger, he would almost certainly have found it far more difficult to curtail the baser passions of some of his people at home. No one can accuse America of having acted in haste.

The impression I was left with was of a people bewildered but certainly not broken. I remember joining a crowd outside St Patrick's Cathedral on Fifth Avenue for a service of remembrance. As the haunting strains of 'Amazing Grace' filtered out into a September evening, New York itself seemed to be transformed. The caricature American, striding ineptly and arrogantly across the world, melted away like the candles held by the mourners. If the terrorists' rage was aimed at an America wilfully exerting its values over nations far away, the people standing outside St Patrick's did not seem to fit the bill. Having myself witnessed some of the disastrous, not to mention deadly, effects of America's actions abroad I was aware of this contradiction. What is it that links a people so determinedly wholesome at home with what their leaders – both business and political – have done in their name in far-away places?

The answer is ignorance. The vast majority of Americans are blissfully unaware of their image abroad. They don't know, perhaps don't care, that in Africa they have made common cause with despots and thugs. They would be surprised to learn that in Asia there are still many workers who associate American companies with the harshest of labour practices. They want the world to join in the coalition against terror, but don't really understand that their present government has turned its back on a coalition of nations determined to save the planet from environmental degradation.

The battle against terrorism has two fronts. One is in that most blighted of countries – Afghanistan. The other has yet to begin. In the months and years ahead America faces a challenge every bit as exacting as the military one it has already embarked on. It will have to break the habits of a generation, and rethink its role in the world.

CHAPTER THREE

AMERICA THE UNLOVED

Brian Hanrahan

Brian Hanrahan has been a foreign correspondent for 20 years, with a ringside seat at many major international events, including the Falklands War, Tiananmen Square, the fall of the Berlin Wall and the Romanian revolution. As Diplomatic Editor for the BBC's international television news channel BBC World, he interprets international affairs from London and travels the globe regularly to report first-hand. In this chapter he considers the resentment that had built up around American foreign policy, and the background to the events of September 11th.

The end of the Cold War left America bereft. For 40 years it had made an enemy of communism, creating certainty in an uncertain world. American presidents might worry about everything from nuclear Armageddon to civil war in Angola, but they had no need to consider their global aims. They had to contain communism, which in practice meant the Soviet Union.

These two superpowers – the Americans and the Russians – made strangely symmetrical enemies. The Russians, like the Americans, fitted the world into an ideological frame. They both based their long-term strategy on belief: for the Americans it was democracy and capitalism, for the Russians it was communism. Both were prepared to take blows to their immediate interests to further what they believed was right. Both were big, powerful nations able to absorb setbacks. They were both intolerant of other nations that didn't share their objectives – but willing to overlook faults in those that did. They demanded their allies accept that they were inspired by the belief that their ideology would make the world a better place.

But with the end of communism the United States lost both a counter-balance and a justification. The strength and self-confidence that had been virtues during the Cold War were now portrayed as vices. Its enemies saw it as an over-bearing, clumsy giant, giddy with power. They expected it to protect the world but complained that it trampled on their ambitions.

It was a problem of perception as much as reality. But as the United States turned in on itself at the end of the Cold War it found neither the energy nor the interest in fighting to protect its image. After all, what did it matter?

It took the catastrophe of September 11th to show clearly how the seedbed of anti-Americanism could breed a fanaticism that ignored all moral restraint. It had delivered one blow of unbelievable proportions and might try to deliver more.

* * * * * *

Before September 11th the United States was deeply unpopular in the Arab world. The root cause of this was its support for Israel. Opinion polls taken among Palestinians show an over-whelming belief that the United States acted only to protect Israel. In April 2001 the Jerusalem Media and Communication Centre found that 95.3 per cent of Palestinians believed the United States was biased towards Israel; 2.5 per cent found it neutral; only 0.4 per cent thought it favoured Palestinians.

This attitude communicated itself throughout the Arab world, and the rage felt against Israel for its behaviour towards the Palestinians was easily transferred to the United States. In some countries, the government explicitly linked the two.

The Syrian Foreign Minister, Farouk al-Shara, complained in May 2001: 'Israel is using American weapons, or weapons it has bought with American money. The United States is fully responsible for the illegal and criminal use of US weapons against Arab citizens; whether they be Palestinians, Lebanese or Syrians.'

It was all too easy for the United States to ignore such

criticism from Syria, Iran and Iraq – all of which were hostile and stood accused of supporting terrorists. But their sentiments were widely heard, and widely supported, around the Middle East.

Even in countries whose governments were supportive of the United States, it was respectable to be suspicious or openly hostile to America. An editorial in the *Jordan Star* as Bill Clinton left office said, 'We loathed his Secretary of State Madeleine Albright... distrusted his personal envoy to the region, Dennis Ross, and derided Secretary of Defense, William Cohen.' The editorial was written, in January 2001, to praise President Clinton for the attention he had given the region. Too often America heard the praise but ignored the accompanying criticism.

In autumn 2000, after the start of the latest intifada, 20,000 Egyptians attempted to break through the frontier with Israel. They were driven back by Egyptian security forces using tear gas. They complained that Israel was killing Palestinian children and youths, and their slogans were aimed as much against the United States as Israel. Although Arab deaths were inflaming opinion, this was no sudden change of mood. At street level, attitudes towards America had been hardening for much of the previous decade.

Until now there had been a clear distinction between hostility towards US government policies, and a respect, even an affection, towards the American people. When the trial of the Lockerbie bombers was going on in February 2001, demonstrators in Tripoli, the Libyan capital, managed to chant 'down with America' while wishing individual foreign reporters 'welcome to our country'.

But after September 11th observers in Cairo and Beirut reported that, along with the genuine sympathy for the victims of the suicide attacks, there was a feeling that now the people of the United States knew what it felt like to be attacked by forces that couldn't be reasoned with.

* * * * * *

The United States had become accustomed to discontent and grumbling. It made decisions that affected the world; inevitably not everyone would approve or benefit. But what has been going on in the last ten years has been fundamentally different and more dangerous. The US approach to both Israel and Iraq has become locked into policies that alienated and angered swathes of Arab opinion. That anger has grown to the point where it may prevent the US carrying through its own policies.

The Arab nations have always been committed to the Palestinian cause, and the US support for Israel has been a constant source of tension. What's dangerous is the way US attitudes to the Middle East peace process have become fused in the Arab perception with its policies towards Iraq. America wants to keep them separate but Arab opinion sees them as one. As the policies lock together, change in either becomes increasingly difficult.

This conundrum was created by President Saddam Hussein of Iraq. He has worked to keep the two policies tied together, constantly broadcasting the same message: that by challenging the might of America he is fighting a battle on behalf of the Palestinians. After a decade of repetition, the message has stuck with many who've heard it.

At the end of the Gulf War, many of Iraq's neighbours privately wanted to see Saddam Hussein toppled. But without their public approval, US President George Bush Senior would not send forces further into Iraq. Western leaders believed the Iraqi regime would either collapse or reform under the weight of defeat. By all the rules Saddam Hussein was finished. His forces were impotent, his weapons systems were being dismantled, his economy fettered. The only rational course open to him was to rebuild under international supervision and emerge tamed, much as Germany and Japan had done after the Second World War.

But the Iraqi president had one weapon left, which he exploited ruthlessly. He let his population die and invited the world's media to watch. By refusing to co-operate with the United Nations, by refusing to buy food and medicine through their channels, he exposed his population to starvation and disease. As children died in their hundreds of thousands, the world watched in horror. And outrage spread through the Arab nations.

As this was beginning, the United States was making good on the implicit bargain involved in assembling the Gulf War coalition. It summoned a peace conference on the Middle East in Madrid. For the first time Israel and all its Arab neighbours sat down together and acknowledged each other; it marked a fundamental change. This ought to have neutralized the Arab–Israeli problem, and left Iraq isolated. But the way things developed, the Arabs were left with a greater sense of betrayal than ever, and doubly receptive to Iraq's constant propaganda.

The Madrid conference meant Israel's right to exist was no longer challenged. It was followed by a deal with the PLO, a peace treaty with Jordan and negotiations with Syria. The United States no longer needed to defend its protégé so fiercely. And yet it became, if anything, even more protective – defending not only Israel's security, but its right to follow any policy decided by a democratic majority.

Some Israeli politicians wanted to press on in their negotiations with the Palestinians, but were held back by Israeli public opinion. As long as the US stood squarely behind Israel, it was impossible to get a majority for the kind of concessions needed to satisfy the Palestinians. A vicious spiral back towards violence began. The negotiations ran into the sand. Extremists who wanted no accommodation gained ground.

Around the Arab world disillusion with America was growing. They believed the United States was backing Israel in blocking a peace settlement. It became harder for America to win support for any policy at all. Some governments didn't trust the US, others were reluctant to be seen supporting it. Certainly none of them was going to stand up in public and defend what it was doing.

And all the time Saddam Hussein continued to pump out his version of the truth. It continued for so long, so insidiously and so unchallenged that for many it became the truth. The

US, they heard, was against the Arab people – the suffering and deaths in Iraq and the suffering and deaths in Palestine proved it.

The festering stalemate over Iraq has been one of the most extraordinary failures of American (and British) foreign policy. For five years it has been clear that the attempt to force Saddam Hussein's hand by blockading his country would not succeed. The policy presupposed that either the Iraqi dictator cared for his people, or that they had the capacity to rise up and overthrow him. But he didn't and they couldn't. Instead he had a golden propaganda weapon which persuaded many Iraqis to support him, and turned many in the outside world against the United States.

Once it became clear that the old policy couldn't work, a new one was needed. Instead the US tried repeatedly to resuscitate the existing approach, even as report after report piled up documenting the humanitarian disaster going on inside Iraq. UNICEF estimated that half a million additional Iraqi children had died while sanctions were in force. No Arab understands how America could allow that to happen as the price of a policy which is demonstrably unsuccessful.

Undeniably the US was faced with a difficult choice. It believed, with good reason, that Saddam Hussein was a dangerous tyrant intent on developing a range of chemical, biological and nuclear weapons which he would be ready to use to extend his personal power. But it was unable to maintain international support for its policy to stop him.

* * * * * *

Throughout the 1990s the US had mostly taken a unilateralist approach to foreign affairs. It was used to getting its own way and was ill-equipped to make the concessions needed to build an international consensus; until now it had not needed to.

The United Nations was the obvious forum to work in – an imperfect and irritating place, but the only one equipped with the legal powers to legitimize major international campaigns.

However the UN had become caught up in American domestic politics and had been treated with almost open contempt. The US refused to pay its fees, and attacked its agencies. (It also used its veto to protect Israel from criticism, further angering the Arab bloc.) Many of the US complaints about the inertia, bureaucracy and expense of the UN were legitimate, but its approach damaged the UN's credibility and made it difficult to assemble support when America wanted it.

On one occasion when the Security Council was slow to pass a resolution the US wanted, the Chinese representative invoked the diplomatic fiction that he was waiting for instructions from his government. Madeleine Albright, at the time the US representative, handed over a mobile phone and told him to get in touch. The Chinese ambassador kept the phone for a polite period, and returned it ostentatiously unused, remarking that he still had not contacted his government. It was hard to imagine who was the most annoyed.

It was a time when America could afford to be irritated and not greatly care about a lack of results. Foreign policy was not high on the national agenda – there were no obvious threats to US interests and no votes in it. The defeat of President Bush so soon after his success in the Gulf War had shown that.

So American politicians became wary about their involvement in foreign affairs. They wanted to do good, but they wanted to do it on their own terms. They shied away from putting their citizens under the jurisdiction of international courts, or risking casualties to sustain other people's peace, or even limiting the US's right to lay landmines if that's what its generals wanted.

They could even argue that America's hard-nosed approach in Bosnia had ended the war there after years of muddled international interventions had failed.

But America's desire to enforce the rules, but not submit to them, irritated many around the world. US allies were no longer willing to take America's good faith on trust now that the Cold War was over.

Nobody had the capability to resist the world's sole super-power but the arrogance of the American approach caused resentment, and foot-dragging in the few cases where the US still needed to muster international support.

By the end of the decade, America's economic success made many of its leaders' public statements sound triumphalist. At the same time, the lengthy public debate about whether America was paying too much to international bodies such as the UN became petty. At one point the haggling was over $31 million, a sum that the American media tycoon Ted Turner eventually paid out of his own pocket. Small change for a billionaire should not hamper policy in the world's richest nation.

American presidents routinely justified US involvement in overseas missions by asserting that America was the world's leader – but the country seemed unable to accept that international stability was of enormous economic benefit to the US and its world trading position, and something that was worth paying for. The argument was rarely heard in public, and rarely made in the media which were devoting less and less space to international reporting.

America was still an enormous and beneficial presence in world affairs, but its image was poor. It appeared indecisive about what it was doing and uncertain about why. Lack of public knowledge hampered efforts to engage America in places where its weight would have made a major difference.

The worst example came in Rwanda. Without knowledge of what was going on, there was no public prod to politicians and they remained reluctant to invest their political capital in somebody else's war. Years later President Clinton apologized for not having 'fully appreciated...this unimaginable terror'.

Policy on Israel was also susceptible to domestic pressure. The Jerusalem Centre for Public Affairs estimated that in California, Pennsylvania and Florida there was a Jewish voting bloc with the potential to swing presidential elections. It also concluded that American Jews as a bloc were 'uniquely swayable', ready to put support for Israel above all other issues.

Overall, it was a time when foreign policy was ill-served

by America's belief in democracy and market forces. Without an overriding principle to guide it, foreign affairs drifted under the influence of cost-cutting and pressure groups.

Perhaps none of this would have mattered at any other time. There was no reason why America should assume responsibility for the world's problems, and it was not ignoble for a people who'd been in the front line of a global battle against communism to take a break. After a pause, and some political in-fighting in Washington, the United States could be expected to return to international politics with a new direction and refreshed policies.

But globalization, the new phenomenon that was generating such economic benefit for the United States, was also doing it enormous harm. The internet and the boom in other media carried America's influence around the world. However, it also boosted the influence of its opponents, who were reaching layers of society that hadn't previously had a voice in politics. And their attack on America's reputation was spreading faster than America could counter it.

Surprisingly, in this new century it was the United States that was being outpaced. America's politicians, so adept at projecting their image at home, had not discovered the need to guard the nation's image abroad.

The war against terrorism will provide – at the terrible price paid on September 11th – a new overarching purpose for American foreign policy. But it will need more than the traditional buttressing by diplomats and armed forces.

If the United States is to employ its great power and global reach, it must convince not just the leaders, but the populations of other countries that it is right. It will need to mobilize their minds.

CHAPTER FOUR

THE MIND OF THE TERRORIST
Fergal Keane

Fergal Keane has reported from some of the world's worst trouble spots since joining the BBC ten years ago from the Irish national broadcasting service RTE. As, successively, Northern Ireland, Southern Africa and Asia Correspondent, he has witnessed death and destruction and people's terror and suffering in many forms. His hard-hitting, often moving reports have touched a particular human chord with viewers, listeners and readers. Here Fergal writes about the different forms of terrorism that he has observed, and analyzes this latest manifestation.

'The heart fed on fantasy, grown brutal from the fare.'
W B YEATS

William Butler Yeats wrote his lines in the bitter context of Ireland's Civil War. I was thinking of them in October as I stood in a crowded stadium in Quetta, Pakistan, listening to one speaker after another denounce the evils of the United States. I was surrounded by young men waving posters of Osama bin Laden and screaming 'death to America'.

I approached a man holding a boy – I guessed his age to be about twelve – and asked if he agreed with the message.

'Most certainly I do and I am teaching him that it is his responsibility to follow the road of jihad.'

Didn't he worry about teaching a child to hate?

'Well, yes of course it is wrong to hate, but in this case it is right.'

This was a man convulsed by violent rage against a country he did not know, except in the cartoon simplicities peddled by the fundamentalists on the platform. What he had been told –

that America was responsible for all the evils in the world – was enough for him to fill his son's mind with hatred, and prepare the boy for jihad. He was not exaggerating. I absolutely believed it was his intention and that of many fathers holding the hands of young boys in that crowd. Abandoned to the passion of the crowd and the comfort of its boisterous solidarity, the mind is swept along a narrow, dark corridor.

There is no prototypical terrorist mind, but there are certainly profound similarities in the make-up and behaviour of many who use terror as a political weapon. I want to explore a number of common influences in the lives of those we call 'terrorist'. Chief among these are the power of simplistic mythologies/ideologies in providing the necessary justification for acts of terror, and the childhood circumstances of the terrorist.

Of course, not all those who become terrorists will have had sad or brutal upbringings. But those who become notorious for their indifference to human suffering are quite often those who have emerged from strange and alienated backgrounds – not necessarily brutal in a physical sense, but damaged in deep ways.

At the outset it is important to make a clear differentiation. There are terrorist foot soldiers and there are the masters of terror. The purpose of this essay is to examine how the big figures, men like Osama bin Laden, are themselves shaped, and in turn shape others. There is a great deal of nihilistic rage floating around in our world, but it takes a person of certain charisma and dedication to shape it into something tangibly threatening. Bin Laden is such a person and he has been helped greatly by history – both the real and imagined history of his region and times.

*　*　*　*　*　*

'The heart fed on fantasy, grown brutal from the fare.' Yeats knew well what he was describing. He was writing in a country that had just experienced the first war of terrorism and counter-terrorism of the twentieth century. From his lonely tower in the County Clare countryside he looked out on a landscape ravaged by two years of savage conflict: assassination, reprisal, house burning, ethnic cleansing. The tactics adopted by the IRA guerrillas of that period would be studied, adopted and adapted by insurrectionary armies across the world as the process of decolonization accelerated. The conflict was watched by the leaders of Arab nationalist groups as well as by members of the Zionist movement planning for the end of British rule in Palestine.

What Yeats referred to was the power of mythology in the shaping of the terrorist's consciousness. To be capable of sustaining a savage war against the enemy, to be able to subject him and his loved ones to a relentless campaign of terror – a war in which the normal rules, the concept of a 'warrior's honour' are abandoned – it is necessary to narrow the mind, make it subject to a very limited range of ideas and influences. So the mythology of a uniquely evil and perfidious Albion became the defining orthodoxy of the gunmen and bombers of Ireland's Troubles.

Just as Osama bin Laden summons up memories of centuries of infidel treachery and oppression to infuse his warriors with passion, so the mind of the average IRA gunman in 1922 was filled with deeply hostile impressions of British culture, frequently encouraged by members of a religious order. The Catholic Church hierarchy – official faith, if you like – condemned the IRA and threatened excommunication of its members. But the view of many local priests was a great deal more sympathetic, and members of the Christian Brothers encouraged a fiercely anti-British line. In a sense they might be compared to the radical mullahs of Islam, in that they combined a conservative religious view with a militant hatred of the imperial presence and its cultural influences.

The nature of the links between the two nations – economic and cultural – ensured that such a one-dimensional picture was ultimately unsustainable, but for a period of some years it was the dominant orthodoxy and elements remain until this day. For terrorism to succeed it demands firstly a rigid adherence to a simple idea. The mind that questions, debates, opens itself to challenging ideas, will prove a source of division for a terrorist movement in the heat of battle. 'There will be time for debate later' is the refrain. Very often the 'debate' takes the form of murderous feuding as one terrorist faction attacks the other for its betrayal of principle.

Sticking to a rigid orthodoxy offers security and justification to people committing acts of terror. In the mind of Osama bin Laden there is no ambivalence about who represents the 'enemy'. Anybody who disagrees with him or who belongs to the infidel countries of the West is a potential victim.

In the Ireland of the 1920–1 period you were either with or against the IRA. The idea that England was the source of all Ireland's troubles, and that all who supported the Crown presence in Ireland were the enemy, allowed the guerrillas of 1921–2 vast latitude in their choice of targets. Consider one murder in my father's home town in 1921.

The village policeman went home for lunch at the same time every day. On Fridays he always had his small boy with him. The child would go to the barracks with his father in the morning and be taken home to his mother at lunchtime. Their slow procession, hand in hand, was one of those sights recognized by every person who lived on the street; they were part of the town's daily narrative, nodded to and saluted in the easygoing manner of country people.

On a September afternoon the policeman took his son by the hand and walked down Church Street. He paused to talk to a local farmer. They stood outside the house of Hannah and William Keane, my grandparents. The conversation was being observed from a lane opposite. As soon as the policeman paused, the watcher walked out and turned right down the street.

His move was a signal for two men who had been looking out the window of Kielys pub, further down the street and out of sight of the policeman. When the watcher walked past they knew the policeman was coming. The two men left the pub and crossed the road, walking the short distance to where the policeman stood talking. As they drew abreast of him they both pulled revolvers out of their coats and pointed them at the policeman. The recorded history does not describe the reaction of the five-year-old boy to this turn of events.

The men opened fire at point blank range and killed District Inspector Tobias O'Sullivan. Watched by his small son, he fell and bled to the death on the street outside my grandparents' house. The men who killed him fled and were never brought to justice. Indeed they were protected by the local community and in later years revered as heroes of Ireland's struggle for independence from British rule.

They were terrorists. They were also comrades-in-arms of my grand-uncle. I do not know if he had any part in the planning of the operation but as one of the leaders of the local IRA he was almost certainly aware of it. My paternal grandmother smuggled weapons for the IRA and passed on intelligence to its hit squads. I have no doubt she did so from an absolute conviction that the cause was just, and killing in its name – an act against the faith in which she had been raised – would somehow be understood by her God. As a child I was regaled with stories of the Old IRA (so named to differentiate it from the Provisionals who were then just accelerating their campaign of bombing and shooting in the north of the island).

On visits to my grandparents' home and the farms in the locality I met many men who had been 'out', i.e. on active service, in the Troubles of 1921–2. My grand-uncle I remember as a gentle and white-haired old man, caring for his cattle and always ready with an ice-cream sixpence for visiting children. I did not know then that he had been a ruthless and dedicated enemy of the police, the British army and anybody who collaborated with them. The version of history I was handed down emphasized the manly and honourable nature of our warriors, and relentlessly demonized the British. It was nonsense. But the adherence to this myth enabled men to kill without mercy and to justify their actions to future generations.

True, the 'Black and Tans' and Auxiliaries – British irregular forces – sent to Ireland by David Lloyd George had a well-earned reputation for brutality. But their enemies in the IRA were fierce and ruthless killers. And in the Civil War that followed, the violence inflicted by Irish men on each other surpassed in horror anything experienced at the hands of the British.

To survive, terrorism needs a constituency of psychological approval. That is the lesson of the last 30 years in Ireland and it is equally the lesson of the violence inflicted on America. Very occasionally a lone maniac or a small group – witness Timothy McVeigh or the Unabomber – will terrorize society as part of a politically motivated struggle. But they act outside any kind of political mainstream and are relatively easily contained. McVeigh's crusade against federal government was based on paranoid fears that had little resonance for the mass of Americans. For groups like the IRA and the terrorists of the Al-Qaida network there is a much broader community of acceptance.

For the most part people will avoid outright expressions of support for the September 11th terrorist attacks, but the 'Americans know how we feel now' school of thought reminded this writer of the 'sneaking regarders' who nodded smugly to themselves every time a British soldier was blown to pieces in Northern Ireland.

The IRA and Al-Qaida both drew their support from deeply held grievances on the part of a critical mass of people. Just as the Catholics nurtured deep grievances against Protestant rule in Ulster, the people for whom bin Laden has become a hero feel a sense of outrage at US foreign policy and the governments it supports in the Middle East.

But there is more to bin Laden's vendetta than rage over American foreign policy, or Israel's occupation of Palestinian lands. While most terrorists feel passionately about a political or religious cause, many of the more extreme are likely to be motivated by the memory of personal slights or humiliations, or the experience of a particularly brutal upbringing.

In the case of Osama bin Laden there is no obvious rationalization of this kind: he was the product of privilege and his earlier years were spent at play among the spoiled princelings of the Gulf states and the Arab diaspora.

Is it too much to speculate that at least part of his hatred of modernity is a hatred of his own background and upbringing, in a very real sense a hatred of part of himself? History has produced many such revolutionaries, men and women whose zeal for their adopted cause outshines that of the most passionate grassroots adherents. Irish republicanism has bred a line of wealthy and educated men – Wolfe Tone and Robert Emmet for example – who took up the cause of the Irish peasantry and ultimately became martyrs. In modern times we can look to the example of a man like Joe Slovo, a white lawyer who might have enjoyed a wealthy lifestyle in apartheid South Africa but who became a military commander dedicated to destroying that society.

But the examples of Irish Republicans and of Joe Slovo differ from bin Laden in two critical respects: unlike the men I have named, bin Laden has no idea of negotiation or compromise. And he is unwilling to recognize any differentiation between combatant and civilian. To do so would render his mind open to compassion. Once the merest hint of pity is admitted, the entire project is undermined.

The problem – for all of us – is that bin Laden is not an isolated fanatic. And for all the ardent protestations of the allied leadership that he does not represent Islam, we must accept that he represents many Muslims. Certainly he distorts the message in a murderous fashion, but a substantial minority of Muslims are willing at least to endorse his world-view. How often did I hear on the streets of Quetta the argument: 'I condemn terrorism but Osama is right about the Americans.'

Most of the people who demonize America and Western values will not become terrorist supporters, but a crucial minority will take further steps, out of the community of acceptance and into that of involvement. They may become active terrorists, they could end up providing funding and safe houses, or they will provide a vocal moral constituency that enables the likes of bin Laden to claim (however erroneously) to be acting for the oppressed of the Islamic world.

It is this last category that one sees crowding stadiums in Pakistani cities like Quetta and Peshawar, or taking to the streets of Jakarta. To the mind of a man obsessed with enemies and their destruction, nothing can be more comforting than the evidence that he and his followers are not lone fanatics, a pathetic minority.

This is by no means to suggest that many millions of Muslims do not have honestly felt and reasonably argued views about US policy in the Middle East. But these are in a different category, a place of passionate but rational argument; these minds do not need to see the destruction of the 'other' in order to feel secure in their own beliefs. A Palestinian like Hanan Ashrawi who has suffered the humiliations of Israeli occupation is still capable of promoting dialogue; bin Laden, who has never suffered any privation that he did not himself choose, would regard such a person as a traitor.

We are wrong to perceive bin Laden's suicide squads as evidence of true belief. I would argue that they represent the opposite, a retreat from the complexities that might challenge dogma and shine light into the dark corridor. For a belief to mean anything it must be tested by argument. Those who have ever had the misfortune to argue with a religious fundamentalist of any kind will know that fear always coils in the heart of apparent certainty.

Suicide bombing – the cult of murderous martyrdom – is an old phenomenon. Bin Laden and his acolytes have taken it to a new level, but they are not the first to use this terrible weapon. The Japanese kamikaze pilots of the Second World War were accorded national adulation and are still described in romantic, mythological terms. To this day one can visit museums in Japan celebrating the glory of 'The Divine Wind'; in no sense is the notion of suicide bombing described as a psychological tragedy.

In Sri Lanka I have interviewed leaders of the Tamil Tigers who are happy to justify the use of human beings as bombs and

who are utterly unconcerned with the devastating consequences of their actions. One of my most vivid memories of my
time as BBC Asia Correspondent was arriving on the scene of a
bombing at the same time as the police. The tableau of ruined
humanity spread across the street was quite impossible to
describe. The bombers and the men who sent them on their
mission were 'true believers' – they did not allow ideas of compassion or humanity, for themselves or their victims, to intrude
into the dark corridor of the terrorist mind.

So it would be wrong to interpret the case of Al-Qaida as
an isolated psychological phenomenon. What differs is the scale
of their atrocity and the use of violence as a 'holy' end in itself.
Simply by inflicting pain the terrorist achieves his goal. Here we
encounter the crucial psychological difference between the
terrorists of Al-Qaida and the IRA.

The IRA's constituency, for example, had no problem
accepting the idea of suicide as a political weapon. But the suicide in question was in the form of a hunger strike. Its purpose
was to act as a moral lever on the British government and, crit-
ically, death was not an absolute certainty. There was always the
hope that the government of Margaret Thatcher would relent
at the eleventh hour and save the hunger striker from death
by granting a series of concessions. The violence of Republican
terrorism may for a long period have been aimed at securing
utterly unrealistic concessions, such as British withdrawal from
Ulster, but from its outset it contained a shrewd political sensi-
bility. The IRA's suicide option directly prepared the way for
Sinn Fein's political strategy; the surge in electoral support that
came Sinn Fein's way after the Hunger Strikes was the launch
pad for the peace strategy that led ultimately to ceasefire and
power-sharing. The IRA's support base would never have tolerated suicide bombings.

I have often tried to analyse why Western terror groups
such as the IRA or Baader-Meinhof have never embraced suicide
attacks. It is difficult to do so without appearing to adopt an attitude of Western cultural superiority. But perhaps part of the
reason must be a very different understanding of the concept of

an afterlife. Those citizens of Western societies who have a religious faith (and those who don't) appear content to make their heaven or hell on earth. They don't believe in placing all their bets on an afterlife that cannot be scientifically proved to exist. To put it in cruder terms: IRA men might believe in heaven, but they aren't willing to bet their lives on getting there by blowing themselves up. The men of Al-Qaida believe absolutely in paradise after death.

It has frequently been suggested that the misery of refugee camps and slums has created a generation for whom the laying down of their life is no great tragedy. In other words, what comes in the afterlife must surely be better than the filthy settlements of Gaza or Bourj el Barajneh. If that were the case, can anybody explain why Afghanistan itself, the most miserable and brutalized country in the world, has not produced a culture of suicide bombing? Or why millions of oppressed people throughout the developing world have not embarked on suicide campaigns? Only a minority of the world's oppressed and those who claim to act on their behalf regard the use of suicide bombing as a legitimate weapon.

Although the promise of a heavenly paradise applies only to the suicide bomber himself, he is willing to ruin the lives of many others on his journey. At the heart of this culture is a narcissistic cruelty, reinforced by a high degree of religious and social acceptance.

As I've said, poverty and oppression are often advanced as explanatory factors. But they do not explain why a group of essentially middle-class Arab men would embark on the biggest suicide mission in history. It is the difference between an admittedly ruthless but ultimately pragmatic psychology, and what the historian Michael Ignatieff has called the 'apocalyptic nihilism' of men with no political programme, only a desire for the destruction of their enemies in a war blessed by God.

What unites these educated men with the semi-literate boys from the desert wastes of Pakistan is the charisma of the warrior–prophet bin Laden. To them he is a military/religious superstar.

He teaches them that the mind of the new 'super terrorist' must be immune to pity and need not be concerned with political compromise or worries about the taking of human life. For, despite the horrors of the IRA campaign and that of groups like ETA, the terrorist groups which evolved in the 1970s did not set out to maximize civilian casualties. There was a general injunction against the deliberate slaughter of civilians. (There were a number of significant exceptions, including the attacks on Jewish civilians by radical Arab groups, and the bombing of Bologna railway station by right-wing extremists in August 1980, which killed 84 people and injured more than 200.) But in the world and words of bin Laden: 'In the name of retaliation there are no innocents.' He seeks a world rid of enemies, and in this sense he is not altogether different from the proponents of genocide. He does not seek an accommodation with his enemies but desires to kill them until they bend entirely to his will. Their surrender can never be anything but unconditional and involves a complete abandonment of their culture and beliefs in favour of absorption by his culture.

By any clinical definition this is psychopathic behaviour. It is no less than one man's vision for the control of human destiny. Yet the terrorists who followed bin Laden's call were not 'mad' in any popularly recognizable sense. They were educated and capable of studying and holding down jobs. They were able to present such a normal facade that their planning and preparation for the crime of the century went entirely unnoticed. Had they not come under the spell of bin Laden, would they ever have wreaked such havoc?

To borrow the words of Primo Levi, survivor of Auschwitz and greatest of all Holocaust chroniclers, the men who followed the suicidal call of bin Laden were held in thrall by a 'monster with beautiful words'. He offered a simple solution to the humiliation and sense of injustice that burned inside men like the suicide terrorist Mohammed Atta. In giving them a reason to live he had given them a reason to die, a cause and also a promise of paradise in the afterlife. The warriors of Al-Qaida are waging something entirely new: war without boundaries or end. Unlike the IRA or the Tamil Tigers or even Hamas, they have no real political programme.

The programme is hatred and this makes Al-Qaida a movement that is more psychological than religious or political. To be sure, the presence of American troops in Saudi Arabia, the continuation in power of a series of despotic Arab regimes in the Middle East and the relentless Israeli–Palestinian conflict provide fertile ground for recruiting angry young men. But it is what happens when they fall under the sway of bin Laden that brings us to the most useful – and for some probably very controversial – comparison.

No leader since Adolf Hitler has been so powerfully able to extend the reach of terror or to seduce so many with his 'beautiful words' and simple promises as bin Laden. The post-war communist world was a construct of fear; nobody could convincingly argue that the leaders of the Soviet Union or of Mao's China controlled their people with a seductive ideology or that they held as their ambition the terrorizing of the entire world. Certainly Mao tse-Tung attempted ideological seduction but the madness of the Cultural Revolution put paid to any illusions the Chinese might have had about his Utopian dream. The mass of the people of the communist world were cowed into terrorized ideological uniformity.

One must of course be careful with Hitler analogies. I have always despaired of those politicians who rushed to compare Saddam Hussein or Milosevic with Hitler. The comparisons were facile, with little regard for historical truth or objective reality, and elevated essentially minor despots to the role of global villains.

For a while Milosevic seduced the Serbs, but unlike Hitler and bin Laden he never believed his own words. Like Saddam he believed in power and patronage. Both men could (and Saddam still does) inspire and orchestrate terror. But their ambitions were limited; for all their destructive ability they were small-time players. They were paranoid and megalomaniacal but lacked any belief in a cause bigger than their own power and wealth.

Osama bin Laden is very different. He has forsaken wealth and power for an ecstasy of righteousness. Like Hitler he can present himself as a messiah for an oppressed people – the dispossessed and humiliated. There are oppressed citizens of the Islamic world who feel all of these things and believe that America, and the secular modernity it represents, are the root cause of all international evils. His movement belongs in an anti-rational universe, where emotion triumphs over reason, a world where anything is possible in the name of righteousness.

I mentioned at the outset the question of more personal influences, in particular the question of childhood and how it shapes the minds of terrorist leaders. In bin Laden's case there are no obvious signs of brutality or neglect. But, despite his family wealth and privilege, he was a comparatively lonely figure, the son of his father's seventh wife. She was a Syrian and so much an outsider that many in the family group called her the 'slave' wife. In many respects his adult life has been a succession of tests, as if he were proving to himself repeatedly the extent of his worth. It has also been a lesson in man trying to control his world.

Because we know so little about his childhood among the many wives and mothers, brothers and sisters and the distant father, an essential part of the picture is obscured. But he is far more than the product of simply political circumstances.

Bin Laden's ability to master immensely complicated financial dealings suggests a brain of considerable ability. But it is not intellect we are considering here but emotional security. That is the key to understanding and perhaps defeating bin Laden. Like Hitler he is rampant in advance, inducing terror by the mere whisper of his warrior's presence (that is precisely what he has been doing to Western society). But his fierce absolutism, his terror of compromise and his need to control a world that cannot be controlled will destroy him in the end. His actions have put him beyond negotiation, not that he has ever countenanced deal-making in any form. Nor are the means at his disposal infinite or the men he has raised as fighters supermen. They are mortals and he is no messiah.

Osama bin Laden is not some prophet who has walked out of a sun-blasted wilderness to lead the righteous to heaven. Nor, despite his own publicity, was he a great warrior leader in the jihad against the Russians. A courageous fighter yes, but no Saladin. When you think of the master-terrorist, think not of a mysterious and deadly figure lurking in some Afghan cave, but of a strange, isolated boy wandering the rooms of his father's mansion, never quite finding the one in which he truly belonged. Bin Laden is neither superman nor arch-devil. He is dangerous and disturbed, but very human. He is of our world and that is what has made him so frightening.

CHAPTER FIVE

INSIDE THE TERROR NETWORK

Gordon Corera

Gordon Corera is a foreign affairs reporter for the BBC's flagship morn-
ing radio programme Today. *He has reported from the US, Europe, the*
Middle East, Africa and Asia. Before that he was the US and World
Affairs Analyst for BBC News. In this chapter he draws together what
is known about Osama bin Laden and the Al-Qaida network.

The mountains of Afghanistan became the focal point for Al-Qaida on its creation more than two decades ago. The origins of the network lie in the years following the Soviet invasion of 1979 when around 35,000 Muslims from 40 countries came to fight in what became the first modern, global jihad.[1] Among those who found their vocation there was the young Osama bin Laden.

Bin Laden was born in 1957 in Saudi Arabia, the seventeenth son of Mohammed bin Laden, a Yemeni immigrant who became a billionaire by winning contracts from the Saudi government to refurbish the holy sites of Mecca and Medina. The young bin Laden fell under the influence of the Palestinian preacher Abdullah Azzam, a passionate advocate of the duty of Muslims to support brothers fighting against the Soviets. In the mid-1980s Azzam created the Office of Services, which recruited and trained Muslims from around the world to join that fight. Osama bin Laden soon showed his skills as an organizer, travelling widely to draw in recruits and funds for the cause, while also using his engineering skills to build and run training camps in Afghanistan and guesthouses in Peshawar, in

Pakistan. These relationships, built in the camps of Afghanistan and the streets of Peshawar, formed the heart of Al-Qaida.

From the late 1980s, as bin Laden began talking about expanding the struggle beyond Afghanistan, across the Middle East and against the West, he and Azzam moved apart. In 1989, as the Soviets withdrew, bin Laden and a small coterie founded Al-Qaida – 'The base'. According to some reports, the structure originated in the need to keep records so that it would be possible to stay in touch with the militants who passed through guesthouses on their way to fight.

Radicalized by their success in driving the Soviets out, veterans dispersed, and countries like Saudi Arabia, which had exported their own militants to fight in Afghanistan and financially supported the cause, suddenly found that the so-called 'Afghans' were returning home more zealous than ever. In some cases, such as Algeria and Egypt, veterans returned to form or reinvigorate groups which increasingly threatened the stability of regimes. With outposts as far away as New York, where around 200 'Afghans' based themselves, the Office of Services and other networks continued to play a key role after the war, maintaining the links that would come to form the global roots of the Al-Qaida network, providing it with a nucleus of hardened fighters.

Bin Laden himself returned to Saudi Arabia where he became increasingly critical of the conservative regime, which he saw as enriching itself at the expense of the people, and, as in Egypt, obstructing the Islamist cause. At this key moment came a pivotal development: US troops arrived in Saudi Arabia in response to Iraq's invasion of Kuwait in August 1990. Their presence near the holy sites of Mecca and Medina was seen by bin Laden as both a prop to the Saudi regime and, more importantly, an affront to Islam which had to be removed.

Since the 1970s, the growing influence of the West on the Arabian peninsula had become a source of discontent as the penetration of Western culture that accompanied the oil boom disrupted traditional Islamic culture, with little of the new wealth trickling down to ordinary people. Ideologically, in forming Al-Qaida, bin Laden drew on the Wahhabi branch of Islam which opposes modernization and calls on followers to live out and create a social order based solely on the teachings of the Koran – always ensuring that the faith is spreading and never retreating or giving up territory. This purist Islam, which has felt increasingly under threat from globalization and Western values, combined with the crucial new ingredient of Pan-Islamism propagated by preachers like Azzam and Sudan's Hasan Turabi. Following the failure of Pan-Arabism, nationalism and Marxism in the Middle East, the belief emerged that Muslims all over the world should be united under a single rule, a newly restored Islamic caliphate. Bin Laden was to become the global messenger for this new cause.

Increasingly concerned with his radicalism, in 1991 the Saudi regime pushed bin Laden out and into the arms of Sudan. Al-Qaida's headquarters in Khartoum were hardly secret – the office even had a receptionist to greet visitors and check their identification. Here, bin Laden set about creating a business network that could both generate money and act as a front for the continued training and building of a network of committed terrorists. Links were so close with Sudan that the President even issued a letter waiving customs dues and searches for Al-Qaida goods brought into the country.[2] A Congressional research report and a US government indictment have pointed to patronage of Al-Qaida from Pakistan and Iran – albeit through those countries' intelligence agencies and associated groups rather than the entire governments.[3]

The arrival of US forces in Somalia in December 1992 proved another pivotal moment. Al-Qaida saw the US intervention as the beginning of an attempt to exert influence throughout the Horn of Africa and even possibly to topple the government of nearby Sudan. As a result, Al-Qaida helped the Somali clans who were fighting US forces and took part in a battle in which 18 US troops were killed. These deaths caused the US to withdraw from Somalia, leading the militants to believe that simply by inflicting casualties they could easily expel the US military presence. Misreading the type of commitment Somalia represented, bin Laden called the US a 'paper tiger' and said he was surprised at the 'collapse'.[4]

By 1996, international pressure forced Al-Qaida out of Sudan, but it found a new home in Afghanistan, which had become the 'purest' Islamic state under the newly triumphant Taliban. In many ways Al-Qaida has been as much the sponsor of the Taliban as the Taliban have been of Al-Qaida, with bin Laden providing assistance to the Taliban's military campaign as well as helping to build roads and infrastructure. Al-Qaida also probably helped to assassinate the Taliban's chief opponent, General Massoud of the Northern Alliance, days before the September 11th attack.

In February 1998 an Arabic newspaper published a statement announcing the formation of the 'World Islamic Front for Jihad against Jews and the Crusaders', a new organization with Al-Qaida at its core. The statement remains its central call to arms and the best document for understanding its ideology.[5] It describes the presence of US troops in the Holy Land, the suffering inflicted on Iraq by sanctions, and the occupation of Jerusalem, as 'a clear declaration of war by the Americans against God, his prophet, and the Muslims'. It invokes its own interpretation of Islamic law to conclude that, 'To kill Americans and their allies is an individual duty of every Muslim who is able, in any country where this is possible'. Faced with the overwhelming military might of the United States, the only option they believed would work was terror.

* * * * * *

At the head of Al-Qaida, Osama bin Laden has been more of a symbol around which to draw Muslim support than some kind of all-powerful terrorist CEO who directs every operation. He may have had relatively little to do personally with the September 11th attacks, and over-emphasising his power risks misunderstanding his network and setting the wrong priorities in disrupting it. Many of the activities carried out under the banner of Al-Qaida are executed with only limited support from the centre, and around bin Laden are a small core of experienced terrorists, any one of whom could step into his shoes, even if they lack the dark charisma and global reputation that he has built up.

Directly below bin Laden is the majlis al shura or consultative council. The exact leadership is unknown but is thought to number between a dozen and twenty men, largely veteran leaders of the Afghan conflict of the 1980s. Only this group has a full understanding of overall operations. A key figure is Ayman al-Zawahari, bin Laden's right-hand man and the ideological force behind Al-Qaida. In many ways he is more experienced than bin Laden, but he merged a large part of his Egyptian Islamic jihad into Al-Qaida when he joined the broader Pan-Islamist campaign against the West. Another senior Al-Qaida member, who was put on the FBI's 'most wanted' list, was Mohammed Atef, a former Egyptian policeman turned military commander, thought to have been a key organizer of the September 11th attacks. The Taliban confirmed that Atef was killed by American bombing in mid-November. The US Treasury department also froze the assets of Abu Zubaydah, another key figure alleged to be involved in recruiting and maintaining contact with cells and groups around the world.

Below the council are four main committees, handling various activities. Membership of these committees overlaps and they should not be seen as part of some kind of formal bureaucracy. The religious committee justifies Al-Qaida's terrorist ideology and activities through the issue of fatwas – Islamic decrees; the military committee recruits and trains people for operations and plans attacks; the finance committee raises money and distributes it to militant groups and cells around the world; the media committee disseminates information.

Around the leadership and protecting the inner core is the 055 Brigade – a unit of seasoned international fighters, veterans of the first Afghan conflict, Bosnia and Chechnya, and numbering up to 5,000. A few groups were effectively absorbed into Al-Qaida itself in 1998 under the broader World Islamic Front for Jihad, and the backbone of the membership is drawn from Egypt (to the point where others have complained of its dominance) as well as Saudi Arabia and to a lesser extent Yemen and North Africa.

Until 1998, Osama bin Laden and his leadership were thought to live in a specially built cave near Jalalabad filled with weapons as well as a library and communications centre with computers, faxes and satellite phones. But after the US cruise missile attacks in 1998, the exact location, if there was any single location, remained unknown. Satellite phones were once bin Laden's preferred means of communication but these were easily monitored – the US National Security Agency (NSA) even played its visitors a tape of Osama bin Laden talking to his mother.[6] But once it was realized that the US was listening and could track locations, satellite phones were discarded in favour of a combination of very high-tech and low-tech means. Because of the loose structure of Al-Qaida, bin Laden has rarely had to communicate with anyone outside his inner circle of aides, largely using hand-delivered instructions that are passed on to senior military commanders and down through the chain to terrorist cells. On the high-tech side, Al-Qaida has begun to use encrypted e-mails which even the NSA has had trouble deciphering. 'We're behind the curve in keeping up with the global communications revolution,' NSA Director General Mike Hayden told CBS News.[7] Al-Qaida may also hide instructions in websites and even taped video broadcasts, and has become expert at spreading false information, with intelligence agencies struggling to pick out the useful information amid the ever-growing din of worldwide communication.

* * * * * *

Below the inner core is a diffuse, loose, compartmentalized net-work of often relatively self-contained cells or pre-existing militant groups that Osama bin Laden linked together. Rather than a bureaucratic hierarchical organization, it is a highly fluid network, flexible enough to work in different cultures and exploit globalization by operating in the gaps between national authorities in policing, finance and intelligence. Despite its image as a global terrorist network, Al-Qaida itself may only number a few thousand members, instead acting literally as a base or clearing house for militants, providing funding, training and members for other groups around the world. Al-Qaida activities have been uncovered everywhere from New Zealand to Thailand, Ecuador to Eritrea. Up to 30,000 trainees have passed through its camps and been sent to more than 50 countries. Many of these militants are not technically members of Al-Qaida, not having sworn the bayat, or oath of membership. But they are 'affiliated' members through their own home-grown radical groups, which are networked to Al-Qaida and can be called on if needed. 'Graduates' bring their new-found expertise and radicalism to the major Islamic insurgencies around the world, back into the Middle East and also deep into the heart of Europe and the United States. This makes characterizing the network a hard task, but it can be divided into a few broad categories.

There is an extremely close relationship, sometimes symbiotic, sometimes almost parasitic, with existing Islamic groups who are trying to overthrow the regimes in secular or conservative Muslim states such as Egypt, Algeria and Saudi Arabia. In Egypt, the links to Gamaya al Islamiya and Egyptian Islamic Jihad are longstanding. In the case of Algeria, Al-Qaida penetrated deep into the Armed Islamic Group GIA in the second half of the 1990s. Thanks to geography, there are close relations with groups fighting in Kashmir as well as the Islamic Movement of Uzbekistan.

Beyond that are the links to Muslim organizations battling for their own state. The relationship with the Palestinians is complex. Palestinians have their own militant groups with far deeper roots than Al-Qaida and focused much more tightly on opposition to Israel rather than Al-Qaida's anti-Americanism. Some Hamas figures also feel that bin Laden has used the Palestinian cause rhetorically but without providing much real assistance. In the case of Chechnya, exact figures are impossible to ascertain, but there are Arab fighters assisting the rebel force and Chechens are trained in Al-Qaida camps.

Further afield there is also support for Muslims perceived as being repressed around the world, including the Lashkar Jihad group in Indonesia, whose founder fought in Afghanistan alongside bin Laden. Its 10,000 members have campaigned to have Indonesia governed by Islamic law and fought Christians in the north-eastern islands.[8] In the early 1990s, Al-Qaida also seems to have operated in the Philippines, helping to set up Abu Sayaff, whose now-dead founder was an Afghan veteran linked to bin Laden.

* * * * * *

Activists are usually recruited informally, either in their own countries through existing networks and mosques, or selected while studying in places like Pakistan. Prime Minister Mahathir of Malaysia told the BBC of just such a group of Malaysian students, recruited in Pakistan, who then returned home to plan attacks on US facilities. The very success of Al-Qaida means it can work on a principle called 'attract and absorb', whereby militants even organize themselves and then contact Al-Qaida to request training. This is alleged to have been the case with former Boston taxi driver Raed Hijazi, who has been on trial in Jordan for trying to blow up a hotel and Christian sites there in December 1999. The relatively independent nature of activities is also sometimes reflected in their amateurishness, such as the attempt to blow up the USS *Sullivan*, which failed when a dinghy was so overloaded with explosives that it sank.

Amed Ressam was an Algerian who moved to Canada and was recruited through his local mosque as a potential terrorist. He was then sent to Afghanistan in 1998 for eight months of training by Abu Zubaydah before returning to Canada and eventually leading the attempt to bomb Los Angeles airport. Ressam and others have described the training received in the camps in some detail. It included learning how to mix together chemical compounds that could be spread through ventilation systems; how to attack power grids and railroads; surveillance procedures, assassination techniques and religious training.[9] Recruits who showed promise graduated to specialist schools for advanced training. Ressam also told the FBI about using syringes to inject dogs with cyanide, and US intelligence believes there have been attempts to experiment with chemical weapons at these camps. There were thought to be a dozen or more Al-Qaida camps across Afghanistan, with at least four devoted to training.

According to Ressam, with him at the camp were fighters from Jordan, Yemen, Saudi Arabia, Germany, France, Turkey, Chechnya and Sweden. Of 100 in the camp, 30 were Algerians who were going to be sent to the US and Europe. Recruits were also taught how to avoid detection by shaving beards, wearing the right clothes and not carrying books that would draw attention to them. Another Al-Qaida member testified that he was told to buy cologne and cigarettes because immigration officers would then not think that he was part of an Islamic group. Instead, 'you look like you are interested in women'.[10] Al-Qaida also produces a number of comprehensive terrorist manuals, some up to 1,000 pages long, which detail everything from how to forge documents and make booby traps, to how to fit into Western society. To do this, almost any compromise is permitted, except for 'drinking wine and fornicating'.[11]

Along with supporting and training existing militant groups, Al-Qaida also establishes 'sleeper' cells which are sent into countries and told to wait. They may spend years slowly working their way into a society before being activated for terror, as happened with the cell sent to Africa for the 1998 embassy bombings. It set up fishing and clothing companies as well as charities and aid agencies, waiting four years before being called to action. As the FBI writes, 'To the casual observer, these individuals would have appeared to live ordinary lives.'[12]

Different cells often carry out the surveillance, planning and execution of an attack, and, once activated, personnel may be sent in from outside the country to carry out the mission. In the case of the targeting of the USS *Cole* in 2000, two suicide bombers arrived in Yemen only a few days beforehand.

Al-Qaida compartmentalizes its activities carefully. Just one or two key organizers will be in contact with figures higher up the chain, and the members of different cells may not know each other or the full extent of any planned operation.

Before and after September 11th, a number of cells were discovered in Europe, and the links between them seem to reveal a far wider network, with arrests in the UK, Germany, France, the Netherlands, Belgium, Italy and Spain. London seems to have been a major base, with dissidents from Arab states maintaining a number of organizations with links to bin Laden, ranging from financial institutions to groups disseminating information and recruiting for Al-Qaida. Many of the European members were also recruited during visits to the UK.

Germany has been another hub, with Hamburg home to one cluster of militants, including the Egyptian Mohammed Atta, involved in planning September 11th. European agencies have uncovered other plans, including attacks on the European Parliament in Strasbourg and US embassies in Rome and Paris. Intercepts of phone calls show a cell in northern Italy boasting of its exploits in Chechnya and revealing its links with Germany, France, Spain, Belgium, the UK and the Netherlands. They talk of supporting other militants in Europe and Algeria by providing travel advice, and false passports and identity cards.[13]

Around the rest of Europe, North African immigrants have proved to be fertile ground for Al-Qaida, which largely operates through existing Algerian, Egyptian and Tunisian militant groups. Among younger, second-generation immigrants there are fewer links to their home countries and more commitment to the Pan-Islamist terrorism of bin Laden. Four thousand 'Arab' volunteers went to fight in the 1992–5 Bosnian war and around 400 stayed after it was over, forging links for future cells in Europe. A team of 50 Arab veterans of Bosnia is being run in the Balkans by the brother of bin Laden's deputy, Ayman al-Zawahari.[14]

Before September 11th, the US believed there were only a handful of poorly organized Al-Qaida cells in the country. 'We really didn't think we had much of an Al-Qaida presence here,' a former head of the FBI's National Security Division told the *Wall Street Journal*. Yet by the end of October more than 1,000 had been detained (though many may prove not to be linked to Al-Qaida).[15] As early as 1995, al-Zawahari travelled to the US to make connections and raise money, but, although they are sometimes referred to as 'sleeper cells', the terrorists who carried out the September 11th attack don't really fit the pattern. September 11th utilized far more accomplished terrorists than some earlier operations and must have been more tightly controlled. The core group of terrorists who entered the US and started taking flying lessons seem to have had the attack already at a planning stage, rather than entering as sleepers to be activated later. The background of these attackers completely contradicts previous perceptions – these were not the desperate young suicide bombers of Hamas but intelligent, often well-educated, middle-class men who could live normal lives and fit into Western society. Mohammed Atta was probably a key organizer on the ground, travelling widely around the US and Europe, co-ordinating with the other hijackers and acting as the contact for other Al-Qaida figures. These men were joined nearer the time of the operation by a group thought to have mainly come from Saudi Arabia whose job it was to control the passengers.

Sixteen of the nineteen entered the country legally, and the attacks exposed serious problems with the ability of the US both to keep undesirables out, and to find people once they got in. Two of the hijackers were already being sought at the time of the attack after being linked to Al-Qaida and the USS *Cole* attack through a meeting in Malaysia in January 2000, but it proved impossible to find them in time. A staggering 475 million people came into the US in 1999.[16] Al-Qaida has exploited the relaxation of border controls and fed off the darker side of globalization, the easy and often illegal movement of people and money and the rise of global communications. Without these, it would be impossible to run a dispersed network like Al-Qaida, and the very complexity of the world increases the difficulty for security and intelligence agencies in keeping track of the network and its activities.

* * * * * *

'Follow the money' – that has always been the advice for those on the trail of illicit activity, but unlike trans-national criminal networks, money is not the raison d'être of Al-Qaida, making it harder to buy people off and to trace its movements. Frequently only relatively small sums are involved – estimates of the cost of the September 11th operation range from $250,000 to $1 million. The Al-Qaida financial trail winds around the world, from the bazaars and back streets of South Asia to global banking centres like London, Frankfurt and New York, mixing legitimate and illegitimate funds and working through the underbelly of the globalized economy. The complex, multi-layered ability to both draw in and then spread money around the world is a central part of Al-Qaida's ability to wield its influence globally and yet also largely remain below the radar of government authorities. As with its global links to Islamic militancy, the finances of Al-Qaida reveal the breadth and depth of the organization around the world.

It is sometimes assumed that bin Laden is self-financing. Stories abound of his inheriting up to $300 million. Even if the figure were that high, he is unlikely to have kept his hands on much of it, since the Saudi authorities began freezing his assets. However, his family funds did provide him in the early days with the ability to establish himself in Afghanistan and in militant circles through acts of generosity, and to begin the building of a global network which could eventually become self-financing.

In Sudan, bin Laden developed a network of largely legitimate domestic and international businesses – holding companies, import-export, currency trading, construction as well as farms. These could generate legitimate income, produce funds for other Islamic groups to win their support, as well as provide cover for terrorist camps and the importation of weapons. The business empire – until the post-September 11th crackdown – was reported to produce and export everything from ostriches to lemons, honey to diamonds.

Wealthy individuals in the Gulf have also provided larger lump sums direct to Al-Qaida and one of the sources bin Laden milked most successfully has been Islamic charities. Money is raised at mosques when the faithful are asked to dig deep into their pockets to help support Muslim brothers suffering in far-off lands: Afghanistan, Bosnia, Chechnya or Kashmir. Most of the money will reach genuine charities for humanitarian aid but some of it has been diverted, either knowingly or unknowingly, to Al-Qaida. Charities help build support bases among the destitute around the world by providing medical relief and religious services which in turn can be infiltrated and used by Al-Qaida.[17] Monitoring and regulating these charities is deeply problematic as many of the suspect organizations also do legitimate work and as a whole these groups form an integral part of the fabric of society in most Muslim countries. A glimpse of the problem came when the Rabita Trust, a well-established group with Pakistan's president on its board, was for a time included on the US list of suspect organizations.[18]

In moving the money, as with moving people, Al-Qaida has worked in the shadows of an increasingly globalized world, building up a vast spread of front companies, false identities and bank accounts across Europe, Asia and the Middle East. Poor disclosure rules are exploited, although in many instances suitcases stuffed with cash are the simplest method. One of the ways in which Al-Qaida has escaped detection is by raising and moving money around the world, using transfers so small that they go unnoticed and are hard for banking and intelligence agencies to track – usually under $10,000, the threshold where authorities start to get interested. In South Asia, the underground 'hawala' banking system, used by immigrants to send money to their families back home, has been exploited by terrorists. With outlets as far away as the US and UK, it leaves no paper trail and billions of dollars flow through the system each year.

Profits from legitimate and illegitimate activities alike are moved through Middle Eastern and then Western banking systems, making the trail horrendously complex for authorities to follow as it becomes lost in the whirlpool of the world's massive financial system. In 2000, there were almost six billion banking transfers in the United Kingdom alone, and 18,500 of these were reported as suspicious. The intricate, global financial architecture that Al-Qaida established over a decade or so is hard to detect and disrupt by traditional tools of financial law enforcement. Trying to stop the money would involve going to the heart of banking and finance in many Gulf states, as well as imposing regulations that would risk strangling the global financial system.

On the ground, Al-Qaida cells survive on cheap hotels and petty crime, making them largely self-financing; they generally receive only small sums from abroad. Everywhere Al-Qaida established cells the members were told to build up their own businesses, both to generate cash and to provide a cover for them to live under. While cash can be requested, smaller, relatively independent cells like those broken up in Canada, Europe and Jordan are effectively left to fend for themselves and become involved in credit card fraud, forgery and bank robberies to raise funds. Bigger operations receive cash infusions from the centre. For September 11th there was a series of $100,000 transfers to Mohammed Atta followed by smaller amounts. They almost certainly came from Mustafa Ahmed, whom US investigators believe to be the chief financier of the operation. Atta then returned the unused cash just before the attack.

* * * * * *

In the days after the bombing campaign against Afghanistan began, thousands of multicoloured posters of Osama bin Laden appeared across the Muslim world. In Bangladesh, for instance, audio cassettes of his speeches, sermons and statements went on sale for 60 cents, translated into Urdu, Hindi and Bengali. Calling for a global jihad, these tapes are played in public places like bazaars, railway stations and bus terminals, attracting huge crowds.[19] One of the ways in which Al-Qaida has grown into a global network has been to become a beacon for radical Muslims around the world – a base around which all those opposed to the US could gather. Bin Laden's most significant role has probably been in shifting militancy from a national to a Pan-Islamic sphere. The more spectacular the attacks, the more devastating the response and the greater the demonization of the man behind them, the more militants seem drawn towards bin Laden as a symbol of resistance to the West.

The compartmentalized, loose-knit nature of the network means that breaking up individual cells may have only a limited effect on the operation of other groups or the network as a whole. The only way to disrupt Al-Qaida is either by infiltrating its core – almost impossible since at the centre is a highly committed, ideological group – or by destroying the entire leadership. Below that head is a body that reaches deep into the Islamic world and also into the heart of the West, from Sacramento to Saudi Arabia, ranging from fully signed-up members to those who may be supporting Al-Qaida without even knowing it. And there is also a vast pool of potential supporters, unhappy with the economic and social dysfunction of their nations, alienated by globalization and modernization, and humiliated by American power. In many Muslim countries, support for bin Laden, while often passive, comes from all levels of society, and Western nations have also been faced with members of their own Muslim communities travelling to Afghanistan to fight.

Although for bin Laden the battle had been going on for years, the September 11th attacks were a major escalation and almost certainly part of a more ambitious plan, based on drawing the US into something that could be portrayed as a war against Islam. In turn, bin Laden's hope was that this could create a new tide of militancy across the Islamic world, overthrowing conservative or secular regimes and ejecting the US from the Middle East, thereby cementing his own role as the figurehead for a new global jihad.

1   'The Taliban: Exporting Extremism', Ahmed Rashid, *Foreign Affairs*, November/December 1999.

2   Testimony of Jamal Al-Fadl in the trial of the Embassy bombers. This is available online at www.findlaw.com/legalnews/us/terrorism/cases.html

3   'Terrorist: Near Eastern Groups and State Sponsors', *Congressional Research Service Report*, September 10th 2001 (the 1998 US government indictment of bin Laden and June 2001 US Grand Jury indictment regarding the 1996 Khobar attack).

4   Bin Laden interview with Robert Fisk, *Independent*, March 22nd 1997.

5   'License to Kill', Bernard Lewis, *Foreign Affairs*, November/December 1998.

6   James Bamford, *Body of Secrets*, Century Books.

7   Interview with CBS, '60 Minutes II', February 12th 2001.

8   'Islam's Holy Warriors', *Far Eastern Economic Review*, April 26th 2001.

9   *Los Angeles Times*, July 4th and September 28th 2001; 'Tactical Insights from the Trial', *Jane's Intelligence Review*, August 1st 2001.

10   Al-Fadl testimony.

11   *Daily Telegraph*, September 21st 2001; *New York Times*, October 28th 2001.

12   Extracted from a declassified FBI report, available on the web at www.pbs.org/wgbh/pages/frontline/shows/binladen/bombings/ summary.html

13   'Arrested Italian Cell sheds light on Bin Laden's European Network', *Center for Public Integrity*, posted online at www.publicintegrity.org October 3rd 2001; 'Italian Tapes Portray Young Arabs Operating on the Edges of Islamic Terror', *New York Times*, October 29th 2001.

14   'Al-Qaida terrorists have positioned themselves on Skopska Crna Gora', *Dnevnik* (Macedonian newspaper), October 19th 2001, sourced by BBC monitoring.

15   'FBI's Biggest Worry: More Al-Qaida cells based in the US', *Wall Street Journal*, October 11th 2001.

16   'Figures from Beyond Border Control', Stephen Flynn, *Foreign Affairs*, November/December 2000.

17   Taken from the testimony of Jimmy Gurule (Under-secretary for Enforcement at the US Treasury) before the House Committee on Financial Services, October 3rd 2001.

18   'Gearing Up for a Shadow Struggle', *Newsweek*, October 8th 2001; *Jane's Intelligence Review*, November 2001.

19   *Dainik Janakantha* (Bangladeshi newspaper), October 18th 2001, translated by BBC Monitoring.

CHAPTER SIX

WASHINGTON READIES FOR WAR

Paul Reynolds

Paul Reynolds was Washington Correspondent for the BBC from 1998 to 2001. He began his career as a foreign correspondent in New York, reporting on the Carter presidency, the Iran hostage crisis and Ronald Reagan's election victory. He then served in Brussels, Jerusalem and London, where he specialized in international affairs as the BBC's Diplomatic Correspondent. His chapter examines the decision-making process in the early days of the Bush War Cabinet.

George W Bush, president for less than eight months, and only after a contested result, had just got out of his car at the Booker Elementary School in Sarasota, Florida. He was there for a visit to give substance to one of the most effective, if unrealistic, lines from his campaign speeches that 'no child will be left behind'. As he was shaking hands with the welcoming party, his Chief of Staff, Andrew Card, told him that a plane had crashed into one of the towers of the World Trade Center. Bush carried on. A presidential event does not get called off without good reason and at that moment there was no good reason, because there was no good information. He went into a classroom where the children were doing a reading exercise. Then Card approached him and whispered that a second plane had crashed into the second tower. Bush's pursed lips were captured by a photographer. America the beautiful had become America the vulnerable.

He waited until the children had finished, then went into a next door room where the Secret Service had set up their communications. He spoke first to Vice President Dick Cheney, who was in the White House; his next call was to the recently appointed Director of the FBI, Robert S Mueller. Then he turned to his staff and said, 'We're at war'. From that moment, what might have been treated as a crime was a *causus belli*. It determined the whole strategy. A statement was quickly drafted. The President would have to say something. He did, but it did not meet the need. He referred to the perpetrators of a catastrophe that millions were already watching on television as 'folks'. Bush's levity of language had let him down again. Then he announced that he was returning to Washington. But he didn't. It was the start of a difficult day for George Bush as he struggled to make his impact when the country turned its eyes to him.

Was Bush up to it? To foes, he was shallow and erratic. He had ridden to power on his name. He had squandered the budget surplus with a tax cut that favoured the rich, and had threatened the world both with environmental disaster, through his abrupt rejection of the Kyoto treaty to reduce greenhouse gases, and with nuclear proliferation, by a pointless pursuit of missile defence. To friends, he had character and principles. He had been a good governor of Texas, and had shown steel when his election campaign had wobbled under challenge from Senator John McCain. In rejecting Kyoto, they said, he had done no more than the Senate, which had already voted against it in principle. And, in so doing, he had demonstrated that he wasn't going to make the mistake of his father, who had neglected domestic policy in favour of foreign. Missile defence, they added, was just that, not a threat to anyone. If he found the right issue, a clear-cut one, he would make a good president.

George Bush has a personal effect on many of the people who meet him. They discover a man smarter than he appears on television. His language is not so disjointed when he talks in private. He has a Texan directness. He pauses between sentences, looking you in the eye. In late October 1998, when he was cruising to re-election as Texas governor, George Bush nibbled fresh popcorn as his bus wound its way around the Houston suburbs. Certain phrases stood out from his conversation, pointers to the future: 'I am a uniter not a divider' and

'I know how to set an agenda and get a strong team around me'. His views of the world outside America seem to have been inherited from his father ('I bought into the whole NATO thing'), with a Republican belief that the American armed forces were not there to carry out humanitarian missions but to be held in readiness to come to the rescue of global order. However, he had the advantage over Bush Senior in being less of the patrician and more of the politician. He saw what mattered most to Americans. He was not an isolationist but he was something of a unilateralist. And another thing was obvious. Although a committed, indeed a born-again, Christian who had not taken a drink for 12 years (and had been faithful to his wife, he told me, unasked), he was no bigot. He was certainly always underestimated. His first opponent for the Texas governorship, Anne Richards, dismissed him as 'Shrub'. She lost.

In November 1990, in Clinton, Iowa, he made a foreign policy speech to try to fill in one of the gaps in his presidential candidacy. It was just after a disastrous interview with a Boston TV station in which he had been asked to name a number of second- or third-rank world leaders with whom he might have to deal as president. His answers were ignorant yet offhand. He was asked who was the leader of Pakistan. The nearest Bush got to that answer was 'General', said with a smirk which at times is his undoing. General Pervez Musharraf was a man he would get to know rather better one day. But I found that he shrugged off that damaging television encounter. The time would come when he needed to know the names, he said, and Americans did not mind a bit of ignorance about foreigners anyway. He and they proved remarkably ignorant about Osama bin Laden.

As Air Force One took off from Florida at 9.45 a.m. that September 11th morning, George Bush was confused, like most Americans. Vice President Dick Cheney at the White House knew far more than he did. And Cheney was telling the President not to come back to Washington. The Pentagon had been hit. The White House had been evacuated. Cheney himself had been hustled down into a bunker, his legs almost lifted off the ground by anxious agents. A fourth hijacked plane was heading for Washington, and, it was feared, the White House or the Capitol building. This turned out to be the plane that crashed in open country in Pennsylvania. At some stage, Cheney proposed, and Bush approved, the formerly unthinkable but now prudent order that it should be shot down if necessary. A fighter pilot, scrambled from Langley, Virginia, too late to intervene over the Pentagon, was then told to 'save the White House at all costs'. The fourth plane might equally have been heading for the CIA, across the river in Virginia; a plot discovered in the Philippines in 1995 had targeted the Agency with a hijacked plane. But nobody knew. It was all too dangerous and chaotic. Washington, the capital of the New World Order, was deserted by early afternoon. Children were sent home early. One mother in Maryland had been working in her basement and had not known of the disasters. She found out only when she wondered why her children were back at an unusual hour. Fighters were on combat air patrol and could be heard in the silence of the streets.

Air Force One headed high up into the clouds to get fighter escort because a new threat had come, to the plane and President. Or at least, it seemed that way at the time. All that had happened, it later turned out, was that someone had phoned in a threat saying that Air Force One would be 'next'. This was passed up the chain, hardening up as it went. Bush was frustrated. If he couldn't return to Washington, he suggested to Cheney, what about Camp David? Cheney was opposed. Air Force One landed at Barksdale Air Force base in northern Louisiana instead. Soldiers surrounded the plane. The base commander wore a sidearm. The President was put into an armoured Humvee, complaining, in 'salty' terms, according to his aide Karl Rove, that he should be going to Washington. Another call to Cheney. Planes were still over the Atlantic, still a risk. Bush wanted a National Security Council conference. Cheney, the old Defense Secretary, suggested doing it from Offutt Air Force base in Nebraska, headquarters of the Strategic Air Command, with secure communications. So AF1 took off again. Nicholas Lemann, a reporter for the *New Yorker*, remarked later that the information available to the administration was worse, or no better, than that available to the television viewer.

At four o'clock that afternoon, eastern time, Bush held his conference call from Nebraska and decided to return to the White House anyway. 'I don't want some tinhorn terrorist keeping the President of the United States out of Washington,' he said with finality and a flash of the Texas vernacular that would catch the public mood over the coming days. There would be criticism of Bush for not getting back to Washington earlier, but in time that dissipated and Cheney got his due for being the wise old owl. Bush landed in the empty city early evening and at 8.30 p.m. he spoke on television from the intact White House.

They were 'remarks' only, little more than a page. They were well-phrased enough and the word 'evil' made two appearances. 'Thousands of lives were suddenly ended by evil' and 'Today our nation saw evil'. Mr Bush, with help from his writers, was beginning to find a voice. From 'folks' to 'evil' in one day was an important semantic step. But although he spoke the words, Bush did not 'ring the bell', as one experienced observer later put it. He had not bound up the wounds, unlike Mayor Rudi Giuliani in New York, whose answer – 'too many to bear' – when asked about casualties, gravely matched the moment. The President would have to do more.

There was one other important sentence in this address, which showed that, already, the administration had moved beyond the limited policy of pursuit adopted by President Clinton after the bombings of the American embassies in Kenya and Tanzania in 1998. Clinton went after Osama bin Laden too, with cruise missiles, but had not acted against the people who protected bin Laden, the Taliban government of Afghanistan. Bush now took the next step. He announced that evening: 'We will make no distinction between the terrorists who committed these acts and those who harbour them.' The commitment turned what he was already calling 'the war on terrorism' into a real war, not just another version of the 'war on drugs' or the 'war on crime'. This decision was not hard to take. Washington had already given notice to the Taliban. A document subsequently published by the British government on October 4th (and approved by the US government), outlining the evidence against Osama bin Laden, recalled: 'In June 2001, in the face of mounting evidence of the Al-Qaida threat, the United States warned the Taliban that it had the right to defend itself and that it would hold the regime responsible for attacks against US citizens by terrorists sheltered in Afghanistan.' The regime would now be held responsible.

At this moment, the dynamics of the 'strong team' which Bush had assembled around him started to work, and in his favour. There was Vice President Cheney, who had been Defense Secretary to George Bush Senior. He had age and experience, was inclined to take a hard line, but not always. Colin Powell, the Secretary of State, had been Chairman of the Joint Chiefs of Staff during the Gulf War. He had invented the 'Powell doctrine' – hesitate before you go in, but if you do go, go in hard. Another veteran Washington figure, with ties to Cheney, was the Defense Secretary, Donald Rumsfeld. Often honest, sometimes mercurial, he was, like Cheney, not always easy to read. And there was Condoleezza Rice, Bush's National Security Advisor. Young, African–American (like Powell), cultured (a piano player), her great strength was in having the President's ear. She too had worked for Bush Senior, had guided the son through his difficult election campaign and was one of the clan. What this team did was to provide the inexperienced President with tempered advice. It also provided the public with reassurance that Bush was not on his own. He didn't mind that. It was the way it was supposed to work, the way he said it would work. And the result was the formulation of a strategy that tried to combine aggression with sophistication.

First, the Taliban had to be given an ultimatum, and time, to hand over Osama bin Laden. This was a diplomatic requirement if countries were to be persuaded to join the 'coalition against terror'. Bush's acceptance of an ultimatum ruled out any immediate retaliation, though he was offered a plan by the military for a cruise missile attack on Afghanistan, Clinton-style. That was no longer enough for him. He wasn't, he let it be known, going to send a million dollar missile to hit a 'camel in the butt'. And there had to be the evidence. Bush told foreign leaders that he would not act until he was sure of whom to blame. One of the curiously weak features of the otherwise sure-footed Bush plan was the refusal to present this evidence in public. John Kennedy had seen the potential for winning over world opinion when he instructed his UN ambassador, Adlai Stevenson, to show pictures to the Security Council of the Russian missiles in Cuba. There was no such moment this time.

The Secretary of State, Colin Powell, did want to publish a document of evidence. After all, there was plenty of it. Osama bin Laden had been indicted in his absence by a New York grand jury for the East Africa embassy bombings. The evidence linking him to those bombings had even been given to the Taliban well before September 11th, at their request, whereupon they rejected it, making their later demands for evidence about the hijacks somewhat insincere. There was very quickly enough to link bin Laden to the New York and Pentagon attacks. This emerged both from the FBI investigation and intelligence sources. Bin Laden himself made videos declaring how much he approved of the attacks and warned of more to come. But Powell was denied by a worried intelligence community and instead had to pass on information to governments in private. And then Britain did the job instead.

The British Prime Minister, Tony Blair, had rushed to Bush's side from the start. The British ambassador in Washington, Sir Christopher Meyer, called this support 'absolutely visceral'. Within two days of the attacks, a team from MI6 and the Ministry of Defence in London had flown over on a military plane, all others being still grounded, and were at CIA head-quarters at Langley going over the evidence on bin Laden. And if Bush did not want the evidence made public, Blair did. He had to present something to the House of Commons which he had called into special session. The texts went to and fro across the Atlantic until the final version landed on the desk of Condoleezza Rice. She said to the British, 'We won't publish, but you go ahead.' It seemed to suit the Americans to do it like this. In the same way, Tony Blair was more open about the war aim of removing the Taliban. The junior partner could afford to be more forthcoming. Blair also promised British military support, including naval, air and ground forces. In due course about 60 British officers went to the headquarters of Central Command in Tampa, Florida, from where the war was to be run.

Bush now had to put together his plan for the war on terrorism. It would be, he declared 'a new kind of war'. It would be multi-faceted. There would be legal, financial, police, intelligence and diplomatic pressure to break up the Al-Qaida network. Indeed, the first shot, he said, had been fired when he signed a document freezing the assets of Al-Qaida suspects and organizations. There would be a Director of Homeland Security, an ominous-sounding office to Americans unused to domestic threats. And there would be a military campaign. Osama bin Laden and his Al-Qaida network had declared war. The Taliban were protecting him. There could hardly be negotiations. But first George Bush had to hold the country together and, in this task, his team counted for less than he did. The public feeling was that America had done no wrong; rather, that a great wrong had been done unto it. Its tolerance and technology had been used against it. There was therefore anger along with the suffering. He had to reflect both. In a memorial service at the National Cathedral in Washington three days after the attacks, on Friday September 14th, he acknowledged the damage done. 'War has been waged against us by stealth and death and murder,' he said. And he acknowledged the suffering: 'We are in the middle hour of our grief.' He was finding his feet.

In New York City, later the same day, he played to his strength – his ability to talk to ordinary people. He stood amid the rubble of 'Ground Zero', one arm round the shoulder of a firefighter, the other grasping a loud-hailer, to talk to the rescue workers. He was able to turn a shout from one of them, that they couldn't hear him, into a memorable response. 'I hear you and the people who knocked these buildings down will hear all of us soon.' This was one of his two finest hours. The other was to come in Congress. He did some other things, too. He met the families from United Airlines Flight 93, which the passengers had tried to save, and he met them in private. He did not parade around funerals. He spoke bluntly at times, declaring that he wanted bin Laden 'dead or alive'. He would 'get them on the run' and 'smoke 'em out'. This kind of language did not go down well with the diplomats but it did with the public. His description of the war as a 'crusade' was a serious mistake, probably born out of historical ignorance, and not repeated. Indeed, this was an area in which the President had to act with sensitivity, and did. He had to speak to millions of American Muslims and to even more millions of non-Muslim Americans, to reassure the first and lead the second, so that an attack from external terrorists (a word for once used in its literal sense) did not lead to internal division. One politician in the South had already said that 'anyone wearing a diaper round his head' should be expected to get pulled over. Bush, in contrast, visited the Islamic Center in Washington, praised Islam as a 'religion of peace', whether he really believed that or not, and invited Muslim leaders to the White House. As Ronald Reagan had done so often, he picked up one anecdote and made it a general example. It was about some 'Christian and Jewish' women who had helped Muslim women, nervous about leaving their homes, go shopping. He used a phrase to describe the Muslim women that had the effect of softening antagonism to people with different habits. He called them 'women of cover'. Like Reagan, he repeated this story many times. And he used it to praise the public mood in America, which, apart from a few brutal incidents of 'revenge', was able to combine patriotism with tolerance.

Congress refused to be bounced into extending the powers of the investigating agencies, as Bush's Attorney General, John Ashcroft, at once demanded. The lawmakers, independent of the executive, took their time. They approved the sensible, like extending the right of surveillance from a single phone number to all phones belonging to one individual (a bizarre restriction which suspects had got round by simply changing their phones). They questioned the draconian, such as the right to hold someone indefinitely over an immigration query, even though such violations were often the only way the FBI, through the Immigration Service, could detain people they wanted to question. Congress was again illuminated by the Constitution.

White House officials were now proclaiming the 'Bush Doctrine'. But what did it actually mean? At its most basic, it meant what he would tell Congress – going after and defeating 'every terrorist group of global reach' and the governments that supported them. But which governments and which terrorists? To the Israelis, a terrorist meant someone whom the Palestinians might regard as a hero, and, indeed, Israeli feelings that its enemies were being excused so angered the Prime Minister, Ariel Sharon, that at one point he implicitly compared Bush to Neville Chamberlain at Munich. Bush, for whom Churchill is a hero, was not pleased.

The fiercest argument was over Iraq. There were those, especially in the Defense Department who saw this as a golden opportunity to deal with Saddam Hussein. They were led by the Deputy Secretary, Paul Wolfowitz, once a Democrat and always a foreign policy hawk. He spoke at a news conference two days after the attack about 'ending states who sponsor terrorism'. Commentators came in from the right to support him. In the *Weekly Standard*, Gerry Schmitt said, 'If two or three years from now, Saddam is still in power, the war on terrorism will have failed.' It was, in fact, a brief argument. It was resolved at a meeting at Camp David the first weekend after the attacks. Powell led the case against attacking Iraq. That could wait, under a watching brief. Iraq would be warned to behave. Phase One should deal with Afghanistan and bin Laden. It seems to have been a lively debate but in the end nobody felt as strongly as Wolfowitz and he was not at the top table. This was a war-fighting administration, but it was also, Bush apart, experienced in the complexities of war. And it decided not to handle more than one at a time. Bush's political instincts about what America and the world might accept came to the fore. He decided that Iraq would not be in Phase One. Powell appeared on the

Sunday morning television shows the next day to announce: 'Our campaign objective is to go after the Al-Qaida organisation and its leader, Osama bin Laden. Its headquarters are in Afghanistan. That is the first phase of this operation. And I obviously cannot comment on what might happen in the future.' There was little dissent outside the ranks of a few on the right. The team had come through for the captain and had rallied round a focused policy that they could all support. So could the country and much of the world. This did a lot to enhance Bush's image as someone who wanted to act with vigour but with care. Iraq was duly warned and remained a crisis in waiting.

Bush and Blair had agreed early on to meet in Washington on Thursday September 20th. That day turned out to be the occasion on which George Bush would speak to Congress and try to elevate his presidency to a mission. He told his presidential counsellor Karen Hughes, a few days before, what he wanted to do and asked for a draft text. She had been his press secretary in Texas. It was hammered out by chief speechwriter Michael Gerson and his team. Bush likes his speeches clear and simple. He rarely contributes to them beyond setting out the themes and cutting things out (he is not used to writing; Karen Hughes wrote the whole of his 'autobiography'). From this one, he cut a quotation from Roosevelt, feeling that this was a speech which had to come from him alone. The speech finally came together on Wednesday September 19th. Congress was told that the President would speak the following evening. When Thursday came, he had set aside a couple of hours for talks and dinner with Tony Blair before going to Capitol Hill for the speech, to which the British Prime Minister, his closest ally, was invited. Blair was late. He had been in New York where he had attended a memorial service for the British victims, and his convoy had been held up in traffic there. His party noticed that policemen from Chicago and San Francisco were trying to sort out the Manhattan gridlock. Then the press with him had been subject to new security measures. Yet Bush did not seem to mind. As soon as Blair arrived and ran up the main front steps of the White House, he was taken by the President into the reception room behind the main hall, overlooking the south lawn. Bush took him to the bow window and for 20 minutes they talked alone. Over dinner, with senior officials from both sides, Bush made clear that states protecting terrorists would have to come to heel, but he also emphasized that the debate about Iraq within the administration was over and that the concentration was on bin Laden and Afghanistan. They also discussed the terms of the ultimatum to the Taliban and which countries might be in the coalition. The Brits were impressed, as they had been when Bush and Blair had met at Camp David in February. Here was a president about to make the speech of his life, yet he was calm and courteous. He ignored an aide who came in during dinner to point a finger at his watch. The President led Blair into the hall to let the Prime Minister make some brief remarks. Shortly afterwards, they left for Congress.

In his speech, Bush responded to the moment with a confidence and passion he had not shown before. He had people around him, worried people, not just the unfeeling camera. The brittleness he often displays in public was not there. The words crafted by Gerson and his team were at times vivid: 'Whether we bring our enemies to justice, or justice to our enemies, justice will be done... The Taliban must act and act immediately. They will hand over the terrorists or they will share their fate... Either you are with us or you are with the terrorists... We will not tire, we will not falter, we will not fail.' By the end, even his foes accepted that, in this speech, he had earned the presidency. He had finally expressed the needs of the American people at a moment when they would wake no more to a glad, confident morn.

In mounting the diplomatic offensive to form a coalition, or series of coalitions, it was clearly vital to prevent the war on terrorism being seen as a war on Islam. There were risks enough in the venture anyway. Some argued against forming any alliances. It would give Bush a freer hand, they said. That was not Bush's way, nor that of the team around him. They felt they needed help. The first American success came in Pakistan, the name of whose leader now became quite familiar to the President. Without Pakistan, there would probably be no air corridors for attacks. Bush was fortunate to have 'the General' in charge, a man who had overthrown an elected prime minister and who was demonstrably intent on deciding matters for himself. Musharraf was amenable to the pressure Washington applied and the inducements it offered. Richard Armitage, the burly Deputy Secretary of State, admitted that the talks with Pakistan had been robust. But they worked. Despite the strong Islamic faith of the masses, Musharraf and the sophisticated Pakistani elite thought Pakistan's best interests lay in being friends with the US, and getting rid of sanctions imposed because of its nuclear bomb. The American got their air corridors and some use of bases. It wasn't everything but it was enough.

Another neighbour of Afghanistan, Uzbekistan, suddenly leaped into world prominence, as the Americans turned their attention there, too. The Defense Secretary, Donald Rumsfeld, paid a visit. The Uzbeks had some handy old bases which had been used for the Soviet operations in Afghanistan. This spin-off from the Soviet Union, which has tried to resurrect a sense of nationalism by reintroducing its people to the glories of Tamburlaine, the fourteenth-century Mongol conquerer, was ruled by the rather old-style Islam Karimov. He had to deal with his own Islamic movement, often violent, and he was no push-over for Rumsfeld. Publicly, at least, Karimov limited his help to allowing one of the bases to be used for search and rescue, but left open the possibility of offering more later. Some Arab members of the coalition had to be coaxed. Saudi Arabia trod a difficult line but in the end the self-interest of the Saudi royal family prevailed, smoothed by a visit from the avuncular Mr Rumsfeld. Some coalition members almost applied, none more so than Russia. President Putin had been the first to get through to Mr Bush and keenly pressed the parallels with what he saw as Chechen terrorism, also supported by Islamic radicals. What a difference a war makes. In January, there was scarcely a ripple of interest in Russia among the Bush team; now the prospect opened up of radically improved relations leading, in the view of some experienced Russia hands, to the achievement of those close ties that were promised so many years ago by Boris

Yeltsin. Other bits of the coalition were easy to bolt on. For the first time, NATO invoked Article Five – an attack on one was an attack on all – and sent its AWACS aircraft to patrol American skies. Americans were thereby protected by German air personnel who made up a quarter of the crews. The most difficult coalition to put together was one to rule Afghanistan after the hoped-for toppling of the Taliban. Bush was slow to realize the need for this, saying at first that he wasn't interested in 'nation building'. But soon a special envoy, Richard Haas from the State Department, was appointed and Washington linked up with the UN representative, Lakhdar Brahimi. Bush decided that the UN had a role to play after all, an acceptance which might help reshape America's view of the world when this is all over.

And there was a domestic enemy as well, an unseen but present danger in the form of *bacillus anthracis*. The emergence of anthrax shortly after September 11th was not immediately explained but its effect showed how disruptive biological warfare, on however limited a scale, can be. The Director of Homeland Security, Tom Ridge, an old friend of Bush, who resigned as Governor of Pennsylvania to take the job, was busier than even he had imagined. Anthrax struck first, and fatally, at the offices of the tabloid newspaper the *National Enquirer* and sister publications in Boca Raton, north of Miami. A letter arrived there addressed to the actress Jennifer Lopez. It was at first thrown into the bin. However, someone retrieved it and opened it, to find some white powder inside. Bob Stevens, a picture editor, was intrigued and, delving into the powder, he found a small Star of David. Within days, he started to feel unwell. On October 5th, he died in hospital. And he died from inhalation anthrax, rare and usually a killer if not caught early. At first, it was described as 'an isolated case'. It proved not to be. Other letters were sent to television news presenters in New York, and to the Senate Majority Leader, Democrat Tom Daschle, a mild-mannered man who should have no mortal enemies. His office was closed but 28 people, including two police officers who came to investigate, were exposed. The next day, I was surprised to find that the whole building, a couple of blocks from Congress, was still open. Yellow tape was blocking off some lifts but only that part of the building which housed Daschle's office had been sealed off. Dozens of staff were lining up off the central lobby, waiting to be given nasal swabs. A bright staffer from Senator Jo Lieberman's office named Jennifer Bond was determined to sound determined. 'Proud to be an American and proud to serve in the Senate' was her attitude. 'And by the way,' she added, 'good for the Brits.' The following day, it turned out that everyone who had even been in that building, media included, was now advised to get swabbed. This involved having an alarmingly tipped swab inserted into the nose till the eyes watered. We were also given a six-day supply of the antibiotic Cipro as a precaution, unlike postal workers who were felt not to be at risk but who were. Two of them died and it was realized how little we really know about the threat from biological attack.

Internationally, the course was set. From the start Bush warned people to have patience. Inevitably there would be set-backs. Support for the enterprise would be tested. So, too, would George Bush. The maturity he had shown in the early weeks did not impress everyone who felt that the real crises were ahead. It was clear from the start that this 'new type of war' would be no repeat of the Gulf War. The British experience in Afghanistan in the nineteenth century, and the Russian experience in the twentieth, ensured that the Americans would not try to invade in the same way in the twenty-first. This would be a campaign of pressure. About nine days before mili-tary action began, Bush had decided in principle that the first part, the air attacks, would have to go ahead. The ultimatum to the Taliban to hand over bin Laden had, as expected, failed. President Bush firmed up his decision on Tuesday October 2nd. On Friday October 5th the new Chairman of the Joint Chiefs of Staff, Air Force General Richard Myers, whom Bush had person-ally selected, told him that the military was ready. It only needed Donald Rumsfeld to return from his overseas trip the next day and give his assessment, for the presidential decision to be formally declared. The bombing began on Sunday October 7th.

CHAPTER SEVEN

AFGHANISTAN'S TRAGEDY

John Simpson

*John Simpson is World Affairs Editor. In his long career in the BBC he
has reported from 110 countries and interviewed more than 150 world
leaders. His assignments have included many key events including
Tiananmen Square, the fall of the Berlin Wall, the Gulf War, the
collapse of the Soviet Union and the end of apartheid in South Africa.
In 1999 he reported from Belgrade throughout the NATO bombing of
Serbia. John has taken a particular interest in Afghanistan since 1980,
reporting from there a dozen times. Here he gives his perspective on this
ruined country.*

This has been a strange war. For many days during the bombing
campaign I sat on the Northern Alliance front line, watching the
tiny silver American planes in the blue sky, then watching a jet
of flame and a cloud of brown smoke go up over another
Taliban position. Taliban soldiers would meanwhile fire off
everything they had into the air, from anti-aircraft guns to
Kalashnikovs, even though the planes were flying twice as high
as the farthest Taliban shell could reach.

The Americans assumed that their enormously expensive
bombs were doing ferocious damage; the Taliban felt the early
American bombing was largely ineffectual because it was so
precise. For them, as for every Afghan, real bombing was what
the Russians used to do: it plastered the landscape, and killed or
maimed everyone within range. These initial surgical strikes,
using the latest twenty-first-century technology, seemed positively effete to them. It was a dialogue of the mutually unaware.
Watching the pillars of smoke go up over the Taliban lines,
I often reflected that the cost of one of these bombs would

probably have been enough to purchase the defection of every single Taliban commander in the trenches opposite. But, rightly or wrongly, that is was not the spirit in which this war was undertaken. The purpose was not merely to win, since everyone took it for granted from the beginning that this would happen anyway; it was to make the point that terrorism cannot and must not be protected.

But, as impatience grew at home and the need for visible success became urgent, the Americans did turn to the heavy bombers. The US Air Force dropped the devastating so-called 'Daisy Cutter' bomb, which produces a fireball and rapidly expanding blast wave many times greater than conventional explosives. They turned again to the venerable but lethal B-52s, which first saw service in Vietnam, to drop complete payloads on the Taliban front lines. Enormously helped by this relentless attack from the air, the Northern Alliance and other opposition forces took towns and provinces across the whole country, often because the Taliban themselves abandoned their defence.

When it finally came, on November 12th, the battle for Kabul was over in a matter of hours. This no doubt came as a surprise to all those who had heard stories of the fanatical determination of the Taliban and their willingness to find martyrdom for the cause; but to anyone who had seen them fight it was only to be expected. The Taliban were never good soldiers. As for the volunteers who had flooded into Afghanistan from the Middle East, from Pakistan and elsewhere, here at least they turned out to be just as feeble. The American bombing demoralized the Taliban thoroughly, and they were also stunned by the speed and ferocity of the Northern Alliance advance. It was so one-sided as to be a total rout.

Once the battle had begun, the Northern Alliance cut through the Taliban defences like a knife through butter. By 6 p.m. on the 12th they had to stop because night had fallen and the fighters were exhausted. The next morning they encountered no resistance whatever. They stopped on the outskirts of Kabul, as they had promised to do. There was no need to enter the city: they controlled it anyway. The Taliban leadership had escaped during the night, leaving the rank-and-file to find their own way out. All in all, fewer than 20 Northern Alliance soldiers were dead or injured; thousands of Taliban must have been killed. As the people of the city came rushing out to greet the news, it was clear that the Taliban were finished.

For the BBC team, which walked ahead of everyone else – soldiers or other journalists – into the city and gave the crowds the news, it was an exhilarating moment. Everyone was enormously stirred up and excited. Two people from BBC Radio who commandeered bicycles to get to the centre of the city had to give up and take taxis instead: the pressure of the crowd was so great that they fell off. After battling my way by foot through a dense mass of people I also stopped a taxi, and climbed into it with one of my television colleagues. Every time we stopped along the way in order to telephone a report to London, a crowd would gather round us and make talking almost impossible. It wasn't entirely a joyful progress: the bodies of several foreign volunteers for the Taliban lay in the streets as we drove through. Hated above all the rest, the Pakistanis and Arabs who had been caught by the crowds had been shot or lynched.

* * * * * *

To travel around Afghanistan is to immerse yourself in a world that scarcely exists anywhere else nowadays: magnificent, complex, perilous, appallingly backward. There is no effective national telephone system, no electricity, and no more than a few hundred miles of paved road in the entire country.

The horse, the donkey and the camel are still the main means of transport. The noise of a jeep or a pick-up truck will bring people out to stare in every inhabited place you pass. The repair of bridges and mountain passes is a matter for local people to look after or not, as they choose. Brigands still set up checkpoints for robbing travellers, though nowadays they carry Kalashnikovs and call it a road-toll.

Strangely, though, Afghans are very well informed. Seventy-five per cent of the entire population, it is estimated, listen to the BBC's Farsi or Pashtu language services, or to other foreign radio stations. The remaining 25 per cent live in a depth of ignorance that is hard for us to comprehend. 'What do you think of the bombing?' a colleague of mine asked a middle-aged man in the market at Faisabad, shortly after the Americans began their campaign against the Taliban. 'Which bombing?' said the man, cupping his ear. 'The one in 1919 or the one in 1926?' China must have been like this in the 1920s and 30s, the era of the warlords; and warlords control most aspects of Afghan life today.

Afghanistan is cursed by its physical position. As an historic crossroads for the movement of peoples, it has a complex population; the two main groups are the Pashtuns and the Persian-speaking Tajiks. The political chaos of the past three decades has also led its neighbours, and other countries, to fish in Afghanistan's troubled waters. Pakistan, India, Iran, Russia, Uzbekistan, Tajikistan, Saudi Arabia, the United States, Britain, France and China have all become involved in one way or another. The plan to run an oil pipeline through Afghan territory, bypassing Iran, encouraged even more foreign meddling. Afghanistan became a battleground for other countries' interests.

* * * * * *

Until the early 1970s, it was a pleasant, ramshackle kingdom, as little concerned with the outside world as the outside world was concerned with it. Britain had long realized that the best way to keep it quiet was simply to bribe the big tribal groups. Later, the British bequeathed their anxieties about Afghanistan, and their methods, to Pakistan and Russia. The Pakistanis were perennially worried that the Pashtu-speakers who lived on either side of the Durand Line – the late Victorian border which still endures – might break away and form a new independent state of Pashtunistan. The Russians were nervous about a resurgence of Islam on the Soviet Union's southern boundary.

Still, King Zahir Shah, who had reigned since 1933, seemed a permanent fixture. Violence was limited to an acceptable level of banditry and the inevitable blood-feuding. Afghanistan had become the main overland route from Australia to London, and Western hippies wandered through it, sampling the local marijuana. Afterwards, it seemed like a golden age.

Sardar Mohammed Daoud, the King's brother-in-law, brought it to an end in 1973. When the King was abroad Daoud, motivated mainly by jealousy, seized power and declared a republic. He made himself president, ruling with the help of leftist army officers. The political structure of the country, which had managed to hang together while the King was on the throne, began to collapse in bloodshed.

Daoud and his entire family were massacred in 1978 in a full Marxist coup; then, with the leftists violently split, the new president, Nur Mohammed Taraki, was murdered less than a year later. The communist system, newly introduced, seemed on the point of being rejected. The elderly leaders of the Soviet Union decided they had to intervene if international Marxism –Leninism were not to receive a serious check. On December 26th 1979, Soviet troops invaded, and the latest president, Hafizullah Amin, was killed in the ruins of his palace. The Russians installed Babrak Karmal as president. He would not last long himself.

Three weeks later, in January 1980, I caught my first glimpse of the country that was to take up so much of my attention during the next 21 years. I followed Lord Carrington, the British Foreign Secretary, on his long trip of reassurance around Britain's friends in central and southern Asia. President Zia ul-Haq of Pakistan, who had long had his fingers in Afghanistan's affairs, received Lord Carrington royally. There were all sorts of subtle reminders of Britain's past, including a trip to the Khyber Pass, where the old fortresses of British India were still in use, and the crests of the British regiments that had served there were still kept freshly painted. Lord Carrington and his press party were given lunch in the officers' mess of the Khyber

Rifles. Then we went to the border at Torkam, and were shown the broad expanse of Afghanistan beyond.

I had never seen so savage and magnificent a landscape, and, caught up in the fierce attraction of it all, I suggested to a colleague of mine that we should quietly slip away and head across the border. He was tempted, but in the end we decided it was too foolish. I was not always to be so sensible in the future.

* * * * * *

Slowly, opposition to the Soviet invasion began to build up inside Afghanistan. There were two mutually hostile tendencies: the religious fundamentalists headed by the subtle, dangerous Gulbeddin Hekmatyar, and the more nationalist faction led by Burhanuddin Rabbani and Ahmad Shah Massoud. And now that Afghanistan was in trouble, the country's traditional misfortune began to show itself: outside countries were becoming involved.

In particular, a new alliance was formed. Pakistan, under President Zia, supported the fundamentalist cause of Gulbeddin Hekmatyar; its highly sophisticated diplomatic corps, an inheritance from British days, worked skilfully to persuade the United States to back him too. The Great Satan was giving its backing to Islamic fundamentalism. It came about because of the excellent relations Pakistan's military intelligence organization, the ISI (Inter-Services Intelligence) had built up with the CIA. Over the years to come, the CIA would follow the ISI's advice faithfully. And regardless of which government was in power in Islamabad and what its policies were, the ISI remained heavily committed to the fundamentalist cause.

The ISI's clinching argument was that Hekmatyar's organization, Hezb-e Islami, was fiercer and more effective than any other mujaheddin group at fighting the Russians. Throughout the 1980s, therefore, the Americans poured money and weapons into Hezb-e, even though the evidence for its success was slender and it never hid its hatred for Western values. It was dangerous, if you were travelling inside Afghanistan, to come across their fighters, and a European cameraman was murdered by the Hezb-e group he was travelling with.

Meanwhile, the genuinely pro-Western forces led by Ahmad Shah Massoud were starved of American weapons and money because the Pakistanis had cleverly persuaded Washington that they were pro-Indian; during the Cold War India tended to side with the Soviet Union. Massoud survived and prospered for two reasons: he had the support of the British and other countries, and he was a highly effective general who defeated no fewer than nine all-out attempts by the Russians to capture his heartland, the Panjshir Valley.

Foreign Muslims – Arabs, Pakistanis, Indonesians, Malaysians – drifted to Afghanistan as well, anxious to fight the Soviet invader. For Western journalists, these foreigners were the most dangerous contingent of all. Once, waiting to get my passport stamped as I left Pakistan to enter Afghanistan at Torkam, I found myself standing next to a tall, fierce-looking Saudi. 'If I find you on the other side of the border,' he murmured, matter-of-factly, 'I shall kill you.' I made sure he didn't find me.

By the mid-1980s, Soviet tactics were grinding the mujaheddin forces down, using their helicopter gunships to great effect. They might have won if the Americans had not decided to supply the mujaheddin with Stinger missiles. Even so, they gave most of them to Gulbeddin Hekmatyar, and Massoud had to get by with the few he could obtain from the Americans, or buy from Hezb-e Islami.

Hekmatyar's later history shows the Americans were unwise to support him: in the mid-1990s, having lost all backing in Afghanistan, Hekmatyar escaped to Iran. His remaining Stinger missiles found their way into the hands of some of the fundamentalist groups which Iran supported. The CIA had to hire trustworthy agents to buy many Stingers back at an inflated cost of millions of dollars each.

But the Stingers changed the balance of the war, and by the late 1980s the Russians, under the leadership of Mikhail Gorbachev, were desperate to get out. The final Soviet withdrawal took place on February 14th 1989. Behind them, the

Russians left a regime headed by the unscrupulous President Najibullah (like a number of Afghans, including the present Northern Alliance spokesman Dr Abdullah, he had only one name). Najibullah, as the former head of Khad, the secret police, was a torturer and murderer; but he was also fully committed to the social emancipation of women and the education of the population. Under his regime, ordinary Afghans probably made more progress than at any time in their country's history. He declared that he was no longer a communist, but his chances of establishing a stable government were never high; and now the mujaheddin declared a new jihad against him.

* * * * * *

In the weeks immediately following the Soviet withdrawal I made a documentary for the BBC about the new battle for power in Afghanistan. When we began, we assumed we would be reporting on the race for Kabul, as the different forces advanced on the city to challenge Najibullah. Instead, it turned into an account of the vicious infighting among the mujaheddin. As part of it, the cameraman Peter Jouvenal (who had frequently roamed around Afghanistan over the previous nine years with the mujaheddin) joined me in a particularly risky undertaking.

On Pakistan's frontier with Afghanistan we came across a small mujaheddin organization called Harakat-e Islami, representing the Hazara people of central Afghanistan. The Hazaras are partly descended from the Mongols who invaded Afghanistan under Genghis Khan in the thirteenth century, and they believe their ancestors were part of the garrison Genghis Khan left behind him when he swept westwards into Persia. To this day, the Hazaras use expressions to their children such as 'Sit up and eat properly, like a Mongol'.

Over the centuries, though, the Hazaras had sunk to the level of an underclass. I found them tough, trustworthy, and very interesting; and when Harakat-e Islami offered to escort Peter Jouvenal and me secretly into Kabul, where they claimed to have infiltrated President Najibullah's feared secret police, we accepted.

It was dangerous; Afghans are justly renowned for their treachery, and Najibullah's security system was extremely good. Yet the offer was a sensational one. They claimed they could drive us round the centre of Kabul in the vehicle belonging to the head of Khad, and would let us interview senior Khad officers who were secretly members of Harakat-e Islami.

After a week's journey across Afghanistan avoiding government posts, just before dawn one morning in March 1989, three men from Harakat led us through the line of small fortresses which ringed Kabul. Within an hour we were being driven through Kabul, just as Harakat had promised, in the jeep belonging to the head of the secret police. During the next three days we were moved from safe house to safe house. We watched as a homemade rocket was prepared, and were taken to see it fired at Khad headquarters.

In the end, though, we were betrayed, and Khad staged a raid on the house where we were staying. Just before it took place, our minders managed to foil it. They smuggled us out to the edge of town, and we made our way back to the mujaheddin lines. It was an extraordinary adventure, and proved one thing: the regime of Najibullah was deeply penetrated by its enemies, and could not last long.

* * * * * *

Three years later, in April 1992, the mujaheddin finally succeeded in capturing Kabul, and Najibullah was given shelter in the UN compound in the city. It was the start of a terrible time for the city. The vicious rivalries between the various mujaheddin groups had never been resolved, and now they broke out in open violence. In 1993, 10,000 people died when Gulbeddin Hekmatyar's fundamentalist forces attacked the government of President Rabbani and Ahmad Shah Massoud. In January the following year Hekmatyar joined forces with the Uzbek warlord Rashid Dostum (previously a general in the communist army) and, without any perceptible justification, attacked Kabul again. Large swathes of the city were destroyed, and once more people died in their thousands.

Ahmad Shah Massoud always believed Pakistan and the ISI had encouraged Hekmatyar to carry out these attacks, in order to destabilize the Afghan government. The ISI, which by now ran Pakistan's policy towards Afghanistan virtually without reference to the elected government of the country, seems to have believed that it was in Pakistan's interests for Afghanistan to be torn apart by civil war; otherwise, it was argued, a breakaway Pashtunistan might become reality.

As for the Western countries that had once been so interested in Afghanistan's fate when the Russian invaders were there, they preferred to forget all about it now. Afghanistan was no longer a Cold War battleground, so it had ceased to matter. It was left entirely on its own. And the worst and most disturbing experiment of all was about to be unleashed upon it by its neighbour.

The word 'Taliban' means religious students. During the years of Soviet occupation, the sons of Afghan refugees who had fled to Pakistan were educated at hundreds of madrasas, or religious schools, along the border with Afghanistan. They were encouraged to feel a bitter resentment against the Russians, and were trained in a peculiarly literal interpretation of the Holy Koran by their teachers. At some point in the early 1990s, the ISI realized that these students would make excellent material for a new force in Afghanistan's continuing war.

Armed and trained by Pakistan, the Taliban made their first foray across the border in November 1994. With Kabul itself the scene of a fierce civil war, the rest of Afghanistan had descended into anarchy. Warlords controlled every road, robbing and murdering travellers as they chose. Near the southern city of Kandahar, a convoy of 31 trucks containing food aid was stopped and captured by bandits. Twenty people were killed in the fighting. This was the Taliban's big opportunity – and the ISI's. A large force of Taliban, wearing their distinctive white turbans, was ferried from Pakistan to Kandahar to rescue the convoy. The resulting battle lasted four days, and cost more than 50 lives; but at last the convoy was freed, Kandahar was captured, and the Taliban were victorious.

It was the start of a legend. The Taliban seemed like a purifying force, rescuing the country from chaos and violence. They moved outwards from Kabul, capturing province after province. At first, even in cities like Herat where the Taliban seemed completely alien, they were welcomed because they seemed to bring peace. But they brought something else as well: the demand that everyone should conform to their extreme code of behaviour. This was not merely an ultra-conservative interpretation of Islam; the Taliban were also militantly Pashtun, and insisted that the inhabitants of the Persian-speaking city of Herat, which had once been part of Iran and had completely different social and religious customs, should adopt the Taliban's cultural norms in full.

And so the women of Herat, who were often emancipated and reasonably well educated, were forced to wear the all-encompassing burka; it was as foreign to them as it would have been to women in India or China. (Later, after the attacks on New York and Washington on September 11th, Peter Jouvenal and I disguised ourselves in burkas to cross the border into Afghanistan. The effect was extraordinary: it was as though we had become invisible. No one gave us a glance, and we found ourselves occupying the worst and most humble places in vehicles.)

The Taliban swept through the city, which was famous for its artistic treasures, cutting the heads off statues and defacing frescos; they believed that any representation of the human figure was a breach of the commandment against graven images. Girls' schools were closed down. I visited one that had been raided a few weeks before; you could see where the teacher's chalk had broken on the blackboard as the Taliban burst in. 'Good morning!' she had been writing in English, 'I am very happy'.

Anyone who owned a television set or a video recorder was obliged to hand it in; television too was an offence against religion. Smashed sets were strung up with video tape at every Taliban post, as a warning to the population. No music of any kind was allowed, no playing cards, no chess-sets, no wigs, no greetings cards, no neckties, no pictures of any living creature, human or animal. Yet the Taliban, especially those who had been recruited in Kandahar, brought other, more incongruous habits with them as they swept across Afghanistan. Many Taliban soldiers wore eye make-up, painted their finger- and toenails red, and teetered around on gold high-heeled sandals. With their long, shaggy beards and Kalashnikovs, this gave them a distinctly unsettling appearance.

They patrolled the streets, beating up men who had cut their beards and women who allowed their burkas to slip and reveal a hand or an ankle. The offenders could then be taken to some public place and whipped. Worse crimes, such as adultery, were punished by shooting. The full force of sharia law was introduced. In Kandahar I went to visit a minister in the Taliban government to ask him about these things. He proved to be an ebullient character called Mullah Balouch, who rather liked the idea of being on television. As long as we didn't show his entire figure, he said, he didn't feel we were breaching the commandment about graven images. This was a relief; we had gone through endless difficulties with a more meticulous Taliban official, who had insisted that all we could show of him was the action of raising a teacup to drink from it; and even then his assistant kept checking obsessively to make sure we were not showing his hand or any part of his face.

'We punish criminals according to the Sharia,' Mullah Balouch explained to us. 'When someone steals or robs, that law decrees that his left hand or right foot should be amputated. If they commit the same crime again, then the right hand or left foot should also be removed, so he can't do it again.' If Mullah Balouch showed a certain relish when he told us this, it was not surprising. The International Red Cross in Kandahar told us that when there was no doctor or surgeon available to cut off the hands of criminals, Mullah Balouch liked to do the job himself. He was, incidentally, the Taliban Minister of Health.

* * * * * *

By the start of 1996 the Taliban advance seemed to have been halted. Ahmad Shah Massoud had re-established control in Kabul; the Taliban's novelty was wearing off. They were not particularly good soldiers, and their main success had been in persuading more experienced groups of fighters to change sides and join them. This was often done with Pakistani money. In March that year the Taliban called a nationwide shura, or conference, of their religious supporters. A thousand mullahs took part; when it finished on April 4th, it had decided three things: to declare jihad, holy war, against the government in Kabul; to press on as fast as possible to capture the capital; and to declare the Taliban leader Mullah Omar Amir-ul Momineen, the leader of the faithful. This meant that his orders were binding on Muslims everywhere.

By chance, I was in Kandahar that day, and the gathering when the shura ended was one of the most remarkable things I have ever witnessed. It had been decided that Mullah Omar should display the cloak of the Prophet Mohammed, which was kept in Kandahar. For us to have stood out in the open with a television camera would probably have led to a quick and ugly death; but Peter Jouvenal, who was working with me again, sat in our minibus filming the ceremony through the window. It was like some great occasion of the Middle Ages. As Mullah Omar held up the cloak, so delicate it was almost transparent, a great sigh went up from the thousands of spectators. Again and again those in the front of the crowd hurled their turbans in the air to touch the cloak, and gain an extra blessing from it. It was the only time Mullah Omar, a reclusive figure who lost one eye in the fight against the Russians, had been filmed for television.

Within six months, on September 26th 1996, the Taliban had captured Kabul. A hit-squad burst into the UN compound, beat ex-President Najibullah and his brother senseless, castrated them, tied them to a jeep and dragged them round until they were dead, then hung their bodies from a lamppost. It was an act of deliberate savagery. In Washington a few hours later, the State Department announced it would establish diplomatic relations with the Taliban; there was nothing objectionable, it said, in the Taliban's intention to establish full Islamic law in Afghanistan. American politicians and journalists who had supported the Central Asian Oil Pipeline Project, in which the American oil company Unocal was heavily involved, generally welcomed the arrival of the Taliban in power. It would, several of them said, ensure peace and stability in the country.

Pakistan, meanwhile, began to benefit from the arrival of the Taliban in power. Pakistani taxis plied for hire in the streets of Afghan cities; Pakistani banks opened everywhere; Pakistani goods were on sale at every market stall. If you wanted to ring a government ministry in Kabul, you had to dial a number with a Pakistani prefix. Afghanistan seemed like an economic province of Pakistan. It was the ISI's greatest achievement, and the CIA, which still listened to what the ISI said, apparently approved.

It took the activities of Osama bin Laden to change the Americans' minds. Bin Laden had never made any secret of his hatred for Westerners. When I encountered him in 1989, he tried to get the group of mujaheddin we were filming to murder us; when they refused, he offered a truck driver $500 to run us over.

Bin Laden gave the Taliban regime millions of dollars – more than they received from any other source. He too had learned that you can get far more by buying the loyalty of Afghans than by any other means. He had become a close personal friend of Mullah Omar, and benefited from the traditional customs of the Pashtuns, known as the Pashtunwali. These forbade the Taliban from handing over guests to an enemy. Even so, several Taliban figures insisted quietly that if the United States asked in the right way, they would force bin Laden to leave the country. The Americans did not ask in the way the Taliban thought was right. Instead, they demanded his immediate handover, and the Taliban refused. The bombs started falling soon afterwards.

* * * * * *

All Afghanistan's problems ultimately come down to two factors: weakness at home, and the interference of outsiders. In the 21 years since I first caught sight of it, I have come to love this country, poor and maimed though it is. To me, a single case exemplifies its position: that of a 17-year-old girl named Zarbibi, whom I first came across in a Kabul hospital. She was brought in on a blood-soaked stretcher, screaming in pain, her foot blown off by a landmine. 'God forgive me,' she was calling out; and even then it seemed grotesque that she regarded herself as being somehow to blame for what had happened. The landmine would have been manufactured by Russia, or India, or China, or even Britain if it was old enough, and supplied by yet another country. All Zarbibi had done had been to step on it accidentally.

Her life was wrecked in that instant. This is a society in which a woman's only hope of a decent life is marriage, and Zarbibi was now unmarriageable. Afterwards, when she had recovered a little, I went to see her. Her suffering seemed to have given her an intense, fragile beauty. She sat in the courtyard of the house she shared with her brothers, her artificial leg awkwardly straight in front of her.

'What can I do?' she said. 'I'm disabled now. I don't want anything. This is my fate – what else can I wish for? I'd like to get married, but who'd want to marry a disabled woman? If the Taliban had let me, I would have liked to go to school. I could have learned something, and had a better future.'

'What,' I asked weakly, 'do you wish for Afghanistan?'

'For Afghanistan I wish peace. A good life. Everything...'

Everything, she might have added, that Afghanistan was too weak to secure for itself. Everything that other countries would not allow it to have.

Now, perhaps, Zarbibi will have a second chance. When the Northern Alliance took Kabul it immediately announced that girls could now be educated, and women no longer had to cover their faces. Less than a week later, Kabul television began its broadcasts after five years of silence under the Taliban. The first presenters to appear were both women, and one at least was wearing make-up. A new world was opening up at last.

CHAPTER EIGHT

MUSHARRAF'S MOTIVES
Mike Wooldridge

Mike Wooldridge was South Asia Correspondent from 1996 to 2001. Previously the BBC's correspondent in East Africa and South Africa, he's now back in our World Affairs team in London. While covering South Asia, Mike worked frequently in Pakistan. His coverage included the 1998 nuclear tests, the conflict that erupted between Pakistan and India in the Kargil region of Kashmir in 1999, and the military coup by General Musharraf later that year. His chapter examines the dilemma that General Musharraf faced after September 11th and how he attempted to resolve it.

I have done interviews in some dramatic settings but Skardu airport in northern Pakistan takes some beating. Tourists fly into Skardu for awe-inspiring views of the western Himalayas. The plane that brings you from Islamabad has the world's second highest mountain, K2, on its nose until it banks to the right to drop down into the valley where Skardu straddles the River Indus. Serious mountaineers fly in to climb some of the most challenging peaks in the world. But it was not tourism or climbing that took me to Skardu in July 1999. It was war – the last one to take place in this region. The man I had arranged to meet, and interview, at Skardu airport was General Pervez Musharraf, then Pakistan's army chief, now the country's president.

To the south of Skardu, along more than 100 miles of mountains and ridges rising to 17,000 feet, Pakistan and India were engaged in their most serious fighting in three decades. A year earlier the two countries had gatecrashed the world's nuclear club. First India's new Hindu, nationalist-led government carried out a series of underground nuclear tests in the Rajasthan desert. Then Pakistan matched them. Both countries subsequently signalled their intention to develop nuclear weapons, and this brief but bloody conflict that erupted in mid-1999 in the Kargil region of Kashmir only heightened international anxieties about the volatility of the region.

The Kargil war began as winter receded along the Line of Control, the ceasefire line from the first war between India and Pakistan in 1948. Pakistan had been created to make a separate homeland for Muslims, when British India was partitioned a year earlier. But the territory of Jammu and Kashmir was disputed, with both India and Pakistan holding sectors. The two countries went to war over the territory in 1948 and in 1965; it was also a factor in the 1971 conflict.

Now, in 1999, shepherds in Kargil spotted groups of armed men who had dug in on the still-snowy ridges on the Indian side of the Line of Control. They were not Indian soldiers, so who were they? India sent in patrols to find out and quickly discovered that the men were there in much greater numbers and much better armed than it first appeared. I am among a number of journalists who can testify to that. In the early days of the conflict I called in at the Dras garrison, which is overlooked by several of the Kargil peaks. We were pinned down by a two-hour barrage of shelling. The only road running along the Line of Control – a lifeline for the Indian military and for civilians alike – had suddenly become much more vulnerable.

Pakistan initially denied involvement in the offensive that was being waged against the Indian forces from the mountain tops. It claimed that all those involved were from the militant groups that had been conducting an armed campaign against Indian rule in Kashmir for a decade: a mixture of Kashmiris and foreigners who supported the Kashmir cause – many of them Afghans. Though it stretched credulity, Pakistan seemed to suggest at first that they had somehow made their way up to their high-altitude bunkers with heavy weapons from the much more precipitous Indian side, unseen by the Indian security forces. India insisted that it was an incursion led and armed by

Pakistan and that the force was mainly composed of Pakistani soldiers. It produced captured identity cards and other documents to support its case.

* * * * * *

The encounter with General Musharraf on the tarmac at Skardu airport was fairly brief. But I suggested to the Pakistan army chief that it was not just India that did not believe the Pakistani line; many people in Pakistan and in the rest of the world did not seem to believe it either. He acknowledged that Pakistani troops had undertaken 'aggressive patrolling' across the Line of Control. There was to be a storm the next day about whether this finally amounted to an admission that it was an intrusion into Indian-administered territory. But there could be no doubting one thing the General said, and it was to assume even more significance a few months later. I asked him whether the Prime Minister, Nawaz Sharif, had been fully briefed on the operations along the Line of Control from the start. 'Everyone was on board,' said the General. And did he approve, I asked? 'Absolutely.' Pakistan was being criticized by many governments for making the region even more of a flashpoint – now potentially a nuclear one – and General Musharraf was not going to spare his political master the flak.

Soon the Kargil war was over, but not the fallout from it. The Americans were so concerned about the rising levels of tension that President Bill Clinton took time out on Independence Day to meet Nawaz Sharif in Washington. Mr Clinton's blunt message was this: the game is up. Pull back all the forces that are on the Indian side of the Line of Control, whatever those forces may be. Nawaz Sharif claimed that the Kashmir issue had been brought out of obscurity and was now on the international agenda. But he also did Mr Clinton's bidding and the retreat followed. The conflict ended with hundreds dead on each side.

What was even more strange about the whole affair was that only a few weeks before the fighting broke out in Kargil, a humble bus had been the centrepiece of an initiative that seemed to hold out hope for reducing the long-standing tensions in the region. The Indian Prime Minister, Atal Behari Vajpayee, had launched the first commercial bus service between India and Pakistan in 50 years, travelling on the inaugural run to Lahore for talks with Nawaz Sharif. They signed a declaration which laid down a road map for overcoming the mutual hostility of half a century since Partition, and proposed steps to avoid a nuclear arms race and the risk of an accidental nuclear war in the South Asia region.

When the Kargil conflict erupted so soon afterwards, Mr Vajpayee said he felt betrayed. The Indian government declared that Nawaz Sharif had been talking peace while preparing for war. In the aftermath of the conflict, India went to the polls and the previously shaky coalition that Mr Vajpayee heads was returned with a bigger majority. In Pakistan, on the other hand, Nawaz Sharif was by now in deepening trouble. There were those who criticized him for ordering the pullout of forces from Kargil under pressure from the Americans, and others who said he should not have allowed such an ill-advised military adventure to have taken place at all. If he had not been party to it from the beginning, the critics suggested, then that simply indicated he was not in control. If he had been, as General Musharraf claimed, that showed his poor judgement.

The writing was probably already on the wall for Nawaz Sharif and his Pakistan Muslim League government when the army staged its coup on October 12th 1999, less than three months after the Kargil war ended. It was a night of high drama. General Musharraf was on board a scheduled Pakistan International Airlines flight returning from Colombo. In Islamabad, Nawaz Sharif was given the news of what appeared to be a coup attempt against him. The crew of General Musharraf's plane were told they could not land at Karachi airport. As the plane circled above the city, events moved fast on the ground. Nawaz Sharif was placed under arrest. General Musharraf's airliner eventually landed with, it was claimed, just a few minutes' fuel left. The army chief took over the country.

As it turned out, it was a bloodless coup. My colleagues

and I drove through the night from Delhi. To our surprise we found the border open and even Lahore, Nawaz Sharif's political base, was calm. I spoke to people who regretted that Pakistan was once again under military rule. But it was also clear that many supported General Musharraf's line that democracy had been a sham in Pakistan and corruption was bleeding the country. Some were quick to point out that every incoming Pakistani leader, elected and self-appointed alike, had said much the same thing. They thought the best course was to reserve judgement and see whether Musharraf, his fellow officers and the technocrats he brought on board delivered any real improvement in the lives of ordinary Pakistanis.

* * * * * *

Pakistan presents many different faces to the world. Islamabad is a spacious, ordered, and leafy city of villas, office blocks, and diplomatic buildings, even if it is somewhat soulless. The capital is now linked to Lahore by a six-lane motorway, one of the most visible legacies of Nawaz Sharif's rule. The motorway is often practically empty but there are plenty of newish cars to be seen on the roads of the larger cities. In five-star hotels, the elite dine well and marry off their sons and daughters in style. In the countryside, the larger landowning families are now likely to have satellite television. Further down the social scale, there are also some signs of increasing prosperity – more motorbikes for personal transport, for example.

But when you talk to those toiling in the fields for the landowners, you discover the rigours of life in Pakistan for most of its 140 million people. On a farm in the southern province of Sindh in 1997, I was interviewing workers about the ways in which they felt their lives had altered in the 50 years since independence. I remember one man checking he was out of earshot of his employer, then telling me that nothing had changed – it was just as hard to make a living today.

The statistics are gloomy. There are some appallingly low literacy rates, particularly for girls and women, and millions of children never see the inside of a school or they drop out early. Either way, many start to work years before they should. Access to health care is woefully bad in many rural areas and there are stubbornly high mortality rates for infants and women in childbirth. Then there are the abuses of human rights that have commanded rather more attention, such as the so-called 'honour killings' of women by male family members who claim they have somehow brought disrespect to the family name.

General Musharraf also took over the reins of power after relentless sectarian killings involving extremist Sunni and Shia Muslim groups. And he inherited another source of volatility and tension which is never far below the surface. Twenty years of conflict, misrule and economic hardship in Afghanistan have left Pakistan with the largest refugee population in the world. Some two million Afghans were living in camps or alongside Pakistanis. But global funding for refugees was increasingly under pressure and, with Pakistanis facing ever greater economic difficulties themselves, there were signs that resentment was growing.

Many Pakistanis feel that their problems have been compounded by the inconsistency of the international community's involvement in the region. When Soviet forces invaded and occupied Afghanistan in 1979, for example, there was a sudden upsurge of Western interest in the region – particularly in supporting the mujaheddin, who were also keen to evict the Soviet 'infidels' from Afghanistan. Pakistan had no problem co-operating with that. It, too, wanted the Russians out of Afghanistan. Moscow was a close ally of India's and the last thing Pakistan wanted was permanent Soviet influence over its northern neighbour as well.

Initially, Pakistan was not exactly impressed by the money the Americans came up with to support it at this time. Washington's first offer was famously dismissed as 'peanuts', but the Americans paid up in the end. With Pakistan's Inter-Services Intelligence (ISI) playing a pivotal role in channelling Western-supplied arms to the mujaheddin, the Russians accepted after a decade that they had lost the battle in Afghanistan and withdrew, humiliated, in 1989. But Afghanistan remained unstable and Pakistan ended up awash with arms and flooded with refugees. Many Pakistanis still claim today that the problems of their own country, as well as those of Afghanistan, have been made worse because, when the Russians pulled out of Afghanistan, the Americans soon lost interest in the region too.

But there was another legacy of the covert war fought in Afghanistan. The then president, General Zia ul Haq, had taken advantage of the conflict to further his own ambitions of refashioning Pakistan into a nation that would be visibly more Islamic. There was to be steadily increasing evidence of the effects of this in many institutions, including the armed forces. And while this was happening, Pakistan was engineering its own descent to semi-pariah status – the nuclear tests, the Kargil conflict and finally the coup saw to that.

* * * * * *

When General Musharraf took over, a country that thought it might have put military rule behind it wanted answers. Was Pakistan now, once again, to be ruled by the generals for years? The army had been in charge for half of Pakistan's existence as an independent nation. Would there be a speedier return to democracy this time, as many governments had urged in their response to the coup? Was General Musharraf more influenced by his experience of the West, or by his Muslim faith? The political class was divided. Some predicted that he would be in charge for at least five or six years; others said two to three years. Many predicted what has already happened: that he would give himself the title of President.

At his first photo-call after the coup, the world learnt of his enthusiasm for Turkey, which derived from a spell living there. He admires it as a secular and modern, but also overwhelmingly Muslim, state. Since the coup, we had seen only the stiff military figure making pronouncements in uniform. Now it was Pervez Musharraf, the urbane family man, accompanied by his wife and clutching their two pet dogs under his arms. Muslim hardliners, who consider dogs unclean, were less than pleased by this domestic scene when it appeared on television and in the newspapers – and they said so.

The international community may have had some sympathy with the idea of a change of regime in a country that had plainly suffered at the hands of too many self-serving politicians. But there are mechanisms that come into play when a democratic government is overthrown. The Americans added to the sanctions that were already in place against Pakistan. The Commonwealth suspended Pakistan from its meetings. I covered the visit to Islamabad by a Commonwealth delegation two weeks after the coup, during which they tried to extract a clear timetable for a return to civilian rule. They were not given one. They also said they wanted to see Nawaz Sharif, who was still under arrest. They were told they could talk to him by telephone. There followed an extraordinary couple of hours. A first attempted call seemed to get lost somewhere in the labyrinth of the hotel's phone system. A new time was set and engineers scrambled to establish and test a telephone conferencing facility in the room the Commonwealth delegation were using. But all to no avail. The deposed prime minister never called. The delegation were told he did not want to.

Eventually, General Musharraf did declare a timetable for the restoration of the National Assembly. It was to happen by October 2002, three years after his takeover. The regime put Nawaz Sharif on trial, charging him with endangering lives by ordering that the PIA airliner with General Musharraf aboard should remain in the air on the evening of the coup. The former prime minister was given a lengthy prison sentence, but was later allowed to go into exile in Saudi Arabia.

One of the developments for Pakistan during this period was a marked pro-India tilt within the international community – as satisfying for India as it was alarming for Pakistan. One of the clearest examples could be seen during President Clinton's visit to South Asia in March 2000. Sufficient time had elapsed since the nuclear tests for the Clinton administration to countenance such a visit to the region. The Americans had been talking for some time of the need for a new, post-Cold War strategic engagement with India, providing opportunities for investment and trade that the US had notably failed to exploit. The talk of India becoming an 'information technology superpower' excited the Americans too. India ended up hosting the President for nearly six days. His visit to Pakistan lasted just six hours. There had been much speculation that Mr Clinton might not come calling at all. General Musharraf put a brave face on it and sought to salvage the notion that the Americans were now more engaged with finding a solution to the Kashmir dispute, so central to Pakistani foreign policy. But, as the world saw it, the Americans had managed to warn Pakistan more starkly than ever before that it was seen as the greater source of instability in the region. There was another alarming development for Pakistan. Its debt burden was mounting steadily. The international financial institutions were not entirely pulling the rug from beneath the economy: collapse could have provoked a far more worrying political situation than a military-led government. But there was pressure on General Musharraf from many directions.

* * * * * *

Then came the September 11th attacks, the naming of Osama bin Laden as the prime suspect, the warning to the Taliban of the consequences of continuing to provide him with sanctuary, and President Bush's challenge to all governments: you are with us or against us in the war on terrorism. Despite the Taliban's policies in Afghanistan, especially towards women, they continued to enjoy support in the madrasas, where they were schooled. I went to a madrasa in Peshawar after the Americans carried out a cruise missile attack on suspected bin Laden training camps just across the nearby Afghan border, in the wake of the US embassy bombings in East Africa in 1998. Rows of small boys were reciting the Koran on one side of the courtyard. In a classroom, older students were discussing issues within the framework of Islamic teaching. After the class I chatted with this group. There was, as I recall, something of a mixture of views on the way the Taliban were running Afghanistan, but many seemed to believe that, if the Taliban had better control of the country, some of the excesses would be curbed. And the students made it clear that they were willing volunteers themselves for what they saw as the causes worth fighting for in the region, including Afghanistan and Kashmir. There was no one willing to denounce Osama bin Laden, at least not publicly. Teachers said the students received no military training, and added that what they did in their vacations was up to them. There are thousands of these schools today in Pakistan. In addition, there are Islamic parties that have supported the Taliban strongly and helped to swell the Taliban's ranks of volunteer fighters. They have also always found willing recruits to pour onto the streets of Pakistani cities for pro-Taliban demonstrations.

That is the background against which General Musharraf decided to give 'full co-operation' to the Americans in their operations against Osama bin Laden and the Al-Qaida network, including the military action. To the Americans, the pledge was crucial. The Pakistani intelligence on the Taliban was unrivalled, the use of Pakistan as a corridor through which to launch attacks on Afghanistan vital. Pakistan's diplomatic links with the Taliban allowed an attempt to be made to persuade them to hand Osama bin Laden over. It was made but – as General Musharraf must have suspected – did not work.

The General told the Pakistani people that the country had, in effect, no choice but to co-operate with the Americans. The minority that came out onto the streets, burning effigies of President Bush, did not agree with him. But most Pakistanis probably did. His biggest threat undoubtedly came not from popular resentment against the decision, but from pro-Taliban elements within the security forces, the army or the ISI – from those who had directly helped the Taliban, even in battle. It has been said that Taliban advances visibly slowed, and they suffered reverses, when Pakistanis working with them were pulled back for some reason. For those in the security forces who had been most closely associated with the Taliban, the idea that Pakistan was now offering to assist in the pummelling they were about to receive from the air must have seemed very strange indeed.

General Musharraf played the India card as he explained his decision, warning Delhi not to attempt to take advantage of the dilemma and the difficulties that co-operation with the Americans caused for Pakistan. Soon he was able to show his people something rather more positive. The Americans lifted the sanctions imposed on Pakistan and India after the 1998 nuclear tests, penalties that had hit Pakistan far more deeply than India. Later Tony Blair was to make a brief visit. It was mainly focused on Afghanistan and Osama bin Laden, but a British prime minister would not have visited Pakistan at this point under any other circumstances. Indeed, the Commonwealth Heads of Government were due to meet in Australia at the time Mr Blair visited Pakistan. Had their meeting gone ahead, Pakistan would undoubtedly have been taken to task for the military coup.

But none of this was ever likely to make much of an impression on those who had taken to the streets, and there was a new intensity to the protests in Quetta and in several other Pakistani cities after the start of the bombing and missile attacks. The government warned that violent protests would not be tolerated, and it brought in the army alongside the police to drive the message home.

General Musharraf said he took the decision to co-operate with the Americans in Pakistan's national interest. He must have been gambling that the outcome will be a government in Kabul that will still give Pakistan greater security on its northern and western frontiers. With India to the east, that has always been a prime concern for Islamabad and was one of the factors that motivated it to foster the Taliban. Another of General Musharraf's gambles is that Pakistan will be able to capitalize on the heightened international interest in the whole region, and the causes of its instability, and may now secure the outside mediation in the Kashmir dispute with India that it has always wanted. The third gamble is that the co-operation with the Americans will bring further economic advantages for Pakistan. If a lasting peace comes to the region, the cruise missiles and American warplanes streaking across Pakistan during the 'war on terror' could be replaced by profitable pipelines between Central Asia and the Arabian Sea. Pakistan is a pivotal country in war and peace.

Yet much does depend on General Musharraf being able to carry his nation with him. On the day he signed Pakistan up to supporting the Americans, I remembered talking to Pakistani soldiers close to the Kashmir Line of Control who were manning British-made artillery that dated back to the Second World War. I could not imagine that these elderly guns would be kept in such pristine condition anywhere else. The soldiers grinned as they told me these were the same guns that would have been used to fire the shells bursting regularly around the hotel most journalists used – just opposite, on the Indian side of the Line of Control. When we sat down to have tea they told me that many officers remained essentially pro-Western by inclination and perhaps also as a result of the Western training and other military contacts that were commonplace in the past. But they also said that now there were many younger officers who seemed much more sympathetic to a radicalized form of Islam.

And the worsening crisis surrounding refugees from Afghanistan threatened to make Musharraf's task even harder. Pakistan had made it clear that its patience with this issue was running out long before the bombing of Afghanistan began in October. I went to the refugee camp at Jalozai, near Peshawar, in early 2001, as the authorities argued with officials of the United Nations High Commissioner for Refugees over what should happen to the camp's 60 to 70,000 inhabitants. The authorities were refusing to let the UNHCR register the Afghans, the camp was desperately and dangerously congested, food was hopelessly inadequate and the government would not allow the refugees to be moved to a better site. Pakistan was even then trying to stop more of them from coming, saying it had borne the burden for far too long. But after September

11th, aid workers predicted tens of thousands of new arrivals, despite the official closure of the border.

Afghans who did make it through the frontier were often bewildered and beyond exhaustion. One man, a prematurely-aged 40-year-old, holding his sick, listless child, said he could do nothing more to help her. 'I can only leave her to God,' he lamented. 'I don't have the money to treat her.' Others, waiting in the no-man's-land between the two countries, grew desperate and angry. Some tried to cut through the wire and were roughly forced back by guards who fired warning shots.

By the end of October at the Jalozai camp there were more refugees, among them 14-year-old Fatima and her aunt – a tough woman, with a challenging, direct stare, who said she had been widowed during fighting in Kabul years ago. Since then she had survived by hand-weaving carpets inside her home. Until a few days earlier, she'd never been outside Afghanistan. Now she too was a refugee.

She explained that she had decided to flee Kabul when her neighbours were killed. 'We heard the explosion in the night but were too frightened to go outside. Some of the fragments flew into our house too. When we went out at daybreak, women were screaming and tearing at their clothes. My neighbour's home was in ruins and she was there, weeping – her husband and two children had been killed.'

Fatima's aunt seemed dazed, but her face took on a sudden fury when she was asked about the international air strikes. 'You can't catch Osama bin Laden,' she said. 'He's up in the mountains with enough supplies to last years. You're punishing a whole country because of one man.'

The desolate, dusty camps provided only the most basic facilities – open latrines and a daily registration process to get a ration of bread. Afghans are a proud people and for some the loss of dignity involved in queuing for handouts of food was painful. But they knew it was the difference between life and death. 'It's a miserable life,' one said, 'but it's all we've got. We just want to go home.'

* * * * * *

General Musharraf's critics said he betrayed his faith by agreeing to support the military action in Afghanistan; he became a tool of the West and sacrificed moral duty for the potential economic gains of co-operating with the Americans. But others suggest he has his own agenda. He came to power as a man with a reputation for an austere lifestyle but also as a modernizer. He soon realized that the process of Islamicization had become so entrenched that he could not reverse it. He wanted to change the blasphemy laws which have been much criticized by Pakistan's religious minorities. He had to back down and he became more careful in choosing the ground on which he challenged the Islamic parties.

Two Pakistani generals have now been asked by the Americans to help them fight an Afghan war. Both have agreed. General Zia ul Haq used it to further his own Islamic agenda at home. General Musharraf, it seems, also wants to turn the co-operation with the Americans to his advantage – essentially to undo what General Zia did in very similar circumstances. Musharraf took one significant step straight away, with a reshuffle in the security forces to ease out and marginalize prominent hardliners.

Looked at in this light, the decision to co-operate with the Americans is indeed critical for Pakistan and has carried with it the highest possible risks. Some say that if General Musharraf does not contain and reverse Pakistan's own tide of radical Islam through the course of action he has chosen – or had foisted upon him – then that check is unlikely ever to happen. But first he has to survive the consequences of his decision. The short-lived war in the mountains of northern Kashmir in 1999 proved in the end to be a blunder for Pakistan. It gained Islamabad no territorial advantage, played into India's hands diplomatically, and cost many lives. Then, General Musharraf was behind the scenes. Now he is centre stage, but in siding with the Americans in a very different kind of war, he risked putting his reputation, and perhaps also Pakistan's political future, on the line.

CHAPTER NINE

THE STREET, THE STATE AND THE MOSQUE – A MIDDLE EAST DILEMMA

Barnaby Mason

Barnaby Mason has been Diplomatic Correspondent, specializing in coverage for the World Service, since 1993. In the early 1980s he was North Africa correspondent, based in Algiers, and went on to become Middle East correspondent in Cairo, covering the end of the Iran–Iraq war, the effects of the first Palestinian intifada, the Islamic-inspired coup in Sudan, and the Gulf War. In this chapter he analyzes the reaction of Muslims throughout the Middle East to the events of September 11th.

'The United States is reaping the thorns that its rulers have sown in the world… When God strikes, no one can stand in the way of His power.'

PRESIDENT SADDAM HUSSEIN on Iraqi television, September 12th 2001.

The crisis that burst on the world on September 11th had some uncanny echoes of the confrontation with Iraq a decade earlier. Then, Saddam Hussein was America's Public Enemy Number One. But this time he was glowering from the sidelines. And he was blatantly out of step with other government leaders in the Middle East; he alone did not condemn the levelling of the World Trade Center and the killing of thousands of people. On the contrary, Saddam Hussein clearly relished the situation. His attitude was elaborated by the Baghdad newspaper, *Al-Iraq*. 'America is tasting what it forced others to taste,' it said. 'America is on fire, and fear and horror have overtaken it…

We are not gloating,' the editorial said repeatedly and unconvincingly, but the message was plain: American arrogance had been humiliated.

These sentiments were extreme. Ordinary Arabs were as stunned as anyone else around the world seeing those unbelievable television images; but for many, mixed in with the shock and sympathy for the victims, was a grim satisfaction that the invulnerability of the United States had been shattered. When asked why they felt this way, Arabs pointed to biased American support for Israel. But as we shall see, the reasons for the pervasive Arab and Muslim hostility to the United States are more complex than at first appear.

There were other responses too in the early days. Many denied that Arabs could possibly have been responsible for so appalling an attack. An odder and more revealing argument was that the Arabs were too disorganized to have carried out such a sophisticated and co-ordinated operation. If it was not the work of American fanatics, some said, then Mossad, the Israeli intelligence service, must have done it.

Middle Eastern governments reacted promptly to the September 11th attacks and – Iraq excepted – spoke with one voice. Egypt described the attacks as heinous and unimaginable; Saudi Arabia said they were inhuman and against all religious values; Jordan spoke of its sorrow at such horrible terrorist acts. These are America's allies, their reaction unsurprising.

But more strikingly, there was strong condemnation from governments at odds with Washington for years, governments it describes as sponsors of terrorism. Syria offered its condolences, denouncing 'appalling attacks' on innocent civilians. Colonel Gaddafi said Libyans should 'console the American people' after horrific attacks that should 'awaken the conscience of humanity'. In his usual eccentric style, he also called for the despatch of humanitarian aid. A few days later, Gaddafi went further and said the Americans had the right to hit back and take revenge – though such action was unlikely to do any good. Even in the Islamic Republic of Iran, where the United States is seen as the Great Satan, the atrocities seemed at first to have transformed the atmosphere. President Muhammad Khatami expressed deep regret at the terrorist killing of large numbers of defenceless American people; some people in Teheran lit candles in the street to mourn them.

The overwhelming majority of religious scholars and Islamic groups in the Middle East also condemned the massacre as contrary to Islamic teaching. Sheikh Mohammed Fadlallah, the spiritual leader of Lebanese Hezbollah, which the Americans class as a terrorist group, said the attacks were not compatible with sharia law.

So the scale of the disaster inflicted on the Americans momentarily transcended politics. The states condemning it included monarchies, theocracies, secular republics still proclaiming a worn-out Arab nationalist revolution, out-and-out tyrannies and less malevolent despotisms, one-party states and multi-party fake democracies. In some countries, Islamic conservatives or militants are influential, even rampant; in others, they are more or less crushed. But in all except non-Arab Iran, they are the only serious opposition to the regime.

The way this works helps to explain Arab reaction to the September 11th attacks and the American military action that followed. It also illuminates the division between the state and the street. The case of Egypt, the most populous Arab country, is particularly revealing.

Egypt is almost the only true nation state in the Middle East, in the sense of a state with a solid identity, long history and continuous occupation of the land. There has been a state on the lower reaches of the Nile since civilization began, and the inadequacies of its modern incarnation have hardly dented the self-confidence of the Egyptians, the sense that they are different from the other Arabs they always claim to lead. The ruling establishment has also shown great cohesion. In 1981, a group of Islamic militants assassinated President Anwar Sadat after he signed a peace treaty with Israel. They were junior military officers, a particularly ominous development in a country where the army is the foundation of the regime's power. But the system held and reasserted its authority. Another military man,

Hosni Mubarak, took over; things went on much as before.

In official theory, Egypt is a multi-party democracy – opposition parties are permitted to win some seats in parliament. But no one believes for a moment that the elections will result in a transfer of power. The violent wing of Islamic militancy is vigorously repressed; those suspected of belonging to it are imprisoned and, according to human rights organizations, routinely tortured. By contrast, the Muslim Brotherhood is mostly tolerated, though technically illegal. As a safety valve, the government allows the non-violent fundamentalists to propagate many of their views, especially on social, cultural and religious matters, and it gives them a platform on state television.

In addition, opposition newspapers are given some latitude to criticize the government, though not the President. More importantly, they are given free rein to attack Israel and to a lesser extent the policies of the United States – especially the influence of the American Jewish lobby. Wildly exaggerated or invented anti-Israeli stories are run by both government and opposition press. Ten years ago, during my time in Cairo, a favourite one was that Israeli prostitutes carrying the HIV virus were being infiltrated across the border to infect the pure youth of Egypt with AIDS. Newspaper cartoonists depict Israeli politicians in crudely anti-Semitic stereotypes – hooked noses, hands dripping with blood – which seem to come straight out of the Nazi era. Columnists defend Hitler or argue that the Holocaust is an exaggeration. All this in a country that signed a peace treaty with Israel more than 20 years ago.

However, the government sets limits to anti-Israeli or anti-American protest. When students demonstrate in the relative isolation of the university campus, they are usually left alone. But if they spill out onto the streets, the police instantly crack down. I once asked an Egyptian journalist why that was. He replied that all demonstrators, whatever their ostensible reason for gathering, were liable to start chanting slogans against the Egyptian government if they got the chance; that might prove contagious and could not be tolerated. The inference is that protest against Israel, however genuinely felt, is often a substitute for complaints about government corruption and incompetence. And the other conclusion is that the authorities deliberately encourage verbal attacks on Israel and the United States in order to deflect criticism away from themselves.

* * * * * *

'Israel and the usurper Zionist regime are the number one state terrorists... America itself, the White House, and the prevalent policy in the United States – most of which is in the hands of the Zionists – they condone these crimes which are perpetrated.'
AYATOLLAH MUHAMMAD EMAMI-KASHANI in a sermon broadcast by Iran radio, September 14th 2001.

Hatred of Israel is a fact, not only in clerically ruled Iran but across the Arab Middle East. It varies in intensity, to be sure. Some Arabs still deny Israel any right to exist at all, more than 50 years after it came into being. Most grudgingly acknowledge that it is here to stay but insist that it must give up all of the extra Arab land it conquered in 1967. In particular – and this is the view of all Arabs without exception – the Israelis must stop their repression of the Palestinians, dismantle Jewish settlements and grant the Palestinians their own state. That is not to say that Arabs in general are especially fond of Palestinians. Let us not have any confusion here: Palestinian refugees have been badly treated over the years in various Arab countries and better-qualified Palestinians who take jobs from locals are heartily resented. But the ideal of Arab unity is an enduring one – the consciousness that on some elevated plane, if not in everyday reality, all Arabs are one. And the Palestinian cause is what Arab hatred of Israel seizes upon, the main way it manifests itself.

In this context, the United States is identified by the Arab world not only as backing Israel, but as doing so in an excessive, one-sided and unjust fashion. Palestinian civilians are killed by American weapons; they are the victims of American policy in the Middle East. A few days after the attacks on New York and

Washington, the Egyptian newspaper closest to President Mubarak, *Al-Ahram*, called on the United States to take an objective look at its foreign policy. If it made a serious assessment of the causes of the hatred the people of the region felt for US policy, the editorial said, it would find that its consistent bias to Israel was the main one. The arguments have been well rehearsed. The United States, even more than other Western powers, is said to apply double standards. It does not allow the Palestinians the right to self-determination, the concept on which its own independence from Britain was founded. It does not insist that Israel withdraws from illegally occupied Arab land in accordance with United Nations resolutions; it says the dispute should be settled by negotiation. On the other hand, when Iraqi forces invaded and occupied Kuwait, the United States used military force to expel them. The Americans have kept an array of UN economic sanctions in force, mainly to compel President Saddam Hussein to give up his weapons of mass destruction; but they turn a blind eye to Israel's widely assumed, though undeclared, possession of nuclear weapons. Amid all the criticism, Washington's efforts over the years to promote a Middle East peace settlement are drowned out, ignored or dismissed as inadequate.

Another Egyptian newspaper, *Al-Akhbar*, took the argument a stage further in the wake of the attacks. It suggested that American indifference to 'Israeli terrorism and brutal practices against an unarmed [Palestinian] population' might have served as a motive for the suicide air attacks. This explanation has been given some credence by commentators in the West, and even indirectly by the British Foreign Secretary, Jack Straw. He told the Iranians – to the fury of the Israelis – that one of the factors helping to breed terrorism was the anger that many people in the Middle East felt at events over the years in Palestine. Of course, Mr Straw did not say the United States was to blame. But for the Arab street, the guilt of American foreign policy had been long established; the argument was familiar and ready to hand. When the man accused of being behind the September 11th attacks – an Arab, Osama bin Laden – suggested that the question of Palestine was central to his cause, he found a receptive audience.

* * * * * *

'How strong this man is! He has a solid faith and power of will. With those he can accomplish the impossible.'
NADA, AN EGYPTIAN WOMAN, contributing to an online Arabic chat room, October 8th 2001.

Osama bin Laden was not the first to play the Palestinian card. In August 1990, a few days after invading Kuwait, an Arab country, Saddam Hussein said he would withdraw – but only after the Israelis had pulled out of Palestine. This linkage was regarded as laughably unconvincing in the West. But to many Arabs, anyone who stood up to the United States, in contrast to their own leaders, was their champion. The Americans helped the process along by casting Saddam as the villain, thus personalizing their confrontation with Iraq. Eleven years on, the Bush administration repeated the tactic: it fixed on Osama bin Laden as the embodiment of terrorism and the chief target of its worldwide campaign. Later it played down the personal angle, perhaps realizing its mistake. By then, however, bin Laden had become a cult figure, the latest Arab hero. His gaunt image was on T-shirts everywhere and his video appearances gave ammunition to anti-American demonstrators on the streets. To be sure, the position of his supporters was logically inconsistent. They cheered when he endorsed the suicide attacks and threatened more of the same – a line widely interpreted as an admission of responsibility – but at the same time insisted there was no proof he was involved.

Within a few hours of the United States launching air strikes on targets in Afghanistan on October 7th, a video statement by bin Laden, carefully prepared in advance, was being broadcast on television around the world. He praised the 'group of vanguard Muslims who destroyed America', and implored God 'to raise them up and admit them to Paradise'. Then he attributed to the suicide attackers a primarily Palestinian motive. They had responded, he said, 'to their oppressed sons and their brothers and sisters in Palestine and many other Islamic countries'. Next, bin Laden castigated Arab rulers for doing nothing about the killing of innocent children in Iraq, before returning to the theme: 'Israeli tanks are wreaking havoc in Palestine – in Jenin, Ramallah, Rafah and Beit Jala… but no one raises his voice or bats an eyelid.' The fact that this is not strictly true (Arab officials do condemn Israeli behaviour) does not affect the main point. Arab governments have long abandoned any thought of direct action against Israel, and are despised by many of their people for failing to match their words with deeds. There was a final Palestinian flourish at the end of bin Laden's video. 'I swear by God,' he said, 'that America…will not dream of having security before we have it in Palestine.'

Osama bin Laden was telling the Palestinians and the rest of the Arab world what they wanted to hear. Astutely, if obviously, he fixed on the key symbol of Arab rage against Israel and enrolled it in the mindset that had produced the devastation in New York and Washington. However, just as with Saddam Hussein a decade earlier, there is evidence that Palestine was not bin Laden's primary concern. In the oath at the end of his video message, he also swore that America would not be secure until 'all infidel armies depart from the land of Mohammed'. And in calling on every Muslim to rise up and defend his [sic] religion, he said: 'the winds of faith…have blown to sweep away evil from Mohammed's Peninsula.' The land of the Prophet Mohammed, of course, was Arabia. And the infidel armies are the American forces stationed in modern Saudi Arabia since Iraq's invasion of Kuwait.

That issue had preoccupied the Saudi-born bin Laden for several years. In 1996 he wrote, even more explicitly, that 'after Belief, there is no more important duty than pushing the American enemy out of the holy land'. Most of the suicide hijackers were alleged to have been Saudis, despite some confusion over false identities. Several of the others were Egyptians.

None, it appears, was Palestinian. The government of Saudi Arabia – with Egypt, the most important Arab ally of the United States – found itself faced with an almost impossible dilemma in deciding how to react. The contradictions are worth examining in some detail.

The House of Saud, the family that conquered most of Arabia in the early part of the twentieth century by cunning and force of arms, founded its long-term legitimacy on religious credentials. To make the point, the King's official title is Custodian of the Two Holy Mosques of Mecca and Medina. That would by itself be a high moral standard for the royal family to meet, but Saudi Arabia also gives special status to the extreme puritanical form of Islam, Wahhabism, which preaches separation from and hostility to non-Muslims. On the other hand, Saudi Arabia's oil wealth brought multiple contacts with the supposedly corrupting West. The ruling family was particularly vulnerable to criticism that it was corrupt, and that it abused its absolute power to enrich itself. On top of that, the government made a bargain with the United States: it guaranteed reliable supplies of oil in return for American protection from powerful neighbours like Iraq and Iran. When that protection took the form of an actual American troop presence on the ground, it enraged the religious right, in effect the only channel for dissent in Saudi Arabia.

Partly to head off the criticism, the Saudi authorities stepped up the promotion of Islamic causes abroad. Besides building mosques and exporting Korans, they had also financed the mujaheddin who fought the Soviet army to a standstill in Afghanistan. And among the Saudis who went to help the Afghans against the Russians was Osama bin Laden. He is reported to have had contacts with the CIA, which was training the mujaheddin. After the Russians pulled out, the Americans lost interest but the Saudis stayed involved. Public and private Saudi money went into the madrasas in Pakistan, which inculcated an ideology close to Wahhabism and whose militant students, the Taliban, were to sweep through Afghanistan and into Kabul in 1996 in four-wheel-drives provided by the Saudis.

It is the American contention that the Taliban regime then

became a sanctuary for bin Laden's network, Al-Qaida, and a base for training terrorists. The Saudi government is said to have allowed Saudi-based charities to channel money to Al-Qaida. So in this scenario, America's closest ally in the Gulf had an intimate hand in creating the launch pad for the September 11th attacks. However, from the Saudi government's perspective the conclusion might be different but equally alarming: that the ultimate target of Osama bin Laden was not the United States, but the House of Saud.

The last thing the Saudi authorities wanted to talk about was any Saudi connection with the suicide attacks. When it became unavoidable, the Saudi Interior Minister, Prince Nayef bin Abd al-Aziz, said they were puzzled by the focus on Arabs, on Saudis in particular; the United States had not given them any material evidence, and there were, after all, hundreds of non-Arab people on the four hijacked aircraft. He also denied that money had flowed from Saudi Arabia to Osama bin Laden.

* * * * * *

'Our rulers, why are you silent? Have you got orders from America?'

STUDENTS AT ZAGAZIG UNIVERSITY in the Nile Delta, October 8th 2001.

Arab anger at the American and British air strikes on Afghanistan quickly made itself felt. The Afghans were fellow Muslims; that was what counted, not the West's explanation of carefully targeted military action. But Arab governments, in sharp contrast to their reactions in September, were hesitant or silent. The Saudis said nothing for a week; then the Interior Minister remarked that they were not happy with the situation. In Saudi terms, that ranks as significant criticism of the United States. There was typical obfuscation of the degree to which Saudi Arabia was involved in American military action; the public line was that Saudi bases would not be used for *offensive* operations against Afghanistan. This formula was designed not to offend the Americans, while providing some defence against criticism from the religious right. One senior Saudi cleric issued a fatwa to the effect that those who supported infidels against Muslims were themselves infidels.

Other American allies in the Gulf tried hard not to say anything officially, leaving the criticism to their newspapers. As the hosts of a meeting of all Islamic countries, the Qataris could not avoid commenting. They said they were sure the United States would not have begun military action without proof of Osama bin Laden's guilt – though they had not seen any. In Oman, students took to the streets in a highly unusual anti-American demonstration. Official unease was palpable in Egypt, the recipient of two billion dollars a year in American aid. After two days, President Mubarak expressed support for 'all measures taken by the United States to resist terrorism' but hoped American forces would not kill innocent civilians.

The other key state in the pro-American camp, Jordan, had difficulties of its own. It is the only Arab state apart from Egypt to have concluded a peace treaty with Israel. King Abdullah, a descendant of the Prophet Mohammed, lined up with the West, saying that terrorism was just as much the enemy of the Arabs and of Islam. In part, he was anxious not to repeat his father's mistake of a decade ago, when King Hussein sat on the fence, expressed some sympathy for Iraq and refused to join the American-led coalition that expelled President Saddam Hussein's forces from Kuwait. But at the same time the Jordanian government is constantly aware that a majority of its population is of Palestinian origin; indeed, that vulnerability is why King Abdullah called for quick action to revive the peace process and find a just solution to the Palestinian problem. Extremism grew in conditions of despair and frustration, he said; peace was the only guarantee of stability.

Jordan allows a certain degree of democracy; the Islamic movement is vocal in opposition. By contrast, in next door Syria, a secular dictatorship, Islamic militancy was ruthlessly crushed 20 years ago. The regime certainly has no time for Osama bin Laden. On the other hand, the focus of its policy, almost its raison d'être, has been virulent opposition to Israel and the recovery of the Golan Heights, lost in 1967. Anti-Americanism has traditionally gone with the territory. Standing beside Tony Blair in Damascus three weeks after the air strikes began, President Bashar al-Assad said the killing of hundreds of civilians was unacceptable. But he did not condemn the whole military operation outright. Mr Assad succeeded his father only in June 2000 and is still feeling his way. On coming to power, he allowed some public debate on political issues, but later clamped down again. Another factor in Syria's somewhat tentative reaction was the fear that it might itself become a target of American military action. The regime played down this danger, but Washington does classify Syria – along with Libya, Iraq and Iran – as a state that sponsors terrorism. Unsurprisingly, President Saddam Hussein of Iraq denounced the air strikes.

The Iranians are a different case. The cry of 'death to America' was revived when military action began, and the spiritual leader, Ayatollah Ali Khamenei, accused the United States of dragging the world into war. The Iranians already resented the American military presence in the Gulf; now they saw it being extended to western and central Asia. But there were other considerations. Unlike any of the Arab states, Iran was Afghanistan's neighbour, with a long history of influence there. It was deeply hostile to the Taliban, partly because the Taliban massacred Afghans of the Shia Muslim minority, and in 1998 killed nine Iranians in Mazar-e-Sharif whom Teheran described as diplomats. So, privately the Iranian government was not unhappy at the prospect of the Americans removing the Taliban from power, and indicated that it was ready to work with them to establish a more broadly based government in Kabul.

To understand Arab reaction, as I have already hinted, it is worth comparing the crisis with the confrontation with Iraq of 1990–1. On that occasion, there was clear-cut Iraqi aggression against a fellow Arab state, even if the Kuwaitis were not popular. Other Gulf governments had good reason to think they were threatened too; that fear overrode domestic opposition and the reluctance to associate themselves too closely with the United States. The military objective was limited and easy to understand, the enemy visible. Egypt and Syria, as well as the Gulf states, sent troops to take part in the war. In 2001, none did. Things were entirely different. The victim of the initial attack, admittedly horrific, was not an Arab country but the United States, regarded with hostility by many Arabs. They did not agree that Osama bin Laden and Al-Qaida were the enemy, nor that the way to fight them was to attack their protectors, the Taliban. Above all, it was a war undertaken in a fog of uncertainty, which, at least in the early weeks of the bombing in Afghanistan, showed no signs of lifting. Arab governments might hope for American success, since they knew they might be bin Laden's next target; on the other hand, joining in American military action might make that more likely, not less.

There was another way in which the situation had changed from 1991, one that had a big impact on the propaganda war. That was the arrival of the Arabic satellite television channel based in Qatar, Al-Jazeera. Given an almost free hand by the Qatari authorities, it airs a wide range of opinion in interviews and discussions of a kind not heard on the state-controlled Arab media. Al-Jazeera also shows much more extensive pictures of events on the West Bank and the Gaza Strip, especially the behaviour of Israeli forces towards the Palestinians. Arab government channels tend not to dwell too long or explicitly on this for fear it might inflame public opinion. With about 35 million viewers, Al-Jazeera has also created an alternative to the Western media. In the Gulf crisis, the main outside source of information available to the Arabs on television was CNN. The dominant point of view was American. Now, as well as other Western channels like BBC World, there is a distinctly Arab television voice. Osama bin Laden was quick to exploit it, sending his video statements to Al-Jazeera and thus getting his message across in full, in Arabic, uncensored by Arab governments and unedited by Western journalists.

As the battle for Arab hearts and minds was joined, Western politicians started appearing on Al-Jazeera too. But the United States also tried, unsuccessfully, to get the Qatari authorities to stop the channel giving so much prominence to bin

Laden. The sight of the self-proclaimed champion of free speech exerting pressure on behalf of state censorship might have been calculated to reinforce the accusation of double standards. It was not the only Western mistake, as President Bush found when he described the war on terrorism as a crusade. In common usage in the West, the word has lost its original force. But in the Middle East, it still resonates; people think immediately of the wars waged by medieval Christians against Muslims to seize control of Jerusalem. The blunder was a gift to bin Laden, who already used the word crusader as a term of abuse for Western aggressors; it seemed to confirm his argument that the Americans were engaged in a war against Islam. The Italian Prime Minister, Silvio Berlusconi, provoked another row when he chose this moment to proclaim the superiority of Western civilization to Islam. Arab newspapers splashed his comments across their front pages and filled columns with indignation. Mr Berlusconi had opened the door to a new religious war, said one; another that he had done a service by revealing what the West really thought. The Arab League and the Egyptian and Lebanese governments demanded an explanation. Mr Berlusconi protested in vain that he had been misquoted. The Americans made another mistake that showed they were not thinking hard enough about the effect their words would have on a Muslim audience. They called the military campaign against Al-Qaida and the Taliban 'Operation Infinite Justice'. To Muslims the phrase was near blasphemous, since only God could dispense such a thing. This was less easy to excuse than Mr Bush's unthinking, off-the-cuff use of the word crusade, as the military campaign title had, it was assumed, been a considered choice.

Mistakes of presentation or failure to appreciate cultural differences were one thing. But there was a deeper difficulty for Western governments in winning the vital war of words. George Bush and Tony Blair argued they were attacking terrorists, not Islam. The terrorists were attacking democracy and freedom – universal values which the West was defending. But that argument rings hollow in Arab ears. Many Arabs would like to enjoy the democracy and freedom the United States stands for; only a minority actually want to live under a rigid, intolerant, puritanical version of Islam that denies women even the right to be educated and bans almost all music. But Arabs do not have the choice: almost all live under governments that monopolize state power and exploit economic growth and modernization largely for the benefit of the ruling elite and its allies. Some are more benevolent than others, more tolerant of limited debate, or less corrupt; but genuine political alternatives are out of bounds. The only channel of dissent powerful enough sometimes to stand up to the state is the mosque, so that is where the Arab street turns. Religious fundamentalists gain support from the absence of democracy, just as they do from the festering sore of the Palestinian–Israeli conflict.

But the question is: why should the hostility that many Arabs have towards their own autocratic governments be turned against the freedom-loving West? The answer is simple: because Western countries, the United States in particular, are the chief supporters of those governments. There may be strategic reasons for that: some of it dates from the Cold War against the Soviet Union, when each superpower was recruiting clients in the struggle against the other; more important nowadays is the desire to ensure continuing large flows of oil from the Gulf to satisfy the appetite of the American economy. But the justification is irrelevant to ordinary Arabs. What they see is Western governments proclaiming the virtues of free expression, fair elections and the panoply of modern human rights, but simultaneously propping up regimes that deny them to their own people. While Western leaders may condemn the so-called rogue states, they hardly ever criticize publicly the abuses in Egypt, Saudi Arabia or other friendly Arab countries: the practice of torture, the repression of dissent, dubious trials, rigged or non-existent elections. The fact that Islamic militants might adopt the same tactics or worse if they came to power alters nothing.

As the most powerful and prominent Western state, the United States attracts the lion's share of Arab hostility. It is also the most pervasive; its economic influence and popular culture reach into everyday life, at once the object of admiration, envy and resentment. No doubt the roots of Arab rage lie even deeper. The awareness of a once great Islamic civilization now fallen so far behind the West in technological and material terms feeds a great historic humiliation. Some commentators have suggested that a fear of the modern world and a hatred of America as its incarnation is central to the motivation of the suicide hijackers. On the other hand, some of them at least were entirely at ease with the *apparatus* of the modern world – with computers, with communications, even with handling airliners.

It is probably impossible to explain the minds of men capable of the synchronized slaughter of September 11th. But the factors examined in this chapter contributed to forming them, and taken together they help to account for the deeply ambivalent reaction among Arabs and Muslims in the Middle East. In short, it is the result of the complex interplay of corrupt regimes, Western intervention and political Islam. There is the long-standing resentment of American support for Israel, whose creation half a century ago remains an unhealed wound. The United States, the embodiment of Western democracy, is seen to deny democracy to the Arabs by backing the autocratic governments that repress them. For their part, Arab regimes encourage their opponents to vent their frustrations on Israel and the United States. It is a mechanism designed to protect themselves, as is the policy of alternately appeasing and repressing Islamic fundamentalists. However, the effect is rather to strengthen the kind of militancy that rejects all contact with the West and sees the world in black and white, in almost apocalyptic terms. As the crisis intensified, the more moderate Arab majority pleaded with the United States not to make things even more explosive by attacking an Arab state. Iraq was the one they had in mind. Any such move would put Saddam Hussein back at centre stage with a bang.

CHAPTER TEN

ISRAELIS AND PALESTINIANS IN THE AFTERSHOCK

Orla Guerin

Orla Guerin is one of the BBC's Middle East Correspondents, based in Jerusalem. Before that she was Southern Europe Correspondent, reporting extensively on the Balkans, and Moscow Correspondent. She had previously worked for the Irish national broadcasting service RTE, covering Eastern Europe and the former Soviet Union. On September 11th, the Middle East was already in crisis over the policies of the Sharon government and the second Palestinian intifada. Orla analyzes the impact of the events of that day on Israelis, Palestinians and the deteriorating peace process.

The noise ebbed away. The phones pleaded for attention, insistent as ever. But the sound was fading, as if the volume was being turned down. Noise never seemed like a comfort, until that moment when it was stripped away. A silence came over us, settling slowly on the whole Jerusalem bureau. We stood together in front of the screens – wordless – and watched the Twin Towers being smashed, like a child's toy.

Two hours on, I heard a familiar Israeli voice from the studio in London. The speaker was the former prime minister, Ehud Barak. He'd been in BBC Television Centre, waiting for a routine interview about his failed efforts to negotiate a final settlement with the Palestinians. He was calm but grave, already wearing the sombre expression that masked every face in the days that followed. 'The world will not be the same from today,' he said. Barak grasped immediately what others would realize later on – 3.47 p.m. in Israel (8.47 a.m. in New York) was the time of death of the world we knew. For a few moments the clock had stopped. When time began to pass again it had a new rhythm, unfamiliar to us all.

It was obvious, even then, that whoever was behind the attacks, and whatever their motive, the Middle East would somehow be part of it all. All we had then were questions: Was this region a staging post for the attacks? The birthplace of the terrorists, or their training ground? Did events and policies here fuel their hatred? In the early moments, we could not be sure. But we knew for certain that Israel and the Palestinians would not escape the fallout, that the trail of bloodshed and destruction that began in America would eventually wind its way back here.

As Israelis crowded around TV sets in shops and offices and coffee bars and schools, there was shock and sorrow. But there was also something more – a profound sense of identification, a quiet certainty that now the world would know how Israel felt. On the morning after the attacks, a leading Israeli daily paper put it like this: 'It is our tragedy, writ large.'

On September 11th, the United States, so proud and so free, became a part of the Middle East – a scene of carnage and sudden death, a place of fear, insecurity and grief. The horror brought down on Washington and New York defies comparison. But Israelis believed that they knew only too well how Americans felt. And certainly they had had a taste. Israel says that since 1993 there have been around 100 Palestinian suicide bombers.

* * * * * *

Two days earlier, I stood on the platform of a train station in the Israeli coastal town of Nahariya, wondering if life could get much worse. (Looking back later it seemed such a naive anxiety, like the fretting of a child.) The Kadisha were working quietly, close to my feet, inspecting every inch of the ground. They are Orthodox volunteers who collect fragments of bone and flesh so the dead can be buried complete, in accordance with Jewish tradition. In Nahariya their task was to gather the remains of three Israelis killed by a suicide bomber.

My day had begun in the parched emptiness of the Jordan Valley, beside a mini-van drenched in blood. It had been ambushed – two Israelis were dead. One of them was a blond-haired school teacher new in her job. Attack followed attack that day; after the Jordan Valley drive-by shooting, and the Nahariya suicide bombing, there was another explosion not far away. In a few short hours 100 Israelis were wounded and five were dead. Israeli missiles struck West Bank targets in response.

We drove back to Jerusalem, wrapped in a kind of cold shock, shaken by so much bloodshed in a single day. On the road we talked about how Israelis live with the threat of attacks. A colleague found a way to make us laugh. He'd been on the beach near Nahariya a few days earlier with his wife and some friends. It was night. They were barbecuing dinner, joking away the stresses of the week. In the distance they saw a torch. After a few minutes a policeman came running up to them, asking if they had seen anyone pass. Sensing their fear, he told them to relax. 'Don't worry,' he said. 'It's just a criminal, not a terrorist.'

Regardless of the suffering of Palestinians – blind to it, maybe – many Israelis believe the role of victim belongs exclusively to them. And it was as fellow sufferers that the Israeli public reacted to America's tragedy. They gave blood, they lit candles, they wept and they mourned. But the Israeli establishment did something else.

Long before the dead could even be counted, some officials were trying to benefit from America's anguish – and its desire for revenge. They began a campaign to convince the world that Israel and America were fighting the same fight. Israel expected to get a lot more sympathy – whatever tactics it chose to use against the Palestinians. This was a miscalculation on Israel's part, one of several to come.

And what of the Palestinians? Did they dance in the streets, celebrating the shedding of American blood? Some did, but not many, and certainly not most. On the grubby, crowded streets of Arab East Jerusalem there was some rejoicing – mainly women and children, gloating on camera. A few hundred more took to the streets in the West Bank city of Nablus, passing out sweets, cheering, firing their guns in the air. But you never saw the Nablus pictures, and neither did we. The lone cameraman who captured the event on tape was tracked down and threatened by Palestinian officials. They confiscated his footage – a crude but effective act of censorship. It worked so well the Palestinian authorities have used similar tactics since.

Where there was joy, it was private – no huge marches, no mass demonstrations. In the usual flash-points – Ramallah and Hebron and Gaza – Palestinians weren't filling the streets. They were at home watching America bleed, live on TV. Word came back that plenty were worried. 'They're on their hands and knees praying,' one contact said, 'hoping that Palestinian groups were not involved in this, and that they won't have to pay the price.'

Yasser Arafat himself hurried to condemn the attacks – one of the first leaders in the world to do so. 'I offer my condolences and the condolences of the Palestinian people to President Bush for this terrible act. We were completely shocked, completely shocked,' he said, and he looked it. He even lay down in a hospital bed in Gaza to give his own blood for America's wounded. (As PR stunts go it wasn't a triumph. The blood was never sent – it wasn't needed. And hospital sources said later that no other Palestinian followed suit.)

But in its dark, despairing hour America was calling on nations to take sides. The Palestinian leader didn't want to pick the wrong one – as he had when be backed Iraq in the Gulf War. This time he was eager to jump on board and support America's 'fight against terror' – as long as that meant terror elsewhere, not the kind of terror practised by Palestinian militants.

Within hours of the Twin Towers attacks both sides in this conflict had reached conclusions. Palestinians expected to suffer because of September 11th. Israelis expected to benefit. Both were right – but not for long.

* * * * * * *

Two days later: Just before 2 p.m. on Thursday 13th I was viewing the damage in the desert town of Jericho, a small cup of Arabic coffee already pressed into my hand. The coffee is compulsory, a ritual hospitality in Palestinian areas, even at the worst of times. My host was Mohammed Khalil Shakbua – a slight man, shrunk by hardships and newly burdened by fresh hate. There was a street sign, in English, just outside his door. He lives, with his extended family, on 'Intifida Street'.

It is claimed that the parched streets of Jericho form the oldest town on earth. Before the Palestinian uprising it flourished on gambling money. But the unrest closed the town's casino and the shekels dried up. Jericho was empty and broke and quiet – the quietest part of the West Bank during the intifada. But that didn't save it.

The night before, Israeli tanks had rumbled into the town, and onto Palestinian-controlled soil, into what's known as 'Area A': territory under sole Palestinian control since the Oslo Accords in 1993. This was the Israeli response to the bloodshed in Nahariya, among other things. After this raid, and another into the town of Jenin, 13 Palestinians were dead. The incursions were the most aggressive in the 12 months of the Palestinian uprising. Israel seemed to feel it had a freer hand since the Twin Towers attacks.

The raids coincided with the eighth anniversary of Oslo. That bitter irony went unnoticed. No one wants to look back at that hopeful moment now. It's like seeing a wedding photo of a smiling bride and groom, long after the divorce has come through.

There was some international protest. The British Foreign Office condemned Israel's incursions, saying the raids were unhelpful and were fuelling tension in the region. Washington too was worried about that. There was a protest by the State Department, but no song and dance.

None of that meant much to Mohammed. He took me to see his balcony, the walls pockmarked by Israeli bullets. 'We were sleeping on the roof,' he said, 'and the bullets passed over our heads.' I asked if he was sorry about America's dead. 'I wish to Allah more of them had been killed,' he said. A neighbour tried to shout him down. 'That is not right, Mohammed, my brother,' he said. 'You know it isn't right and it will bring trouble for us all.' But Palestinians like Mohammed had no tears for America, only for himself.

As Jenin and Jericho and later Ramallah were hit hard by Israel, Palestinians accused Ariel Sharon of exploiting America's torment – striking against them while the eyes of the world were elsewhere. Israel's leader was busy trying to convince the world that all terror was the same, that there was no difference between Osama bin Laden and Yasser Arafat. He began referring to Arafat as 'our bin Laden'. But in American eyes the old war-horse of Israeli politics was going too far – and not for the first time. Soon it was Sharon himself who was coming under pressure from the White House.

George Bush urgently needed to cobble together a coalition – just as his father had done before the Gulf War. But this time the enemy was global terrorism. America needed global support; it had to woo moderate Arab states. Most of all it needed a ceasefire, not an escalation of the conflict, in the Middle East.

Yasser Arafat was told to control the gunmen. Ariel Sharon was told to stop provoking the Palestinians and to agree to peace talks, but he wouldn't be rushed. Palestinian attacks had not stopped. In one ambush a 28-year-old Israeli woman was killed. Holding out for absolute quiet, Sharon postponed peace talks five times in ten days.

For once America needed Israel's help, and it wasn't happy to be kept waiting. The White House was losing patience with Ariel Sharon. So too was his own Foreign Minister Shimon Peres, the great champion of peace, who sounded weary and exasperated. 'America has stood beside us for 53 years,' he said. 'Now it's our turn to stand beside them.'

The word from the White House was that George Bush was furious – he wanted co-operation from America's traditional ally, not aggravation. Relations started to chill. 'We're living in a new world,' one American source said, 'and Sharon just doesn't seem to get it.' In fact Yasser Arafat understood that much sooner than his Israeli counterpart.

Eventually a truce was forced on both sides. Washington made them do a deal, for the sake of its broader aims. The Israeli–Palestinian conflict was no longer occupying centre stage. It had been reduced to a small piece of a bigger puzzle.

In late September, at the grandly titled 'Gaza International Airport', Yasser Arafat and Shimon Peres came face-to-stony-face for peace talks. There wasn't even a handshake until photographers asked for one. The aim was to shore up the truce. Washington was desperate to keep it going, though few here had much faith in it. ('Ceasefire' in this conflict usually means 'reduce fire', not stop it.) But George Bush was trying to buy time to build his coalition.

At the very moment Arafat and Peres were talking peace, a few miles away one more child was going to his grave. Mahmud Jalal Kishtak was carried into a morgue, his slender body placed on a slab. Between his two eyes was a tiny red mark, so small it was difficult to believe that this was what killed him. But it was the entry wound of a bullet that tore off the back of his head. Mahmud was 16, and Palestinians claim he was killed by Israeli troops.

After the Arafat–Peres meeting, Palestinian violence did not come to a full stop. But in the five days that followed there were 19 Palestinian dead – and none on the other side. Israel was using excessive force, claimed the Palestinians, even at this sensitive time. Israel countered that this was all a question of self-defence.

On one of those late September days, I stood on a blackened, battle-scarred roadway in Ramallah and watched Palestinians carry away their latest casualties. The trouble happened in the usual place – 'the fashionable clash spot' as a Palestinian colleague puts it. (The intifada has its own humour. The deserted hotel on this stretch of road is now called the '5 Stones Hotel'.)

This was September 28th, one year to the day since Ariel Sharon insisted on touring Jerusalem's most disputed holy site. His sweep around the Temple Mount (known to Muslims as

Haram al Sharif) was not the cause of the intifada but it was the event which lit the match.

One year into their uprising, the Palestinians had not ended the 34-year Israeli occupation of the West Bank and Gaza. They had nothing to show for the intifada but their dead.

On this bitter anniversary another Palestinian child, a ten-year-old boy, was killed near his home on the West Bank. A year before, the whole world knew about Mohammed al Durah – the first Palestinian boy to be killed in the intifada. He died in terror, cowering behind his father's back. In the 12 months that followed, Palestinians say they lost 150 children. In the same period, 28 Jewish children were killed.

By October 2001 the intifada had taken close to 900 lives, the vast majority of them Palestinian. There was burning Arab anger at that death toll. Now, as never before, that mattered to George Bush because he needed Arab support. The American leader who had tried so hard to steer clear of the Middle East was getting sucked right in. The Twin Towers attacks had brought the Israeli–Palestinian conflict to him.

As the anniversary passed, Washington was leaning hard on both sides to lower the temperature. No one speaks aloud of an 'acceptable level of violence' – it sounds too offensive. But such a concept exists. The mission was to keep the bloodshed down to that level. But it did not save the lives of a fun-loving and gentle Jewish girl aged 19, and her boyfriend aged 20.

* * * * * *

Arik Harpas was woken by the commotion outside. He opened his eyes expecting to see his two daughters, but while he had been dozing they had gone. There was noise and confusion. Someone told him Palestinian gunmen were inside the settlement, shooting in all directions. Arik – a paramedic – rushed out to help the wounded.

The first thing he saw was a body crumpled on the ground. He recognised the upturned shoes; they belonged to Assaf Yitzhaki, the boyfriend of his daughter Liron. She was lying a few steps away. The couple had been standing together, hand in hand, when the killers appeared. Liron had tried to run but she was chased, pursued into the small back garden of a neighbour's modest, white house. Arik wanted to treat his own dying child, but it was too late. Liron died in her father's arms.

She and her boyfriend were killed by militants from the Islamic extremist group Hamas. Yasser Arafat had signed up for the ceasefire but they had not. Protected by the night, they had crawled through long grass to approach the settlement of Alei Sinai – a sliver of beach-front in the Gaza Strip where Jews live on occupied Palestinian land. Before their mission, the militants left the now obligatory suicide video tape. One was grinning, in a kind of ecstatic trance, at the prospect of killing Jews. He was just a teenager himself.

When morning came, Arik Harpas stood outside his home and told me about the loving child he had lost. There was great dignity in his grief. 'Liron was very gentle,' he said, 'and beautiful. She had just started her military service. She wanted to travel to America, and to get married – all the usual things.'

He showed me pictures of his smiling middle child – joking with friends on a bus, relaxing at the beach, and in a boat at sea – during what turned out to be her last holiday. 'When I saw her last night, I said to the doctor, "Take my life. Take my life and give it to her." But he could do nothing.' Arik was fighting back his tears and struggling to find words in English. He told me about his trip to the morgue. 'When she was inside the fridge,' he said, 'I went to her and I kissed her goodnight.'

Arik's brother, Oz, took me to see the place where Liron was killed. He walked in the footsteps of his niece, tracing the path she had taken as she tried to escape. 'They were two young people in love,' he said of Liron and Assaf. 'Now they will stay together, and they will stay young for ever.'

A few hours later, and a short distance away, Israel was hitting back. Six Palestinians were killed by Israeli fire. And they were mourned with promises of revenge. Every bullet fired by either side had become a problem for George Bush. Washington was already in danger of losing the ceasefire it needed so much.

And America was about to face an extraordinary attack – from Israel itself.

* * * * * *

Israel's Prime Minister looked relaxed on his way to the podium, slowing down to shake a few hands, a smile flashing on and off his face. When he spoke it was not off-the-cuff. His words were scripted. And when he delivered them to the waiting cameras, it was in English, not in Hebrew. He wanted the international media to broadcast his message straight away – that Israel would not be sacrificed as Czechoslovakia was sacrificed to Adolf Hitler in 1938. 'Do not try to appease the Arabs at our expense,' he said. 'This is unacceptable to us. Israel will not be Czechoslovakia. Israel will fight terrorism.' A few hours later he sent tanks, infantry, helicopter gunships and bulldozers into the heart of Palestinian territory in the West Bank city of Hebron.

The massive military operation was in response to Palestinian attacks. By daybreak five Palestinians were dead. Hours later we found the tanks still in position – one parked right outside a house on Rashad Al Jabri street, as if it was the family car.

Sharon was hammering home his message: there would be no more holding back for the sake of George Bush and his coalition. Days before he'd had a nasty surprise from the White House. Seated in the Oval Office, George Bush announced that a Palestinian state had 'always been part of a vision' for Middle East peace, so long as Israel's right to exist was respected.

The move had been carefully choreographed. It followed leaks to two daily papers about a new American peace initiative. Officials claimed the White House had been on the verge of unveiling it, before the attacks in the USA.

Talk of American support for a Palestinian state alarmed many in Israel. So Sharon waded in with his accusation of appeasement, an allegation that hit Washington like a slap in the face. And produced a swift rebuke. It came from State

Department spokesman Ari Fleischer. The tone was unusually blunt: 'The President believes that these remarks are unacceptable,' he said. 'Israel can have no better or stronger friend than the United States.' US–Israeli relations were becoming another casualty of the Twin Towers attacks.

Yasser Arafat, by contrast, was beginning to benefit from September 11th. His dream of a Palestinian state now appeared to be getting a little closer. But in the meantime he had to deal with a problem in his own backyard.

* * * * * *

When Osama bin Laden announced in his video broadcast, 'I swear to God, that America will not live in peace before peace reigns on Palestine,' Arafat's officials dismissed his remarks as a belated attempt to hijack the Palestinian issue. Our cause is not his cause, they said. But the tape was trouble, nonetheless, for Arafat, and for America. Bin Laden's remarks had great appeal on the Palestinian street.

One day after the broadcast, Gaza was ablaze. Students from Gaza's Islamic University – a stronghold for the extremists of Hamas – went out to protest against the air strikes. Chanting 'Long Live bin Laden', they poured onto the streets. They came under fire from their own police. Three people were killed, including a 12-year-old boy.

Yasser Arafat did not want the world to see this – the worst internal Palestinian fighting for years. Local TV crews were warned off by Palestinian officials. Many carried on filming anyway, in spite of the risks. Palestinian police made sure we couldn't reach Gaza. Hours passed amid smiles, apologies, even offers of hospitality. But they maintained their armed refusal to let us across the border into Gaza. 'Orders all the way from the top,' I was told. But we managed to obtain the footage anyway. By nightfall, Palestinians were torching one of their own police stations.

After a day of bloodshed the Palestinian Authority held peace talks with Hamas. They agreed to calm the streets for the sake of 'national unity'. And Arafat's many security services helped to make that happen.

Exactly one week later he stood with Tony Blair in Downing Street, as the Prime Minister echoed America's endorsement of a Palestinian state. Mr Blair went one step further, talking about the need for a 'viable' Palestinian state – code for the Palestinians getting more territory in any final peace deal. Yasser Arafat was being well paid for supporting the coalition, and forcing bin Laden supporters off his own streets.

It was the legendary Israeli diplomat and former foreign minister Abba Eban who said of the Palestinians that they 'never miss an opportunity to miss an opportunity'. Less than 48 hours after Yasser Arafat's warm welcome at Number 10, Palestinian gunmen carried out an attack which ended a life and turned the clock right back.

* * * * * *

The tourists were being herded onto their bus when we arrived, police snipers keeping watch from the hotel roof. The visitors had come from Canada, South Africa and America on a trip organized by the Jewish Agency. Inside the Hyatt Hotel in East Jerusalem they had seen far more than they wanted to.

Over breakfast Rehavam Zeevi knew he was being watched. He told his wife 'an Arab' at another table kept looking his way. Zeevi had been staring into the face of his killer, or one of them. The assassins tracked him as he made his way back to his room. They left Israel's tourism minister dying in the corridor – where he was found by his wife.

Two days earlier he had said he would be leaving the Israeli government because Ariel Sharon was too soft. Zeevi wanted a tougher line with the Palestinians; instead he died at their hands. His killing was claimed by the Popular Front for the Liberation of Palestine, a radical group opposed to the Oslo Accords and opposed to peace. They said it was to avenge Israel's own assassination of their leader Abu Ali Mustafa seven weeks before.

In the 53-year history of the state of Israel, this was the first time a cabinet minister had been killed by Palestinians. It was clear that a handful of bullets had changed everything.

Israel warned that Yasser Arafat would be treated as America was treating the Taliban, if he did not hand over the killers. He refused. (To do so would probably have meant a Palestinian civil war.) Officials announced that Zeevi's assassination was 'Israel's Twin Towers', giving some hint of the kind of retaliation that would follow.

While Israel buried Mr Zeevi with full state honours, on the West Bank a father was burying his beloved daughter, with a homemade wreath and a Palestinian flag. Nabil Ward, a major in the Palestinian security services, stood crying in the street, in his green uniform and red beret. His big frame was crumpled like a boxer in the ring, as he called his daughter's name aloud. She was a 10-year-old called Reham, killed in her striped school uniform after Israeli forces pushed onto Palestinian-controlled soil in the town of Jenin. When she lay in the morgue, beneath a white sheet, he rested his head on her stomach – a father's last goodbye. Israel did not accept responsibility for the killing. But the commander of Israeli forces in the area was suspended for 'overstepping his responsibility' – a rare instance of a soldier being disciplined.

And Jenin was only the start of Israel's retaliation.

* * * * * *

The bullets penetrated the arched window in the middle of Sunday morning mass. Inside Bethlehem's Nativity Church, said to stand on the birthplace of Christ, the faithful ran for cover. Afterwards one of the local priests, Father Ibrahim, dug into a pocket in his brown robe and produced the two bullets. He believes they came from the Israelis.

Bethlehem has an ancient community of Palestinian Christians. For them, that Sunday was a time to bury the dead. They came in numbers for the funeral of a 23-year-old woman called Rania Murrah. She was young, beautiful and married.

Palestinians claim she was killed by an Israeli bullet as she went to buy milk for her children.

There were shades of Sarajevo in the little town of Bethlehem – wild gunfire on every corner, civilians getting killed by stray bullets. An altar boy was shot dead on Manger Square just after leaving the church. Israeli tanks were prowling the streets, troops going house-to-house. Palestinian gunmen put up what resistance they could.

Like Jenin, Bethlehem had been reoccupied by Israeli tanks and troops – Ariel Sharon sent his forces into six of the eight major towns in the West Bank. Israel said it had no choice because Yasser Arafat was refusing to hunt down terrorists, including the killers of the tourism minister. Israel was hoping to make a link to America's actions in Afghanistan, to convince the world that they were fighting the same kind of fight.

The White House did not accept the comparison. After seven days Israel had lost no troops, but there were 40 Palestinian dead in Bethlehem and other towns reoccupied by the Israelis. Palestinians claim most were civilians. Washington told Ariel Sharon that his tanks must leave 'immediately' and must never come back.

Israel announced that the army had captured wanted men, before bowing to American pressure and leaving Bethlehem. On a black and desolate Sunday night, I watched the first armoured personnel carrier make its retreat. The only sound was the grinding of its tracks. There was no fanfare, no elation on either side. The Israelis had been heavily criticized for an incursion that turned into a wrecking mission. And the Palestinians were worried that having done it once, Sharon would be back.

* * * * * *

Long before the attacks on America, I interviewed a senior figure in the Palestinian leadership, a pretender to Arafat's throne. Mohammed Dahlan is the well-dressed and well-spoken security chief in Gaza. Israelis who negotiated with him in the days of Ehud Barak dubbed him 'The Kid'. I asked for his thoughts on what lay ahead. 'The Israelis and the Palestinians,' he said, 'we are going together to hell.' The descent feels a lot quicker since September 11th.

The Twin Towers attacks have created a new international landscape. The Middle East now matters far more to the Bush administration, but as part of the bigger picture. With America and Britain fighting their own war, this conflict has been relegated to the status of a small domestic dispute.

Yasser Arafat is hoping for a payback over the longer term, calculating that his support of the coalition will get him closer to a Palestinian state. Maybe so. It's possible that the Palestinians could be the big winners in all this. But it's also possible that Arafat may be left waiting.

When Arab co-operation is no longer so crucial, President Bush could revert to a hands-off approach to the Middle East. America could disengage. The two sides may be left to their fate, to keep 'washing blood with blood', as the United Nations Middle East envoy Terje Larsen has grimly put it.

Israelis are concerned that Washington will be more preoccupied with its own problems and less with theirs. Israel's elder statesman Shimon Peres understands this in a way that Ariel Sharon may not. 'They aren't thinking about how to defend Israel, but how to defend themselves in a crazy war,' he said.

But the anger of many Arabs is fuelled by American's policies in the Middle East. The suffering of the Palestinians is lodged like a splinter beneath the flesh of the Arab world. That is one of the lessons of September 11th. Without peace between Israel and the Palestinians, America could continue to be a target for Islamic extremists, for the next generation of bin Ladens. Washington's long-term interests would be well served by an agreement.

When the dust settles, will there be a real impetus to deal with the Middle East? Or will America and Britain forget unfinished business here, after their war against terrorism is declared a victory, or runs out of steam? Without concerted American pressure, there will be no resolution. Even with it, a settlement may be beyond reach.

CHAPTER ELEVEN

PUTIN'S OPPORTUNITY

BRIDGET KENDALL

Bridget Kendall was the BBC's Moscow Correspondent from 1989 to 1994 before moving to the Washington bureau for four years. She is now one of our Diplomatic Correspondents, based in London. She maintains a particular interest in Russia and East–West relations on which she is a recognized authority. Here, she explains President Putin's reaction to the attacks on America, and the potential long-term consequences of his alignment with the anti-terror coalition.

Voronezh: On September 11th 2001, America was the last thing on Galina Ivanovna's mind. It was late afternoon and there was no radio or television in the bookshop where she worked. So when her shift ended she hurried home, preoccupied as usual with worries about how to make her meagre wages go far enough and what would become of her only son Slava. She was proud of him. He knew about computers and was fluent in English. But in their dilapidated, struggling town over 200 miles south of Moscow, what hope was there of a job for a shy young man with a history degree? At least, thank God, he had escaped being called up by the army to serve in Chechnya.

It was only when she stepped inside a shop to get some food for supper that she realized something was wrong. People were huddled in groups, talking in shocked undertones. 'Have you heard what happened in New York?' they whispered to each other. At home she found her elderly mother sitting in front of the television, mesmerized. The main channels had all dropped their scheduled programmes – one of them even ditched a live football match – to carry raw American television footage, voiced over in Russian by their Moscow presenters. Soon Galina could not tear herself away from it.

'It was terrifying,' she said. 'The last time our TV did that was in 1993, when Boris Yeltsin bombed the Russian parliament. You had to watch, but it was awful and somehow unbelievable. And this time it was even harder to grasp it was real.

'Pictures from America always look so dramatic, so unlike our drab Russian life. It was like some sort of Hollywood film. But I knew it was true. And I fear it will change everything...'

* * * * * *

Moscow: In the Russian capital Muscovites were similarly horrified. But many felt closer to America's tragedy. Only one year before, a bomb had gone off in the underground entrance to one of Moscow's busiest metro stations near Pushkin Square, killing a dozen people and leaving others with horrendous injuries. And a year before that, a bomb in a Moscow suburb had demolished an entire eight-storey block of flats at 5 a.m. Families were killed as they slept in their beds. There were only two survivors. The rubble of the destroyed building had been replaced by a memorial to the victims. The people of Moscow knew about terrorism all right.

On the busy Garden Ring Road that loops around the city centre, six lanes of constant traffic roared past the American embassy. It was only a couple of years since crowds of angry Russians had gathered here to throw bottles and other missiles at the windows, protesting at America's role in NATO air strikes against the Serbs in Yugoslavia. Now the ground outside the embassy was a carpet of flowers. More flowers were stuck in the railings. There were even candles and the odd icon in a small gilt frame. 'This tragedy touches us all,' said one man.

'Russia will never be the same again,' said another.

Not all Russians felt so unequivocal. 'Well, now they know what we've been through,' said one woman.

* * * * * *

The Kremlin: When President Vladimir Putin first heard news of the attacks, he reacted swiftly. He got on the phone to Washington DC and spoke to Condoleezza Rice, the National Security Advisor – the first phone call to the White House from any foreign leader. He despatched a telegram to George W Bush, declaring that these 'barbaric acts' were a challenge to the whole of humanity and should not go unpunished.

'We understand the feelings of the American people better than anyone,' he added in a televised address from his Kremlin office. 'We know from our own experience what terrorism can do. We feel your pain and support you.'

He declared he was ready to act jointly with NATO and offered to pool intelligence. He ordered Russian flags to be flown at half-mast and a nationwide moment of silence.

And to avoid misunderstandings, since US defences were now on high alert in case of further possible terrorist attacks, he called off a series of far-reaching military exercises that had been planned for that week. They involved Russia's strategic bombers flying over the North Atlantic, Pacific and Arctic Oceans in mock attack against NATO planes that were supposedly planning an assault on Russia. An ambitious war game, but it no longer seemed appropriate. When the real enemy turned out to be kamikaze hijackers heading for skyscrapers in civilian airliners, old Cold War scenarios suddenly seemed hopelessly outdated.

Mr Putin had his own motives for moving so fast. Within hours he and his ministers were not only echoing American suspicions that an international network of fanatics led by Osama bin Laden was the most likely culprit; the Russians insisted they had concrete proof to link him to Russia's own terrorist problem. For over a year Vladimir Putin had been trying to persuade the Americans and their Western allies to join forces in making international terrorism a priority. He must have felt in some way vindicated. In his eyes the United States was the second victim. The first victim was Russia. And the reason for that was Chechnya.

*　*　*　*　*　*

Russia launched its second war against Chechnya in the autumn of 1999, just as Vladimir Putin was finding his feet as Kremlin leader. A relatively inexperienced bureaucrat who had trained as a spy and never stood for public office, he was unexpectedly singled out by President Boris Yeltsin. Out of nowhere he became his successor.

But within weeks of taking over, Mr Putin was personally insisting on launching a large-scale attack against the tiny rebellious republic. His Kremlin advisers warned against it. They remembered the disastrous first Chechen war a few years earlier. But Mr Putin was adamant. He was incensed by the 300 or so deaths that had resulted from the explosion at the Moscow apartment block and other bombings like it. Many Russians were unsure who to blame. But he was almost obsessed with the idea that it was the work of Chechen separatists in league with militant Islamic fighters. He believed their plan was to foment revolution across the many tiny autonomous republics of the North Caucasus that made up Russia's vulnerable border in the region.

In fact when the Chechens began their revolt against Moscow in 1991, there was little talk of Islamic government. Their eccentric leader at that time was Dzhokhar Dudayev, a former Soviet Air Force general, who was married to an Estonian, and who waxed his moustache and sported a black Homburg hat and a trench coat. He proclaimed a political vision that was mostly driven by personal ambition and largely secular. An undercurrent of Sufi mysticism may have helped fuel Chechen defiance, but their main grievance was historical, not religious. After the Second World War, Joseph Stalin had exiled the entire nation to the northern wastes of Kazakhstan, accusing them of collaborating with Hitler's Germany. Many perished in the cold, harsh conditions. After Stalin's death they were allowed to return to their homeland in the Caucasus.

When in 1991 they saw a chance to shake free from Moscow, their main aim seemed mostly to be motivated by a desire to run their own affairs and grow more prosperous. You would not have called it a Muslim country. Attitudes to women were relaxed. Chechen hosts invariably greeted guests with toasts of local cognac or vodka. Religion in those days was a subject most of them barely mentioned.

But by 1999, in Mr Putin's view, Chechnya had changed. It had turned into lawless bandit country, rife with kidnappers, an embarrassment and a danger to Russia. Islamic fighters from abroad had joined the ranks of Chechen freedom fighters, creating a new security threat that could not be tolerated. 'We'll wipe them out, if we have to follow them into the shit house,' Putin announced through gritted teeth. On hearing that, Russians turned up the volume on their televisions: they were not used to such blunt language from their president.

* * * * * *

But Mr Putin was now two years into his war in Chechnya, and visibly frustrated. Criticisms of the war infuriated him. He wanted more understanding from the West and less carping about human rights abuses. He wanted the world to recognize that this was a war against terrorism. He wanted more international collaboration to cut off the foreign funding he believed was fuelling the rebellion.

Russia's savage aerial bombardments had allowed his troops to take over the northern plains, but they failed to dislodge a hardened core of rebels who retreated into Chechnya's high mountains. In the spring of 2000, the capital Grozny was practically razed to the ground by carpet-bombing and finally seized by Russian troops. The official version was that war was now over and a period of reconstruction could begin. But it was an open secret that the conflict continued. Eighteen months later, sometimes dozens of Russian soldiers a week were being killed in ambushes and attacks on checkpoints. Life for troops was almost as miserable as it was for the tens of thousands of Chechen refugees made homeless by the fighting. Hapless, hungry Russian soldiers would let anyone through a checkpoint for a chunk of bread or a few cigarettes. Many were teenage conscripts not long out of school, or jobless youths who had only signed up to fight out of desperation. The failure to subdue the Chechens was dramatically illustrated only days after September 11th. Rebels managed temporarily to seize parts of the second biggest city, Gudermes. Hours later they shot down a Russian helicopter, killing ten senior officers, including two Russian generals.

Then there was public opinion. Inevitably the Russian people were becoming weary of the conflict. At first, President Putin's tough stand against Chechnya had been applauded. But for how much longer? During the first Chechen war Boris Yeltsin saw his popularity plummet to a two or three per cent approval rating. The war in Chechnya could not go on for ever.

* * * * * *

Fly a thousand miles east of the Caucasus, to where the former Soviet border meets Iran, Afghanistan and China, and you find the five Central Asian republics. Since securing independence after the collapse of the Soviet Union in 1991 they had evolved differently, though with dubious democratic credentials. Three presidents were the same leaders who once ruled their fiefdoms as communist party bosses on behalf of the Politburo in Moscow. Only in mountainous Kyrgyzstan was President Akayev from a different background, a former nuclear physicist, and even his reputation came under fire when national elections were widely criticized as less then free and fair.

In the oil- and gas-rich deserts of reclusive Turkmenistan, President Niyazov enjoyed the unrivalled authority of a 'President for life'. Alongside the camels and carpet bazaars, communist-style posters and statues testified to an officially sanctioned personality cult.

Tajikistan remained the poorest country, so riven by tribal quarrels and ravaged by drought that it barely functioned. The gaudy traditional dress of most Tajik women – red, blue, green and yellow-striped silk tunics and trousers – stood out in stark contrast to their miserable, dusty living conditions. The least stable of the five republics, it was most closely tied to Moscow.

Kazakhstan, by far the largest in geographical terms, used its new independence to strike deals with foreign companies to develop its extensive oil fields. But radiation from former nuclear testing grounds and other environmental hazards of the Soviet era still contaminated parts of its vast territory.

Unexpectedly, the most politically independent of the five proved to be Uzbekistan. Ruthlessly authoritarian, President Karimov had pulled out of a collective security pact with Russia two years before. Once the bridgehead for the Soviet invasion of Afghanistan, Uzbekistan was no longer prepared to do Moscow's bidding – though a recent spate of bombs blamed on Islamic militants in the capital Tashkent had created new bonds with Russia and a new reason to worry about what was happening next door in Afghanistan.

Russia still regarded the five Central Asian states as its southern security belt. Many of its citizens still lived there, trapped on the wrong side of borders when the Soviet Union disintegrated, unable to leave because they had no money or no place in Russia to move to. The constant worry was that any uncertainty in Central Asia could prompt a flood of terrified refugees into Russia proper. Or worse, it could encourage Islamic disaffection to spread to Russia's heartland. The gold domes and icons of the Russian Orthodox Church might suggest Russia was an overwhelmingly Christian nation. In fact it is now generally acknowledged that one out of seven citizens is a Muslim.

Fear that the power of Islam might subvert Russia's control over the region has a long history. It lay behind the disastrous decision by the ageing leaders of the Soviet Politburo to invade Afghanistan in 1979. They reckoned an Islamic government in Afghanistan might export revolution to communist Central Asia. But going into Afghanistan was a humiliating failure. When the Russians finally pulled their tanks out in 1989, up to 15,000 soldiers had been killed. And resistance to the Soviet invasion had turned Afghanistan into a breeding ground for Islamic militancy.

In the years that followed, Russia's unsolved dilemma was how to influence events in Afghanistan without new losses. Under no circumstances was Russia prepared to get sucked into another Afghan nightmare. But it also wanted to protect its interests.

In August 1998, when President Clinton launched missile attacks on Sudan and Afghanistan in retaliation for the bombing of US embassies in Kenya and Tanzania, President Boris Yeltsin said he was outraged. Russia's argument was that unilateral military action must be on the basis of international approval, preferably through a United Nations Security Council resolution, and anyway no nation had the right to show such blatant disregard for another country's sovereignty.

However, by the summer of 2000, President Vladimir Putin was sending rather different signals about Russian policy in the region. At the G8 summit in Okinawa he declared that the world faced what he called a 'crescent of Islamic terrorism' which stretched from the Philippines through Afghanistan and Chechnya to Kosovo. At the time it was a claim that sounded faintly implausible, a pretext to justify Russia's brutal war in Chechnya.

But by now Putin's government was openly declaring it had reliable information that Osama bin Laden's Afghan bases were training rebel fighters for Chechnya. Top Kremlin officials warned the Taliban rulers that Russia itself was considering missile strikes against terrorist bases in Afghanistan in reprisal. In fact the threat remained rhetorical. When the Taliban hinted they might respond with a counter-attack on Russian interests in Central Asia, the Kremlin hurriedly backed off. It seems that was a gamble too far for Moscow.

The volatile republics of Central Asia were a potential powder keg in Moscow's view. Since Tajikstan nearly split apart during a civil war in the 1990s, thousands of Russian border guards had been stationed on its frontier with Afghanistan. But Russian forces were in no position to take on any other major role in the region. Bogged down in the war in Chechnya, beleaguered by a decade of cuts and economic mismanagement, they had enough on their plate.

And this perhaps explains why, in the weeks that followed the attacks of September 11th, American intervention in the

region was first rebuffed and then positively encouraged by
Mr Putin.

To begin with, his own military chiefs objected. 'I see no
grounds, even hypothetical, for a possible NATO deployment in
Central Asia,' said his defence minister. To grant the United
States a toehold in Russia's back yard by allowing it to station
troops in Central Asia would surely jeopardize Moscow's long-
term interests.

But there were other considerations. For a start, Russian
influence over the leaders of the Central Asian republics was
relative. It turned out Uzbekistan had been in negotiations
with the Americans for far longer than the two countries were
at first prepared to admit. The Americans apparently offered
generous terms for Uzbekistan's foreign debt. They had promised to help Uzbekistan and Kazakhstan clean up a germ
warfare site left behind by Soviet military scientists on the notorious Resurrection Island in the middle of the Aral Sea. Among
other things the island was a testing ground for weapons-grade
anthrax.

President Putin had limited options. There was no way he
could match the promises of American aid. And anyway, in the
short term, US involvement was useful. After all, he too wanted
the Taliban and Al-Qaida removed. He could not do it on his own.
The Russian people would never agree to send troops into
Afghanistan again. Crippled Afghan veterans begging on street
corners were a constant reminder of the price Russia had paid
last time.

How much better to let the Americans shoulder the burden
of the war, while benefiting from their presence on the border.
In these troubling times, a stabilizing American military presence
in Central Asia was not a challenge, but extra protection.

* * * * * *

Russia's paranoia about how to keep its country safe is nothing
new. Stretched across 10 time zones, with a population of 140
million, it boasts an economy that is smaller than that of the

Netherlands. Yet it needs to guard borders that encompass a sixth of the world's land surface. And the disintegration of the Soviet Union at the end of 1991 left its security arrangements in tatters. For months afterwards, Russian soldiers were unsure what country they were supposed to defend. Was it still the Soviet Union, the country they had sworn allegiance to? And if not, where were the frontiers of their new country? What was left of the former military might of the Soviet superpower?

So it is not surprising that after September 11th, Russia felt exposed. The terrorists had targeted America, but Russia too felt vulnerable. President Putin's personal guards were reinforced. Aircraft were banned from flying over Moscow and St Petersburg. Extra troops were despatched to protect the country's nuclear installations. And Russian air defences were put on heightened alert. In a telling interview, one senior officer told a Moscow newspaper that Russian air defence forces could not in fact guarantee the country full protection. Along with the break-up of the Soviet Union, the old Soviet air defence system had fragmented. What was left, he warned, was a patchwork of depleted radar and missile facilities that might easily miss an incoming enemy aircraft. 'There are gaps along Russia's borders through which a dozen Boeings could pass undetected,' he said.

Alongside compassion for Americans was barely concealed panic. If the United States, with all its wealth and technology, could not protect itself from this terrible enemy, what was Russia to do? By the morning of September 12th it was written all over the newspaper front pages. 'The world has collapsed!' went one headline. 'Armageddon now' warned Russia's main business daily. 'Third World War' claimed a popular tabloid. At currency exchange kiosks on the Moscow streets, the mighty US dollar, for so many years the nation's surrogate national currency, began to fall heavily. Russians were used to seeing their own rouble's value plummet in times of trouble. But this was the first time they had begun to question whether stashing American dollars under their mattresses was the right way to keep their savings.

After a day or two the currency fluctuations corrected

themselves. But the knee-jerk market reaction signalled a deeper readjustment. The United States had turned from victor into victim. For all Russia's resentment and envy of its former Cold War rival, this blow to American infallibility also undermined Russia's own sense of security.

'There is no superpower left now!' proclaimed one Russian paper, at once triumphant and bewildered. Instead it was Moscow that was offering to fly out rescue workers and medical supplies to New York to help with the disaster. And it was the American ambassador who came out onto the steps of the US embassy in Moscow to tell the Russians how moved he was by their sympathy.

The world had suddenly become a lot scarier.

* * * * * *

In the comfortable dacha land of Peredelkino and Nikolina Gora, the charming, leafy settlements an hour's drive from Moscow, where writers and academics traditionally spend their summers, few of Russia's literati would disagree with the notion that their country is part of Europe.

That was Mikhail Gorbachev's vision when he dismantled the old Cold War edifice. Letting loose the Soviet client states in Eastern Europe to seek their own political destinies, he called for a new 'Common European home', to provide a security roof for all European nations, the Soviet Union included.

Gorbachev's vision never happened. When the Warsaw Pact fell apart, most of its members queued up to join NATO. Post-communist Russia was left on the edge, the loser in the Cold War, a failed superpower with an ever-expanding NATO military alliance creeping towards its borders.

'If Estonia joins, NATO's frontline will be less than 200 miles from St Petersburg,' noted one retired Russian general recently. Those generals who remembered the deals done as the Cold War ended were especially angry. They complained that NATO had promised not to expand eastwards and not to act offensively. So why, they grumbled, should they trust an alliance that was still signing up new prospective members, including former Baltic states which were once part of the Soviet Empire and should by rights be in Russia's sphere of influence? And why had NATO ignored its pledges and without provocation launched an aggressive bombing raid on Yugoslavia?

But, if the military top brass are hostile, that is not true of all Russia's political elite. Even before September 11th, think-tank experts and government advisers were musing on the idea that if Russia's natural home was in Europe, why not join the European Union one day, and for that matter, why not join NATO?

President Putin himself has said something similar on several occasions. 'Why not?' he says. 'I don't rule it out if NATO evolves in a more political direction... Everything depends on what is on offer.'

It is hardly surprising that Vladimir Putin should look to Europe. He was born and bred in the most Western city in Russia: St Petersburg, imperial home of the Russian tsars, originally built by Peter the Great to give Russia a window onto Europe. Putin's only foreign posting as a KGB spy was to Germany. Admittedly he was stationed in Dresden, in the communist East. But for a young man from the USSR with no previous experience of the outside world they were formative years. They left him fluent in German and with a warm admiration for Germanic discipline and efficiency.

But there are other more practical reasons for knocking on Europe's door. Despite the row over NATO expansion, Europe looks a good security bet.

'Put yourself in our shoes, look at our borders in all directions,' says one of Russia's more liberal politicians. 'In the east you have China with its vast population eyeing empty Siberia. Then there is Afghanistan and Central Asia, a tinderbox. And more potential conflict in the Middle East and Caucasus. But to the west, we have Europe, much more stable, even if there is trouble in the Balkans. It may be less than two decades since the massed armies and nuclear missiles of the Soviet Union and NATO faced each other across the Iron Curtain divide. But from our point of view Europe is our most reliable ally.'

The events of September 11th reinforced a desire to reconcile security differences with Europe and the US that was already there. The Russians still beg to differ with George W Bush's Missile Defence Shield and his plan to withdraw from the Anti-Ballistic Missile Treaty. But even before September 11th he and Vladimir Putin were signalling that they were looking for a compromise. So when at their November summit they declared that they would both slash the number of nuclear warheads they held, while still disagreeing about Missile Defence, it was no more and no less than experts had been predicting. What was different was the back-slapping warmth on show as they dined on steak and catfish at George W Bush's Texas ranch. 'A lot of people never really dreamed an American president and a Russian president could establish the friendship we have,' declared Mr Bush proudly.

Security is only one reason to look westwards. The economy is another. Vladimir Putin was blessed from the start of his presidency with high oil prices which provided much needed revenue. But, in the longer term, prospects could be much more dismal if oil prices fall and Russia fails to attract large-scale foreign investment to turn around bankrupt enterprises and shore up the nation's crumbling infrastructure.

Already there were signs of a possible heating crisis in parts of Siberia – a grim thought when the winter freeze is so fierce, burials have to be postponed till the spring thaw, and outside daytime temperatures regularly fall to below minus 40 degrees centigrade. Television reports were showing shivering people forced out of freezing apartment blocks to huddle round campfires in the snow, because the town heating system had broken down. No one seemed sure how widespread such a problem could become, but foreign investment to overhaul parts of Russia's energy system was urgently needed – if Western businessmen could ever be persuaded to brave the risks of Russia's Wild West capitalism.

Against this background, the crisis of September 11th offered valuable opportunities.

The quid pro quo that Russia wants for signing up to the US-led campaign is help in speeding up accession to the World Trade Organization and forging closer economic links with Europe. Already Russia has secured an agreement to hold monthly meetings with the European Union, a degree of co-ordination Brussels does not even offer to its American allies.

* * * * * *

When President Putin made his first big entry onto the international stage as Russian leader in 2000, he arranged his schedule carefully. Immediately before meeting G8 leaders at their summit in Okinawa he paid a highly publicized visit to the communist pariah state of North Korea. It allowed him to announce to his fellow summiteers that he brought with him a new negotiating offer on North Korea's controversial nuclear programme.

When he finally fixed a date for a face-to-face meeting with the new American president George W Bush, after months of strained US–Russian relations, Mr Putin did not want to look too eager. He came to the hunting lodge they had chosen in Slovenia straight from China and a regional summit meeting with President Ziang Zemin. A month later the two former communist giants, Russia and China, signed a new treaty of friendship.

Even after the attacks of September 11th, the Russian leader refused to be pigeon-holed. As he shook hands in Brussels on closer links with NATO and the EU, back in Moscow his ministers were signing a new agreement on lucrative arms deals with the defence minister of Iran, a country still accused by America of sponsoring terrorism. These were surely deliberate gestures.

Mr Putin's message is that Russia does not want to be taken for granted by the West. It longs to be treated as an equal partner, as befits its size and status. An anti-terror coalition is all very well, but that does not mean Russia is ready to tailor its own interests to suit America. And after September 11th Vladimir Putin is likely to be even more impatient with any

Western criticism of what he does in Chechnya, or any attempt to sell Russia short in the diplomatic carve-up that will decide Afghanistan's future.

Just over ten years ago the Soviet Foreign Minister Eduard Shevardnadze, standing alongside the then US Secretary of State James Baker, pledged Moscow to a new partnership with Washington to fight its old Soviet ally – Saddam Hussein of Iraq. At the time President George Bush Senior claimed it was an historic moment, the start of what he labelled 'a new world order'.

That strategic realignment never really delivered its full promise. Back in Moscow, there were furious suspicions that the Kremlin was making too many concessions. Moscow was in danger of turning into America's poodle, or worse, a beggar dependent on Western aid handouts.

Vladimir Putin is unlikely to forget that history lesson. Recent research by American political scientists revealed that a surprising number of Russians think of America as an enemy. Even in the few weeks that followed September 11th, attitudes hardened. Pity for American victims of terror did not translate into backing for American air strikes. Many Russians were appalled when NATO bombed Yugoslavia. The American bombing of Afghanistan looked uncomfortably familiar.

When Russian communists came out onto the streets of Moscow to mark the anniversary of the Bolshevik Revolution, as they do every November 7th, they waved anti-American placards and openly accused President Putin of selling out to the West. To be sure they were mostly elderly pensioners, the sad remnants of the once all-powerful Communist Party, but it was such criticism that first signalled Mikhail Gorbachev was in trouble.

And the unexpectedly swift collapse of the Taliban regime in Afghanistan was also an excuse for Russian scepticism. 'They'll retreat to the mountains to wage a full-scale guerrilla war,' predicted one veteran of Russia's war in Afghanistan. 'Remember what happened to Napoleon in 1812,' warned another military veteran. 'Lured to Moscow by Russia's General Kutuzov, the mighty French army was trapped by a deadly winter...' Communists, military men, there are plenty of Russians whose secret hope is that the Americans and their allies might still get bogged down in a messy, unwinnable war in Afghanistan – proof, if it were to happen, that it was Afghan fiendishness, not Russian incompetence, that led to their own humiliation there.

That said, there is a good chance that the events of September 11th offer Russia and Mr Putin a real opportunity. If fighting terrorism does stay the world's top priority, perhaps this latest crisis could mark a major geopolitical shift, a chance finally to move beyond Cold War rivalries and suspicions.

'For the first time since 1945, Russia and America have a common foe,' was the refrain that echoed in Moscow in the days following September 11th.

US–Russian relations had undergone a 'seismic sea change of historic proportions', was Colin Powell's verdict.

Maybe, but ahead there are plenty of pitfalls.

CHAPTER TWELVE

BLAIR STEPS FORWARD

Andrew Marr

Andrew Marr is the BBC's Political Editor. He enjoyed a long career as a print journalist, becoming Editor and then Editor-in-Chief of the Independent *newspaper before joining the BBC. He has written three books on British politics. In the weeks after the attacks on America, Andrew accompanied the Prime Minister as he travelled over 30,000 miles to show support for the USA, and to help build the international coalition against terror.*

On the morning of September 11th, Tony Blair was in Brighton – and in trouble. It was a curious kind of trouble. He might have expected to be still basking in the golden lustre of his second overwhelming election victory. True, a worryingly small number of people had actually voted in the election. But by most conventional standards he was already the most successful prime minister Labour has produced, the first to have won a full second term.

Yet somehow, that morning, it didn't feel like that. Success has always been hard to define in the shifting scenery of political life and is becoming more so. Mr Blair had discovered himself more powerful than liked. He was facing great mistrust over his plans for public service reform. His government gave every appearance of dither and delay on the great question of when to try to adopt the Euro. Valued members of his staff were quietly planning to leave him to pursue other careers. The fresh bloom of optimism he'd enjoyed in 1997 could not be recreated so many resignations and let-downs later. Mr Blair was a worn leader; the satirists' acid had bitten deep.

Within hours of the US attacks, much of this seemed to be

changing. The Prime Minister was decisive, shot through with energy and certainty. He cancelled the speech he had planned to give to the Trades Union Congress; uttered a short, stark statement about the attack being not on America but on us all; and rushed by train back to London with his aides. He must have recognized almost immediately what he had to bring to the crisis: his instinctive pro-Americanism; his relative experience as a world leader; Britain's unusual place in the structure of global power; his actorly fluency; and, not least, his religious certainty – which included, by luck, an interest in the Koran stretching back five years.

So while President Bush was still fumbling for an initial response and juggling serious warnings about his own security, Mr Blair was shaping, in a few bold strokes, his answer to the question drawn in black smoke and dying words over Manhattan. Britain would stand unshakably 'shoulder to shoulder' with America. This was about terrorism, not Islam. It was a world threat. There should not be a wild, indiscriminate or immediate military response. Later, as the crisis developed, he added to those thoughts. But they remained his basic analysis.

By the time he was speaking to the Labour conference a few weeks later, he had expanded it into a hugely ambitious and moralistic vision of the need for a world remade. The speech, in Brighton, marked a pivotal moment in his political life. It is the most important speech in its range and ambition, and technically the best, that the Prime Minister has given.

Among its most resonant passages was this: 'In retrospect the Millennium marked only a moment in time. It was the events of September 11th that marked a turning point in history, where we confront the dangers of the future and assess the choices facing humankind. It was a tragedy. An act of evil. From this nation, goes our deepest sympathy and prayers for the victims and our profound solidarity with the American people. We were with you at the first. We will stay with you to the last…'

There followed a trenchant analysis of the need for a ruthless prosecution of the war against bin Laden; an eloquent restatement of his now-familiar theme that Islam, properly understood, was a 'tolerant, peace-loving' religion; and the most aggressive attack on left-wing anti-Americanism any Labour conference can have heard. Later in the speech, Mr Blair promised that the West would not allow further Rwandas and would intervene to prevent war-related tragedies developing in Africa, as in the Balkans. In its final stages, he took flight: 'The starving, the wretched, the dispossessed, the ignorant, those living in want and squalor from the deserts of northern Africa to the slums of Gaza, to the mountain ranges of Afghanistan: they too are our cause. This is a moment to seize. The kaleidoscope has been shaken. The pieces are in flux. Soon they will settle again. Before they do, let us reorder this world around us.'

The speech won plaudits from the anti-Blair *Daily Telegraph* on the right and from long-time Blair critics on the Labour left. Commentators struggled for parallels. It seemed Gladstonian in its high moral tone, religion-tinted language and rolling ambition. Others found it Churchillian in its defiance and self-confident analysis of global issues, though we should not compare them as men – Winston Churchill was a very different character from Blair and the scale of the peril they faced equally so. There are circumstances, including a successful end to the war against terrorism and a new effort to aid Africa and Asia, in which Blair's Brighton speech could come to be seen as a prescient imaginative leap – comparable in scale to Churchill's 1946 'Iron Curtain' speech in Fulton, Missouri.

But, as Chou en Lai remarked when asked about the effects of the French Revolution, it is a little too early to say. The sweep of Mr Blair's ambition and his moral fervour could equally well come to be seen as an example of embarrassing hubris. If the world coalition should break down over aid, refugees or any other myriad likely points of dispute, or if Britain were targeted by a terror attack on the same awful scale as New York, then the pieces of the Blair kaleidoscope could quickly look like the fragments of shattered illusion. Big ambitions – in political speeches, as in ordinary life – imply big risks and the possibility of big failures.

Beyond the public talking, most of Mr Blair's activity in the first few weeks after the attack centred on diplomacy. During four early trips, he covered 30,000 miles – visiting Berlin, Paris, New York, Washington, Brussels, Moscow, Islamabad, New Delhi, Geneva, Oman, Egypt, Syria, Saudi Arabia, Jordan, Jerusalem, Gaza and Genoa. As if that wasn't enough he then went back to Washington, on an overnight Concorde visit, to brief President Bush.

During the initial trips, Mr Blair leant on a formidable range of personal contacts built up painstakingly over the years. Since so much of his early achievement was based on personal contact, it is worth rehearsing them. Though he had been very close to President Clinton, and remains so, the Prime Minister had worked hard to build trust with President Bush. There were problems over European defence strategy and the two had different political philosophies. But Mr Blair is nothing if not open-minded – some of his colleagues think he is far too open. Though his first visit to Camp David had seemed a little awkward, he supported the National Missile Defence programme in principle while other Labour figures were hostile. He returned to London telling colleagues that Bush should not be underrated and that he had chosen a first-rate team. When others in Britain were jeering at the President's initial reaction to the attack, Blair did his best to slap them down. He got his reward in front of Congress when the President turned to him and said, 'Thank you, friend' for British support. That in itself was an extraordinary moment, a classic example of how the terrorist act has accelerated and compressed ordinary political life.

In Europe, Blair's relationships are much older. Still a fairly young man, he is a veteran leader in today's EU. Germany's Chancellor Schroeder is someone Mr Blair has been working increasingly closely with on tricky future-of-Europe questions. Lord Robertson at NATO is an ex-cabinet colleague and former British defence secretary; Chris Patten, the EU's External Affairs Commissioner, is one of the few Tories the Prime Minister feels close to. The relationship with President Chirac of France will never, however, be warm.

With Russia's President Putin, it was a great deal easier: the British Prime Minister had been among the first outside leaders to visit him, even before he took up office. That was at a time when the former KGB man was being widely derided or cold-shouldered and the Russian leader has not forgotten Mr Blair's gamble. The two men say they get on well and give every indi-cation of doing so. (Bizarrely, they apparently grumble together about their media coverage.) During his October visit, Mr Blair had the rare honour of being asked to the Putin family dacha in the Gorki district of Moscow.

In Pakistan, the former chief of the defence staff Lord (formerly Sir Charles) Guthrie was used to open doors. He and General Musharraf have been friends for more than 20 years. They quickly made contact after September 11th and Lord Guthrie was placed by the Pakistanis beside Mr Blair during the Islamabad talks. According to one who was there, 'it was Charles says this, and Charles that, all night.' In Oman, British influence remains very strong and there are close, interwoven military links at many levels. The country is a pivotal one in the Gulf region, bordering both Yemen and Saudi Arabia.

The Brighton speech gives some indication of the scale of Mr Blair's global ambition. His urgent international diplomacy with other leaders gives a sense of what he had to work with, the personal store of political capital at his fingertips. But what exactly was he doing?

An early, perhaps somewhat cynical, response is that he was doing exactly what previous post-war British leaders have done, which is to try to use the UK's position between the US and the rest of Europe, and her historic links with other world regions, to seize a leadership role in a crisis. Way back, we had the toe-curling vanity of Harold Macmillan's era when the British were to be the (cultured, worldly-wise) Greeks to the Americans' (powerful, brash, naive) Romans. Long after the illusion-punc-turing disaster of Suez, however, the Foreign Office continued to purr about Britain 'punching above her weight' or being 'a bridge across the Atlantic'. Much of the time these seemed rather light, ineffectual punches, and the bridge seemed a rickety one. The EU continued to integrate and the US looked increasingly west, seeking fresh relationships for the Pacific age. But there were moments when London's diplomatic preening seemed to match reality. Margaret Thatcher's close relationship with President Reagan in the final stages of the Cold War was one. Her famous warning to the older President Bush not to go 'wobbly' at the start of the Kuwait crisis was another. Tony Blair's own pressure on the Clinton administration over Kosovo was, just about, a third.

The weeks of early Blair diplomacy seemed more dramatic than these. Not only was he clearly working closely with the US administration; he had his own agenda, which was subtly different, and was weaving it in all the time. There is no doubt that Mr Blair and the people around him enjoy the warmth of the world spotlight; politicians are attracted to that dangerous glow like proverbial moths to candles. He has levered himself up from the relative obscurity of British public service reforms to a place at history's elbow. However tired he sometimes looks, he is infused with energy and purpose as a result. Presidential honour-guards, late-night palace dinners and swerving, siren-garlanded motorcades have something of the same effect on politicians as a glass of breakfast champagne might have on the rest of us. Under Mr Blair's direction, and for better or worse, this crisis has also become a British Moment. Resentment has been breaking through in Belgium, which held the EU presidency at the time of the attacks. In Paris they were tapping their noses and muttering, just wait. The smaller countries of the EU were close to open revolt at his failure to consult them. He held the requisite meetings, eventually, for the sake of politeness. But his mind was elsewhere. Small European countries, without a specific military contribution, simply did not count

At one level, his task was straightforward. To minimize the danger of the 'war against terrorism' – both the military danger and the risk of it becoming a generalized conflict of Islam against the West, as Osama bin Laden intended – it was necessary to maximize the size and strength of the coalition. Muslim countries were hugely important, none more so than Pakistan and Saudi Arabia. Getting the support of Pakistan meant, in turn, reassuring her deadly enemy, India. It also meant finding a formula for the future government of Afghanistan that was acceptable both to the pro-Northern Alliance Russians and the anti-Northern Alliance Pakistanis. At some moments, the dizzying spread of the coalition seemed almost surreal. Despite Iran's support for Hezbollah, Jack Straw was despatched to Teheran. At this rate, said the satirists, Al-Qaida would be applying to join the coalition against terrorism too.

Many of the key conversations could only be had between coalition-joiners and the US President. But Bush's first job was to rally America, rather than to engage in long overseas visits, so much of the face-to-face work devolved to Tony Blair. Downing Street resists the idea that he became in any sense Washington's messenger-boy; the relationship, advisers insist, is more equal and closer than that suggests. Rather, he is like a military scout, going out ahead of the main body of the army, but also able to influence the route it takes. He shared much with Washington, including the moments of surprise, as at the breakthrough of the Northern Alliance.

Here, however, we come to the kernel of the Blair–Bush relationship and to questions that cannot be fully answered until they are out of office and their private papers unveiled – perhaps not even then. To what extent, and where, has this British prime minister influenced the US President? Mr Blair denies, repeatedly and vehemently, that he has 'moderated' or 'softened' the Bush line, either over early reprisal attacks, or over widening the targets of US anger to include Iraq. The two men think alike, he insists. To portray Mr Bush as someone who needs restraint is offensive, Blair's people add. It isn't like that. Whenever it has seemed that Washington 'hawks' such as Donald Rumsfeld or, from the outside, Pentagon adviser Richard Perle, are gaining influence in the administration, the Blair team respond quietly that 'we don't think that's where the President is…and he takes the decisions.'

The trouble is that the more Mr Blair insists he doesn't influence Mr Bush, the more observers may conclude that he actually does. People who are really influential don't tend to boast about it, because that diminishes trust and therefore influence; boasters, by contrast, are often people being edged out of the inner circle. There is a persistent belief that Mr Blair is acting as a kind of outer buttress to, or auxiliary support for, the more moderate factions inside the Bush administration – above all, Colin Powell at the State Department and his supporters. In practical terms, this has meant emphasizing the coalition rather than America alone; emphasizing the need for a multi-track response, including humanitarian aid and diplomatic initiatives across the Middle East, not simply the military attack; and by trying to keep the focus limited to the Taliban and Afghanistan. The phrase used, *sotto voce*, by one British source, is that they want 'so far as possible, to de-Americanize the response'. It is not something one can imagine anyone even muttering in public, but that 'so far as possible' is the key. In the end, Mr Blair and his people accept this was an atrocity that took place in the emotional heart of the United States and the US would do whatever it thought necessary to avenge it. At no point did Mr Blair even nod to the case for a pause in the bombing.

Britain has a cotton rope around Gulliver's thigh. It might yet snap, either because an irate Gulliver suddenly strides ahead, or because an anxious Britain tries to tug the giant somewhere he just won't go. Where are the danger points? The most obvious one is Iraq. Whenever Mr Blair has talked to Arab leaders – from Saudi Arabia, Egypt, the Palestine Authority, Oman, the United Arab Emirates – he has been warned of the coalition-shattering effect of going after an Arab country like Iraq. Regimes that are controlling, but nervously, hard-line Islamic anger about the bombing of Afghanistan, fear they would lose control if the attack was broadened. Mr Blair himself is strongly seized of the view that bin Laden intended to provoke wider attacks, and thus to foment uprisings across the Gulf against the hereditary rulers – perhaps returning himself in triumph to Saudi Arabia as the House of Saud collapsed, in a rerun of Ayatollah Khomeni's return to Iran in 1979. So, while the public language was studiously neutral, to avoid making unnecessary enemies in Washington, the strong private view in Whitehall was that an attack on Iraq would be disastrous.

During Mr Blair's visit to the huge October British military exercises in Oman ('our biggest exercise since…well, Boadicea, I think,' as one senior officer put it), his spokesman released details of an internal Whitehall paper on Britain's war aims. This spelt out a first phase of the anti-terrorist actions, clearly limited to Al-Qaida and the Taliban. There would then be a second phase, which would concentrate on the funding, ease of movement, harbouring and protection of terrorists across the world. But, said the spokesman, any attack on a sovereign country during that second phase would have to be based on '100 per cent proof of guilt', on the approval of the United Nations under international law, and on the need to maintain the widest possible coalition. These points, particularly the last one, seemed designed to go as far as possible to reassure Arab opinion that Britain would not support a swivel of the attack towards Baghdad, without risking an open row with Washington. Could Mr Blair rethink? After all, breaking with the President over something like that would be a shattering diplomatic blow.

If the Taliban could be removed relatively quickly, without much bloodshed, and bin Laden and friends brought swiftly to justice, then there are some signs the Iraqi question could be reconsidered. But London is intensely alive to the danger of a general uprising throughout many key Arab countries. When, therefore, there were signs from the Bush administration that the mysterious first wave of anthrax attacks in the US was being linked to an Iraqi intelligence agent, alarm bells started to ring across Whitehall. The terse, tight-lipped official response was that Britain saw no evidence of an Iraqi link, either to the events of September 11th, or to anything subsequently. This writer has been told very privately that if it came to a US attack on Iraq, 'we might very well walk away; we might say no'.

As I write, that remains by far the most dangerous-looking fissure. It is not, however, the only potential danger point. One of the more mysterious and subterranean aspects of British diplomacy has been the intense effort in Moscow. After Mr

Blair's visit, followed by several follow-up phone calls, both the Deputy Prime Minister, John Prescott, and the Defence Secretary, Geoff Hoon, were sent for further talks. It is openly admitted in Downing Street that 'the Russians were being incredibly helpful. They are offering things that no one would have believed possible before September 11th.' But what are those 'things'? And what are they looking for in return? President Putin's mid-November visit to America, when the US announced dramatic cuts in its nuclear arsenal, was part of the answer. But there will be more. Apart from a virtually free hand in Chechnya – Mr Blair has become ready to describe 'many Chechens' as 'terrorists' – it would be surprising if Moscow were not looking for a deal both on missile defence and on limits to NATO's expansion eastwards. NATO has already offered Mr Putin a special relationship but with the whole security shape of the world in flux, Mr Blair will have to be very adroit to avoid worrying the Republican defence establishment in America.

These Russian deals match many others being quietly done around the world by Britain and other countries trying to stitch the coalition ever more tightly together. Behind the fine words of solidarity and mutual grief, many nations' leaderships have been forced into hard choices about backing the US, and wish to extract something in return. In some cases, the price demanded is relatively easy to pay; Pakistan, for instance, won a resumption of defence contacts and the promise by Britain to champion Islamabad's case in the International Monetary Fund, as well as substantial new aid for refugees on the northern border. Given that Britain, along with the rest of the EU, is the major financial donor to the Palestinians, it has been a natural match to American pressure on Israel in trying to restart the agonized Middle East peace process.

These are among the things Mr Blair was saying to political leaders. But what about the people? In particular, what about the millions of impoverished, angry Arabs and other Muslims who were unimpressed to find the Americans, Europeans and Israelis allied with their autocratic and repressive governments in a war supposedly being fought for 'freedom and democracy'? As he travelled, the Prime Minister became more seized of the great gulf in understanding between the West and the Arab world generally, and the need to respond with what one of those close to him described with brutal directness as 'propaganda'. Osama bin Laden was, it seemed, something of a master of propaganda himself, with his video-taped calls for jihad sent to Al-Jazeera; Mr Blair responded by offering to be interviewed by the TV station. He followed this by giving interviews to other outlets such as Abu Dhabi Television, as well as penning articles to be translated into Arabic and disseminated round the region.

Quite what militant-inclined Muslims in the slums of Cairo or the cities of northern Pakistan made of lectures from a Christian prime minister about the proper interpretation of the Koran is hard to say – if the Blair articles ever reached them. But his lines of argument were interesting and may have resonated among middle-class Arab opinion. First, he emphasized that bin Laden had a clear political objective, which was to topple all the main Gulf regimes, imposing Taliban-style regimes everywhere. Second, he pointed out that the Al-Qaida statements since September 11th were virtually an admission of guilt – something that matters particularly in a culture where justice is a stronger concept than personal freedom. Third, he rammed home again that most readings of the Koran found the terrorist actions wholly un-Islamic. And finally, he tried to refute the widespread belief that Britain and America were hostile to the Arab world. They had defended Muslims in Kosovo against Orthodox Christian Serbs; they were doing their best to restart the peace process to bring justice to the Palestinians.

This account of Mr Blair's behaviour after the attack has been almost entirely focused on his work outside Britain. He was able to spend relatively little time on 'the home front' because of the remarkably widespread support he was getting. Early polls showed that the public were overwhelmingly in favour of attacking Al-Qaida and the Taliban, even if it led to reprisal attacks in Britain and the loss of British lives in Afghanistan. The Conservative opposition, under its new leader

Iain Duncan Smith, offered total support, even being uncomplaining when their annual Blackpool conference was badly disrupted by one of the three special recalls of Parliament that Mr Blair asked for during September and October. The Liberal Democrats were slightly more cautious, emphasizing their concern for civil liberties and the developing humanitarian disaster in Afghanistan; but they too were basically supportive.

The breadth of domestic support allowed David Blunkett, the Home Secretary, to announce a raft of new measures on asylum, detention, Europe-wide arrest warrants, deportation and policing, without there being a great political or press protest. These went far enough to require a derogation from Article 5 of the European Convention on Human Rights, on public emergency grounds. One other obvious source of serious dissent, the organized Muslim communities of Britain, received a powerful and sustained programme of reassurance from the Prime Minister, including personal meetings, support for Islam, and the promise of a new law against religious harassment. Early protest demonstrations were loud and passionate but they were neither very large nor politically difficult for Mr Blair.

All of this became a little harder to sustain the longer the military campaign continued. Between mid-October and the breakthrough a month later, the few voices of Labour dissidents were joined by a widespread rumbling of worry and unease on the Labour benches. Mr Blair had won his unexpected friends on the left by emphasizing the central importance of humanitarian aid and coalition-building, and his determination to avert famine, not simply wage war. But as the harsh Afghan winter came nearer and the US seemed to be running out of targets, patience among the critics began to wear thin. Though most people remained more frightened of Al-Qaida than worried about the plight of Afghans, there was a rising tide of questioning about the real war aims and the oft-repeated assurance that this was a war against terrorism, not against Afghanistan. Below the surface, opinion polls showed that British Muslim opinion was alienated from the war.

But abroad as well as at home, Mr Blair has been fighting

to hold together a grand coalition of opinion far wider even than the 'big tent' politics he espoused in his earlier years. This common undertaking tries to draw in, at its outermost edges, both the Iranian government and Italy's prime minister, Silvio Berlusconi; it includes both Moscow's KGB-man-turned-president and his old enemies in Pakistan; both Yasser Arafat and Ariel Sharon; both Western Muslims and angry Western liberals; the Labour left and a distinctively right-wing Conservative leader. So long as the enemy is clear, the danger great, the means trusted, the time limited, and the human cost not too severe, then such a grand coalition can hold. And perhaps a bit beyond then too. Both Mr Blair and his Chancellor, Gordon Brown, believe that a post-September 11th and post-Bin Laden world can also be a more engaged, fairer and interwoven world. They think a more ambitious economic, health and education effort by the United Nations, the World Bank and other institutions, backed by many billions of extra dollars for many years ahead, can help prevent tomorrow's terrorists, in the slums of African, Middle Eastern or Asian cities. The Prime Minister's grand dream of a new world order is ambitious but is not yet ridiculous. Much depends on whether the United States under a Republican president can be persuaded to go along with this liberal world-view. Mr Blair is a leader of remarkable talents, not the least of which is his unfashionable belief that mere politicians can do decent deeds in a wicked world. It may be worth a try.

CHAPTER THIRTEEN

EARTHQUAKE IN THE GLOBAL ECONOMY

JEFF RANDALL

Jeff Randall is the BBC's Business Editor. Previously he was City Correspondent for the Sunday Telegraph, *City and Business Editor for the* Sunday Times, *and the launch editor of the* Sunday Business *newspaper. He was also a director of Times Newspapers in the mid-1990s. Jeff was reporting the global slowdown long before September 11th and writes here about the effects of the terrorist attacks on the contracting world economy.*

When two flying bombs crash through the upper floors of a twin-tower skyscraper in New York's financial district, the business world changes for ever. Those firms whose premises were destroyed and employees slaughtered can begin to recover and try to start again. But the way in which they operate can never fully return to how it was before the attacks.

Sir Martin Sorrell, chief executive of advertising group WPP, explains: 'Anguish on such a scale does change your life. Five thousand people were killed. If you think that each of those had 150 or 200 acquaintances, that is a huge number of people sharing that anguish in a direct and personal way.'

Even Wall Street, with its formidable resilience and gung-ho attitude to work, cannot rewind the clock. It will, of course, remain a powerhouse for trading in stocks and shares, bonds and currencies; the capital of international finance. In that sense, lower Manhattan has not been cowed by the terrorists. But its skyline has been reshaped and so has its mindset.

Companies have reassessed the downside of high-rise

premises; travellers on all forms of transport have inevitably become more wary; security has been stepped up at offices, shopping malls, bus stations, subways and airports; financial institutions have rethought lending policies; insurers have re-priced the risks they cover; and consumers have re-evaluated their lifestyle priorities.

For many Americans, not just New Yorkers, the adjust-ments forced on them by the events of September 11th are very apparent and unlikely to be temporary. 'Business as usual' has taken on a different meaning.

In other countries too, companies and their customers are coming to terms with a seismic shift in the commercial landscape. At one end of the scale, change equals not much more than a minor inconvenience. For instance, new rules mean that airline passengers in the US are now limited to a single piece of carry-on luggage. A small price to pay for enhanced safety, but a lasting reminder that the days of treating internal flights as bus rides in the air have passed into history. At the other end, opening the mail in government buildings has become fraught with danger.

Of the sectors damaged by the suicide killers, air travel has been hit hardest. The images of destruction remain fresh in people's minds long after the event. All over the world, the appeal of flying has been diminished. British Airways' chairman Lord Marshall said the industry had been plunged into 'crisis', a sentiment echoed by many of his airline counterparts.

Immediately after the attack, airline analysts predicted a 50 per cent fall in domestic American traffic for 2001–2 and about a 25 per cent reduction in the transatlantic market. If these forecasts initially seemed alarmist, it quickly became clear that the outcome could be even worse, with international air-transport profits being devastated by a collapse in demand. Six weeks after the attacks, the Association of European Airlines said that transatlantic traffic had fallen by 36 per cent.

Aviation job losses have piled up, as carriers slash their workforces in a desperate attempt to align costs with vanishing revenues. US airlines in particular have pushed through draconian cutbacks, with Continental, United and American shedding tens of thousands of jobs. American, which had two aircraft hijacked in the raids, would have lost nearly $1 billion in the third quarter of 2001 without its share of the $15 billion of special aid that the federal government pumped into the industry.

Around the world, airline companies were knocked over like dominoes. Swissair collapsed, but was then revived, Aer Lingus was bailed out by the Irish government, and Lot by the Polish government. Belgium's Sabena airline filed for bankruptcy. British Airways' finances are stretched to near breaking point, as are those of its British rival, Virgin Atlantic.

Throughout Europe, flag-carriers, such as the Netherlands' KLM and Scandinavia's SAS, are cutting routes and flight frequencies. In the end, several of the weaker state-owned carriers are likely to merge in order to survive.

The severity of the aviation downturn, which few analysts expect to be short-lived, also threatens aircraft and aero-engine manufacturers. Boeing, the world's biggest plane maker, has cut 30,000 jobs and Britain's aero-engine supplier Rolls-Royce another 5,000. Boeing's chairman, Phil Condit, said his industry's plight will be 'ten times worse' than during the Gulf War.

The Geneva-based International Air Transport Association estimates that the final tally for job losses in the airline industry, resulting from the World Trade Center attacks, will reach 200,000. IATA, which represents 275 airlines, reckons its members' aggregate losses will be $7 billion in 2001, and sees little prospect of a swift recovery.

When people stop flying in large numbers, the impact on other industries, most notably the leisure business, is immediate and costly. Fear is the travel sector's biggest enemy. Hotel companies throughout the world, but especially in America, are cancelling construction projects for 2002 and 2003 amid a glut of unfilled rooms. More than 17 million Americans work in travel and tourism-related industries, with an annual payroll of $159 billion – and many of these jobs are in jeopardy.

A month after the outrage, hotels in Washington DC were reporting that occupancy levels had fallen to 50 per cent from a more typical 80 per cent in early autumn. Some of America's leading tourist spots have suffered a 75 per cent drop in attendance figures. On some days in October, Florida's Disney World was all but empty. And if the war against terrorism has made Americans less keen to travel within their own country, their appetite for going overseas has been affected even more.

In Britain, tourism chiefs estimate that £1 billion of business will have been lost over the last quarter of 2001, threatening up to 75,000 jobs in the sector. Americans make up about 20 per cent of the 25 million visitors to Britain each year. BAA, the British airports operator, suffered a 20 per cent decline in passenger volumes through London's Heathrow alone after September 11th and through October. It took four years for the British tourism industry to recover from the effects of the Gulf War, and most analysts believe that this time the damage will last longer.

Tourism, of course, is a two-way street and the sharp drop in Americans and Britons going abroad has had a disproportionate impact on those regions that are heavily dependent on tourism. About £150 million of bookings from the UK were cancelled in the four weeks after September 11th, leaving areas such as the Caribbean with a massive shortfall in revenues. Two-thirds of all winter bookings to the West Indies were scratched. Not surprisingly, places like Dubai in the Middle East have been even harder hit by tourist cancellations.

Less obvious routes and destinations have suffered, too. Eurostar, the operator of train services between Paris, Brussels and London, calculates that terror in America has sliced about 20 per cent off its passenger numbers, with bookings from the US down by 70 per cent. This fall has dashed the company's hopes of breaking even by the end of 2003.

* * * * * *

Prior to September 11th, the US economy had been buoyed by irrepressible consumer confidence. Long after the corporate sector had starting cutting back investment (down 15 per cent in the second quarter of 2000) in anticipation of a global slow-down, the American public had continued to spend freely, believing that the country's ten-year boom had further to run.

The attacks on New York and Washington wiped out that optimism overnight. Just two weeks after the outrage, a survey of 5,000 American households recorded the largest month-on-month drop in consumer confidence since 1990.

From the heights of 'irrational exuberance', as US Federal Reserve chairman Alan Greenspan described it, to genuine fears for personal safety amid anthrax attacks on government personnel and others, the change in mood prompted millions of Americans to slam the brakes on personal spending.

In a masterpiece of understatement, a spokeswoman for Macy's in New York, one of America's biggest department stores, said, 'you could say we're not as crowded as you might think'. Many US shoppers simply stopped shopping. And their retrenchment pushed an already weakening economy over the edge.

As *Fortune* magazine reported on October 15th: 'Forget any talk about whether there will be a US recession. It's here.' That prognosis was later confirmed by Lawrence Lindsay, the White House chief economic adviser.

With Japan stagnating and Germany slowing rapidly, struggling US companies cannot rely on robust export sales to ride to their rescue. The US feel-good factor, for so long a feature of American commercial life, has evaporated and jobless figures are rising.

In October, the *Wall Street Journal* warned of 'an end to America's late-1990s golden era of low unemployment', as workers headed for the unemployment offices in numbers not seen for a decade.

As if this were not bad enough, Americans are weighed down by record borrowing. Consumer debt as a percentage of personal disposable income is close to 15 per cent, its highest level since 1986. At the beginning of September 2001, the average American household owed more than $8,500 on credit cards alone. According to David O Beim, Professor of Finance and Economics at Columbia University, the possibility of a massive rise in consumers defaulting on their debts is the factor most likely to turn a modest US recession into something much more serious.

There's little doubt that the American economy was riding for a fall before the World Trade Center was wrecked. The country had to face the music for the late-1990s' boom in telecommunications and technology that sucked too much investment into new-economy and internet projects, many of which turned out to be worthless.

London fund manager Legal & General estimates that $750 billion was poured into the world's telecoms companies between 1996 and 2000, and that about half that was 'thrown down the drain'. It was 'the modern-day equivalent of the South Sea Bubble', L&G said, 'the worst period of financial destruction in modern financial history'.

In a separate report, McKinsey, the management consultancy, concluded that much of the $1,240 billion invested by US businesses in information technology between 1995 and 1999 may have been wasted, when the internet boom turned to bust.

Somewhere along the line, these colossal managerial mistakes, which led to trillions of dollars of shareholder value being blown away, would have prompted a serious US downturn. Indeed, industrial output fell for 12 consecutive months up to September 2001, the longest run of negative numbers since 1945.

The terrorist attacks made matters much worse, however, by undermining consumer confidence, disrupting trade flows, and imposing massive extra costs on a US corporate sector that was already tottering under $4.7 billion of debt – an all-time high.

Investment bank Morgan Stanley estimates that additional security measures alone will cost the US freight industry $20 billion a year. The US Economic Strategy Institute reckons the final bill will be even higher, with American output being hit by $110 billion in the 12 months after the outrage.

The crisis provoked the US government and central bank into drastic action. Between them they provided the American economy with its biggest single peacetime package of fiscal and monetary stimuli. In October, President Bush unleashed $75 billion of tax cuts and federal spending, saying 'we've just got to be aggressive'.

The Federal Reserve backed this up with three quick interest-rate cuts, making it ten between January and November. The House of Representatives even passed a bill allowing the US Treasury to sell the country's first war bonds since the Second World War.

Whether this will make America's recession short and sharp, rather than long and painful, is hard to say at this stage. But the scale of what the US economy is up against can be gauged by estimates from *BusinessWeek*, the US magazine, which reckons that in New York alone more than 100,000 jobs will be lost as a result of the attacks, and the city will lose about $90 billion in output during the next three years.

Moreover, the disaster may encourage some firms to abandon their downtown offices for good, seeking cheaper accommodation in other parts of New York. For instance, Wall Street stockbrokers Lehman Brothers have left their headquarters near the bomb site and moved four miles away to midtown Manhattan. 'The city will never be quite the same again,' said *BusinessWeek*.

America's economic distress has created massive problems elsewhere in the world. Not only is it the biggest importer of goods and services, it is also has more inward investment than any other country. The United Nations warned of a 'vicious cycle of downward adjustment' rippling out from the battered US economy, which will have a disproportionate impact on the world's poorest economies. And Oxfam said that the aftermath of September 11th is 'creating an economic disaster in developing countries'.

Disentangling the direct effects of the attacks from business weakness that was already evident before the strikes is not easy, but poor countries are hardest hit because many of them rely on exporting commodities, such as coffee, the prices of which dipped sharply after September 11th.

The negative impact has been felt by the richest countries

too. Germany has been worst affected, with automobile makers Volkswagen and DaimlerChrysler halting investments and preparing investors for greatly reduced profits.

Though growth rates have slowed in Europe, there are signs that economic activity could pick up more quickly on the continent than in the US. That's because Europeans are not as exposed to stock markets as American investors (who buy and sell shares more actively than any other people) and therefore suffered a smaller reduction in wealth as a result of share prices that fell sharply between early 2000 and autumn 2001.

* * * * * *

Stock markets typically anticipate events 12 to 18 months ahead, which explains why it is not unusual for share prices to fall when business conditions seem benign and vice versa. If traders suddenly conclude a company's profits will suffer next year, they mark down the price of its shares today. In that sense, they keep ahead of the game.

But no stock market sage could have foreseen the events of September 11th. It was impossible to price into shares the impact that such devastation would have, because attacks on that scale were unimaginable to most investors. Once the bombers struck, there was mayhem in world markets, as the investment industry scrambled to recalculate the value of shares.

The New York Stock Exchange was paralyzed and closed for business until September 17th, its longest shutdown since the Great Depression. That closure added to the markets' confusion, as there was no way of knowing just how American investors would react to attacks on their home soil.

Elsewhere on September 11th, the response was uniformly grim. In London, the FTSE-100 index of leading shares suffered its biggest percentage fall since the crash of October 1987, closing 5.7 per cent down at 4,746, a three-year low. The next day, September 12th, Tokyo's Nikkei index plunged 6.6 per cent to 9,610, ending a session below 10,000 for the first time in 17 years. The situation was similar all over Europe.

When the New York Stock Exchange finally reopened, six days after the World Trade Center was destroyed, there was hope and fear in equal measure. Some pundits talked about the possibility of a 'patriotic rally', with American investors buying US shares, even though they knew that prospects for corporate profits had been severely dented. Others hinted nervously at a 'wipe-out'.

Before the bell was struck to recommence share dealing, both the US Federal Reserve and the European Central Bank tried to shore up sentiment with a half-point cut in interest rates. I watched the opening action from a trading floor at NatWest Stockbrokers in the City of London. British dealers, many of whom had lost friends when the towers collapsed, were willing the New York index to go up, not for financial gain but as a way of defying the terrorists.

The combined effort of central-bank rate cuts and stockbroker goodwill was not enough, however. As soon as trading began, financial gravity kicked in: market-makers' computer screens turned crimson, reflecting a sharp fall in share prices.

By the end of the day, the Dow Jones industrial average index had dropped by 684 points to 8,920, its biggest-ever one-day points loss, down 7.1 per cent. It was a hectic session, but by no means a catastrophic one. After all, the US markets had been closed for four trading days and the scale of the downward adjustment in share prices was bound to reflect that.

In the view of many professionals, the stock market 'looked for the bottom' on that day and found it. 'We feared it would be worse than it was,' a trader told me. From that point, the debate about stock markets and share prices moved on to focus largely on the competing forces of falling interest rates (which normally boost share prices) and corporate profit warnings (which undermine them).

The vital questions still are: can central bankers, by reducing the cost of borrowing money, help companies offset the damage done by a collapse in consumer confidence? If they can, will investors conclude that lower share prices represent a buying opportunity? Or, will investors decide that share prices had been overvalued long before September 11th, and that there is still a long way for them to fall before they return to levels that reflect good value?

The fact that there is no consensus, not even among professional economists, makes for a lively market. For trading to exist at all, there has to be a divergence of opinion between buyers and sellers.

What is unarguable, however, is that if share prices remain well below the peaks they reached at the beginning of 2000, there will be a negative effect on consumer wealth, further eroding confidence not just of direct investors but of all those savers whose pensions and insurance plans depend on stock market performance.

The hardest factor of all to price into shares, but nonetheless one of the most critical, is uncertainty. Markets hate uncertainty and often assume the worst. Military action against targets in Afghanistan and bio-terror in America create doubts, which inevitably lead to risk aversion among investors.

When that happens, they tend to return to the store of value that's perceived to be the safest rather than the one offering the greatest potential reward. Thus cash is preferred to shares, which explains why US investors pulled a net $32 billion from equity funds in September 2001, a record monthly withdrawal.

Even after October's stock market rally, with the Dow Jones index climbing back above 9,300, the 2001 bear market in US shares ranks among the biggest in history. This occurred despite falling interest rates and low inflation.

Historical comparisons give a perspective on how severe that share-price slide was. From the peak of prices in April 2000 to the trough in September 2001, the US stock market, as measured by the S&P 500 index, fell by 35.9 per cent. After the Great Crash of September 1929, however, US shares fell by 84 per cent and did not reach their trough for 33 months – in June 1932.

So for how long can the bad news go on? When will markets get back to their peaks? The honest answer is: nobody knows. According to *Fortune* magazine: 'If you hear anybody offering confident answers to any of these questions, cover your ears.'

Even in the most severe bear markets, share prices do not go down every day, or indeed every month. As Mr Greenspan told the US Joint Economic Committee on October 17th: 'Nobody has the capacity to fathom fully how the effects of the tragedy of September 11th will play out in our economy.'

What can be learnt from history, however, is that the largest stock market falls in America and the United Kingdom have generally been followed by sharp rises. Booms tend to follow busts. That's the good news.

The bad news is that there is no evidence of this pattern in Japan, where the main stock market index reached almost 40,000 in the late 1980s and 12 years later had fallen by 75 per cent to about 10,000. But neither the US nor the UK has an economy like Japan's, where the banking system has been enfeebled by corruption and years of bad loans.

* * * * * *

If airlines are the businesses worst affected by September 11th, then insurance companies are not far behind. The blow delivered by the hijackers changed the rules of insurance cover, especially for the transport and property sectors. Not only do all the world's leading insurers face massive pay-outs, but they have been forced to reassess the size of the risks they can take on.

The cost of insuring high-rise buildings has soared. In the words of one insurer, 'the unthinkable became reality'. French insurance giant AXA said that high-risk property insurance premiums would have to go up by 80 per cent. This clearly hurts landmark skyscrapers, such as London's Canary Wharf tower. Aviation insurance premiums have increased tenfold.

Initial estimates of the World Trade Center insurance cost were put at $15 billion, but once the full extent of the damage began to emerge, forecasts for the final insurance bill soared to more than $50 billion. This dwarfs the $20 billion paid out in the aftermath of Hurricane Andrew, which devastated America's east coast in 1992.

Lloyd's of London, the British insurance market, initially

calculated that its net payout would be $1.9 billion, but that assumed it could recover most of its claims on US reinsurers. Not all of the reinsurance companies involved, however, are expected to survive the financial drain of the New York catastrophe. So, just as Lloyd's appeared to be recovering from a long period of uncertainty, the terrorists have created complicated new problems. Putting on a brave face, Lloyd's chairman Sax Riley told the BBC that Lloyd's 'capital base will be able to absorb this loss'.

For the world's media, New York's nightmare has turned into the biggest running story since the Gulf War. Newspapers, magazine groups and broadcasters have pumped up their editorial budgets to cover huge additional costs of in-depth reporting not just from America, but Afghanistan, Pakistan, Israel and Europe.

While world events on this scale attract millions more readers to newspapers, viewers to television, and listeners to radio, the incremental costs invariably outweigh any financial benefits from enhanced circulation and audiences. Each of the major US television networks incurred extra costs of about $1 million a day in the weeks immediately after the attack.

Worse still, many advertising campaigns were frozen or abandoned, as companies slashed expenditure in response to worrying times. In the days immediately after September 11th, some American TV commercial stations were running without any advertisements at all, costing the TV industry $300 million in lost revenues.

Rupert Murdoch's News Corporation said it suffered a $100 million decline in advertising income as a result of the attacks. Dow Jones, owner of the *Wall Street Journal*, warned that advertising volumes would fall by up to 45 per cent in the fourth quarter of 2001.

In Britain, Pearson, owner of the *Financial Times*, reported a 40 per cent decline in advertising revenues after September 11th. Marjorie Scardino, the company's chief executive, told shareholders: 'This is already a lot worse than the advertising downturn in the early nineties. It took a real nose-dive from the week beginning September 10th... We're assuming advertisement booking at the current very low level through 2002.'

Supporting that gloomy outlook, Gerry Murphy, chief executive of TV company Carlton Communications, said: 'People do not know how to deal with the short-term effects of September 11th. It's a confidence call.' The picture was the same all across Europe, with media shares, such as France's Havas Advertising, falling sharply on fears of a collapse in revenues.

Oil traders have had a roller-coaster ride. Minutes after the bombers struck, oil prices jumped sharply on the expectation of conflict in the Middle East, but fell back a few days later when it became clear America's economy was heading for recession. As a result, the price of gasoline at some US outlets fell below $1 a gallon for the first time since 1999.

The International Energy Agency reckons that world oil demand could fall by 600,000 barrels a day to 76.2 million because reduced air travel has cut the need for jet fuel, and economic growth prospects have been lowered for 2002. Prior to the attacks, the IEA was expecting demand for oil to grow by 500,000 barrels a day. In October, the oil price stabilized at $20–1 a barrel, some way below the $26 target price set by OPEC.

Another sector badly affected is luxury goods. In austere times, the last thing nervous consumers need is a jewel-encrusted watch or a diamond-studded belt. Fashion house Gucci was quick to issue a profits warning, rival Prada cancelled its stock market flotation, and shares in Bulgari, the jeweller, fell by 30 per cent in the wake of the bombings.

Of course, for many badly managed companies, the shock of September 11th has provided credible cover to slip out gloomy news and invent excuses for directors' mistakes. Not all of the hundreds of profit warnings that have emerged since the attacks were directly related to those events. In many cases, companies were already in trouble, but for some unscrupulous managements the opportunity to defray blame for poor performance was too good to resist.

In such a febrile atmosphere, it's the businesses with the heaviest borrowings that come under the greatest immediate pressure. Default rates on US corporate bonds have already gone past levels seen in the 1990–1 recession.

In good times, stock markets are inclined to turn a blind eye to debt mountains. Rising operating profits hide a multitude of sins. But when the crunch comes, it's often a case of 'can't pay' rather than 'won't pay', and over-borrowed companies unravel quickly. For instance, Polaroid, the photography company, filed for bankruptcy in October, weighed down by $1 billion of debt.

Research from Dutch bank ABN Amro concludes that 'as confidence evaporates, the debt burden on many companies is becoming a major concern'. Nowhere is this more obvious than at Marconi, the crippled British telephone equipment company, which clocked up debts of £4.4 billion. September 11th turned its prospects from difficult to dire.

With so many companies cutting back operations, the flow of mergers and takeovers has all but ground to a halt. Indeed, several bids that were in the pipeline have been scrapped or the terms altered. This has prompted investment houses, accountancy firms and other financial advisers to lay off highly paid deal-makers in large numbers.

Even the mighty Goldman Sachs and Merrill Lynch were forced to cut hundreds of jobs. Those fee-hungry investment bankers whom the novelist Tom Wolfe called 'masters of the universe' have discovered that they are just as susceptible to redundancy as blue-collar factory workers when the business world is turned upside down by a group of fanatical killers.

* * * * * *

When bad times grip the global economy, it's often hard to see how the tide will be turned. But we should remember that no single act of war, however terrible, can plunge the world into recession for ever.

The atom bombs dropped on Japan in 1945 devastated its economy and shattered its citizens' confidence. Yet by the 1960s, against all the odds, it had recovered much of the lost ground, and by the end of the 1980s, Tokyo's stock market temporarily overtook New York's as the world's biggest.

Germany was also wrecked by the Second World War, yet thanks to a combination of massive financial aid from the United States, and the industry of its people, the country bounced back quickly to become one of the world's three biggest economies and the locomotive of growth within Europe for much of the 1970s, 1980s and 1990s.

Even a relatively underdeveloped country such as Vietnam, pulled apart by conflict in the 1960s and 70s, was able to restore its battered fortunes and enjoy rapid growth from a very low base in the 1990s. Human spirit does overcome appalling events.

History tells us that the questions arising from September 11th should not be about *whether* the world of business and finance can rediscover the momentum that propelled Western economies to new heights of prosperity in the 1990s, but when and how.

The timing of revival will depend a great deal on how long the military action goes on and to what extent the terrorists can eat away at American consumers' morale with threats of further attacks or biological warfare.

Even the darkest clouds have silver linings, however. At a relatively trivial level, flag-makers in America have experienced unprecedented demand. More lasting benefits to other sectors should come from the increase in US federal expenditure on construction projects and security equipment.

Shocks such as September 11th prompt businesses and governments to take positive action that they otherwise might have put off. Necessity fosters invention. Companies shed costs, look for other efficiencies, and think about new ways of improving themselves. Old complacencies are swept away, as fresh ideas are brought to bear on tackling the threat of terror.

The ripples from the World Trade Center have only just begun. The spirit of free enterprise invariably finds ways of turning the impact of evil deeds into opportunities for human achievement. Across the world, corporations big and small are working to a completely rescheduled agenda as a result of September 11th. Some will fail, but many more will emerge stronger, leaner and fitter.

CHAPTER FOURTEEN

FIGHTING AN UNENDING WAR

JONATHAN MARCUS

Jonathan Marcus became Defence Correspondent for the World Service on the eve of the Gulf War. He has reported for the BBC from the Gulf, the Balkans and the United States, and specializes in international security issues and strategic affairs. He discusses the limitations of an all-out military answer to terrorism, and considers the options facing governments as they try to defeat this new adversary.

Sun, sand and the threat of virtual violence. Some four years ago I found myself bouncing across the Mojave Desert in a US Army Humvee, a latter-day jeep used by the military for a variety of roles. This was Fort Irwin in California – a training range about the size of Wales – where a new prototype military formation dubbed Force 21 was going through its paces. Heavily digitized, with tanks and armoured vehicles packing on-board computers as well as weaponry, the new information systems were intended to give the Pentagon an unbeatable edge on the battlefields of the twenty-first century. As ground attack aircraft thundered overhead, pyrotechnics exploded and the tanks churned up the desert sand, it all looked mightily impressive. But the real warfare of the twenty-first century has turned out to be rather different from the exercises at Fort Irwin. There was nothing here about passenger airliners being turned into guided missiles or anthrax spores being released in the very heart of the nation's capital.

To be fair, the battlefield experiments of which Force 21 was a part were only one element of a wider effort to modernize America's military machine. Earlier administrations have picked around the edges of defence reform. But from the moment he arrived in office, President George W Bush promised one of the most far-reaching defence reviews in America's history. The new Defense Secretary, Donald Rumsfeld, had inherited a military machine that, despite some cuts, was essentially a scaled-down version of the forces the US deployed to fight the Cold War. There was a great deal of talk about a second military revolution ushered in by new information- and intelligence-gathering systems. (The first military revolution was linked to the arrival of gunpowder and the larger military organizations of the seventeenth century.) But in terms of the new technologies, each of the armed services seemed to be ploughing its own furrow. Impressive exercises were held to demonstrate the applicability of the new information systems to different levels of war-fighting. However, the whole project seemed to lack a fundamental guiding principle. Just who were the Americans training to fight? Could military force alone be leveraged to win any conflict in an increasingly complex and interdependent world? Furthermore, in an age of 'asymmetric warfare' would any opponent in the future be as stupid as Saddam Hussein and put their armoured divisions in the field to face America's technologically superior forces?

This term 'asymmetric warfare' has emerged as one of the buzz words of the US defence debate. It refers to the war of the militarily weak against the strong. If America's conventional armed forces were just too formidable even to be confronted, let alone defeated, then a potential enemy would have to explore other avenues of attack. In a society whose essential nervous system depended more and more upon computers, cyber attack was flagged up as one of the major asymmetric threats. Hackers, it was feared, might seek to take down air traffic control computers or those handling credit transfers in the banking system. Many pundits raised the spectre of a cyber attack from out of the blue resulting in an 'electronic Pearl Harbour'. The other great fear was terrorism, especially the possibility that some shadowy organization might get hold of biological, chemical or even nuclear weapons. Thus, even before the attacks on New York and Washington, 'homeland defence' had become a second focus of the emerging US defence debate. The Bush administration's cherished plans for a missile defence system were one element of this new emphasis upon defending the continental United States itself.

There was of course a certain irony in Donald Rumsfeld being chosen as the man to carry out the Pentagon's post-Cold War spring-cleaning. He was something of a first division cold warrior himself, having served as the youngest-ever Secretary of Defense in the Ford administration, back in the 1970s. Nonetheless Mr Rumsfeld set about his task with zeal; too much zeal as it turned out. He insisted that no area was sacrosanct. Fundamental questions would be asked about both the relevance and shape of America's armed forces. How far could they meet the challenges of the twenty-first century? Some tentative conclusions were reached: Asia was to be the new focus; some key equipment projects would have to be trimmed. But well before September 11th, it looked as though Mr Rumsfeld's efforts were running into the sand. The secrecy and scope of his review alarmed both the military top brass and many key figures on Capitol Hill. Within the Washington belt-way the rumour mill began to turn. Rumsfeld, it was said, had handled military reform badly, and newspaper columnists openly speculated about his replacement.

What a difference just a few weeks make! The opening of the military campaign transformed Donald Rumsfeld's political fortunes. This was no gung-ho warrior claiming rapid success; his calm, deliberate manner and command of detail at Pentagon briefings restored his reputation. But the key test for Donald Rumsfeld will not be the multi-faceted war on terrorism, which may well continue long after he has retired: it remains defence reform. Can he provide the United States with the armed forces it needs to fight this struggle, perhaps for decades ahead? The attacks on the World Trade Center and the Pentagon demonstrated that US strategists were right to flag up asymmetric threats and homeland defence as two key areas badly needing attention. But the US still needs to decide how best the military, alongside other institutions, can participate in this fight, and it needs to choose the appropriate military tools.

The military campaign that opened on October 7th began with a small-scale reprise of the concerted air war that had been played out over both Iraq and Serbia. The initial targets included airfields, air defence sites and command posts; and Pentagon briefings showed the predictable imagery of attacks from precision-guided weaponry. But this highly conventional opening was the prelude to an unconventional follow-up: the use of special forces to raid deep behind enemy lines. The aim was to throw the Taliban regime off balance and ultimately, through a gradual stepping up of the pressure, to force it from power.

Even a few weeks into the campaign, it was already clear that some of its special circumstances were feeding into the Pentagon's review process. The lessons were equally applicable to Europe's fledgling joint defence effort, especially if the Europeans had the ambition to deploy credible military forces capable of engaging in, rather than just supporting, US-led operations. The key areas in which lessons had to be learnt relate to the application of air power, the essential role of intelligence-gathering at the tactical level, and the new emphasis upon covert operations using special forces.

The first weeks of the campaign underlined many of the lessons of earlier air wars and provided ammunition for both sides in the argument over the respective merits of sea-based, as opposed to land-based, air power. Despite the huge American build-up in the Gulf region, distance and political sensitivities meant that the bulk of the initial sorties were carried out by carrier-borne strike aircraft operating from the Arabian Sea. For several years a battle has raged in the Pentagon – essentially between the Navy and the Air Force – over the best way of conducting distant operations. The Navy has championed carrier-based air power, a solution that carries its own airstrip everywhere it goes and can be deployed irrespective of local politics or favours. The US Air Force, on the other hand, has argued for expeditionary air power: the ability to deploy large mixed groups of aircraft to far-flung bases and to sustain them there throughout a campaign. The Air Force has also championed the long-range manned bomber capable of operating from bases in the United States with a global reach. Both the advocates of the carriers and the long-range bombers have had their cases strengthened by the Afghanistan conflict. The advocates of shorter-range tactical air power operating from land bases have not: a factor that could have important implications for the future shape of US tactical air power with two contenders – the F-22 Raptor and the Joint Strike Fighter – vying for limited funds. Both may still be purchased, but the numbers and balance of the force may change.

The initial week of operations also demonstrated the limitations of carrier air power. Some targets were over 700 miles away from the carriers positioned off the Pakistani coast. This is an unusually long distance over which to mount sustained carrier-borne operations, affecting both the tempo of operations and the strains on the crews involved. It was sufficient given the relatively small-scale start to the air war over Afghanistan, but the pressure has shown, especially on the vital S-3 Viking refuelling aircraft operated from the US carriers. Overall though the utility of carrier-borne air power has been underlined, especially for operations that involve delicate political calculations, underscoring the determination of key European countries like Britain, France, Italy and Spain to maintain a carrier capability.

The air campaign over Afghanistan has employed large numbers of precision-guided munitions. Even though it has been relatively small-scale compared to other recent operations, after some two weeks of action, stocks of certain key munitions were shown to be limited. The expenditure rate for the satellite or GPS-guided Joint Direct Attack Munition or JDAM was very high. The US Air Force initially husbanded its stocks of conventional air-launched cruise missiles, so Pentagon planners depended on the naval Tomahawk, fired from both US warships and Royal Navy submarines. Britain's initial contribution may have appeared slight, intended largely to demonstrate engagement alongside the Americans rather than having major military impact. But the additional flexibility offered by the presence of the British boats was more than welcome. America has many global commitments and a finite stock of weaponry available at any one time, and Britain is the only one of America's NATO allies to have this kind of long-range maritime land-attack capability. As the Kosovo war demonstrated, few of America's major allies have yet invested in air-launched precision-guided munitions. And as the Afghan crisis showed, even the world's one remaining superpower can face shortages of critical equipment. (Witness Britain's useful assistance in both air-to-air refuelling and photo-reconnaissance, and NATO's despatch of AWACS radar aircraft to help patrol the skies over the United States.) Defence reform is not an issue for the US alone. NATO and the EU have talked a great deal about improving defence capabilities, but a number of governments have consistently failed to honour the pledges they have made. Many NATO countries can barely field a few infantry battalions for peace-keeping missions, and the future of coalition operations is going to depend upon America's allies doing significantly more.

Precision-strike is one critical capability, but of equal importance is the ability to find targets and then to hit them quickly before they move. The US military characterizes this as the time it takes to get the information from sensor to shooter. One of America's newest weapons systems has already been used over Afghanistan. The armed Predator – an unmanned aerial vehicle (UAV), previously used simply for reconnaissance – can now both spot targets and attack them with Hellfire missiles. Informed sources suggest that at least two such Predators were lost during the early stages of the conflict. This type of system is still in its infancy but it is a dramatic example of the direction in which military technology is going.

Just as in earlier times when a general sat on his horse surveying the battle from a convenient hill top, so today information is still the key to success. The United States has focused extraordinary intelligence-gathering resources on Afghanistan, from satellites to manned aircraft and UAVs. But these assets are also in short supply, and much of the initial additional funding going to the Pentagon has been set aside for both the Global Hawk project – the very latest long-range unmanned reconnaissance vehicle – and to buy more Rivet Joint electronic intelligence-gathering aircraft. These are also areas where modern and compatible European assets could assist significantly in future coalition operations.

The Afghan crisis has turned a significant page in America's post-Vietnam military history. The Pentagon has shown a willingness to put ground troops 'in harm's way', to trade fire with Taliban forces on the ground. For many years after the Vietnam War, American generals and politicians were said to be 'casualty averse', fearful of the impact any losses would have on public opinion at home. To my mind this casualty aversion was often overstated. It was probably stronger on the part of the politicians than the military top brass. It was as often as not due to the failure to argue the case successfully with the public (why exactly were the Americans in Somalia, for example?). Lucky outcomes have also meant that the public has been unused to seeing body bags. (Nobody imagines that the Americans were unwilling to suffer casualties in the ground war to liberate Kuwait. But as things turned out, the ground war was so brief that casualties were few, often caused by accidents or friendly fire.)

A greater willingness to deploy ground forces, however, begs the question of just what sort of troops to deploy. Afghanistan has demonstrated the importance both of elite Special Forces like the US Army Rangers and the British Special Air Service, but equally of well-trained specialized units like the troops from the US 10th Mountain Division or the Royal Marines. Such troops are essentially light infantry: highly mobile and self-sufficient. Much more attention needs to be given to such formations to enhance their agility and to increase their fire power. The United States Special Forces are a small army in themselves, but other countries may well seek to expand their own elite formations and to increase their ability to operate alongside allied units. Britain too may need to take a hard look at the way its ground forces are organized. Indeed the progress in the Northern Ireland peace process may facilitate some changes that were not possible in the past. Continuing commitments in the Balkans and elsewhere impose huge strains. Increasing the size of the SAS itself is probably not an option: the pool from which it is drawn is relatively small in Britain's professional armed forces, and the SAS might only be expanded at the risk of diluting its highly tuned skills. Better for Britain, perhaps, to take a leaf out of America's book, where the bulk of its so-called Special Forces are effectively the premier league in a two-tier military system. Some in Britain have advocated expanding either the Parachute Regiment or the Royal Marines, and building upon their already highly special-ized roles.

But the ability to wage sustained expeditionary operations is only one aspect of the war against terrorism. Of equal and perhaps even greater importance is homeland defence, with its several elements – military, political, legal, medical and so on. The terrorists' war did not begin on the streets of Manhattan or at the Pentagon. There were the embassy bombings in Africa and the attack on the USS *Cole* in Aden harbour. But the attacks in the United States were of such a scale and audacity that they took the terrorist threat to new levels. Experts debate whether this really represents a strategic challenge to Washington and its allies. It is not an existential threat, as perhaps was Soviet com-munism, but its impact can be huge – just look at the economic ramifications of the events of that one day in September, and the further disruption and concern prompted by the anthrax attacks that followed.

In the aftermath of September 11th, the United States went on full alert. Fighter jets flew combat air patrols over key cities. By mid-October well over 32,000 reserve military and National Guard personnel had been mobilized to assist in the anti-terrorist campaign. The Quadrennial Defence Review, pub-lished just a short time after the attacks in New York and Washington, inevitably became just an interim statement of the administration's thinking on defence matters; but it did put homeland defence at the top of the list of the armed forces' missions.

Homeland defence is clearly not the job of the military alone. Indeed, since the late-nineteenth century there has been a legal doctrine that has kept the federally controlled US military from engaging in domestic law enforcement activities. The Deputy Defense Secretary, Paul Wolfowitz, for one has already called for this convention to be reviewed. But as he admitted when presenting the defence review to the Senate Armed Services Committee, the Pentagon is 'at a very early stage of figuring out what the role of the Department of Defense might be, for example, in responding to a major act of terrorism with weapons of mass destruction'. The armed forces do have a number of capabilities that could prove helpful in terrorist emergencies; indeed the US Marine Corps has already established highly effective mobile units to deal with chemical or biological incidents. These units are now being rolled into a larger Marine Corps anti-terrorist brigade, with its focus firmly on operations within the United States itself.

A key element of homeland defence is likely to remain missile defence. Defending American cities against a potential ballistic missile attack has become almost an article of faith for the Bush administration. Defense Secretary Donald Rumsfeld has campaigned for it with almost missionary zeal. Many liberal experts, sceptical about the cost and mindful of the technological hurdles still to be overcome, argue that the events of September 11th prove once and for all the irrelevance of the idea. Even if there is a small potential missile threat from a rogue state, they argue that the Pentagon's costly plans would have done nothing to stop passenger aircraft being transformed into guided missiles loaded with people and fuel.

But the advocates of missile defence are likely to be similarly confirmed in their beliefs. Much of the focus on the ballistic missile threat stems from a perceived sense of vulnerability, and September 11th has proved that Americans have every reason to feel vulnerable. Given that missile technology is spreading, it is almost inconceivable that President Bush will choose to give up defences against missile attack. The new relationship with Russia promises to ease some of the diplomatic strains that a decision to deploy missile defences would create. And many of America's NATO allies, not least Britain, seem to be tilting more in the direction of accepting the merits of such a system. Clearly, though, America's plans may suffer significant delays, not least because of the numerous defence programmes competing for limited funds.

A reorganized Pentagon has an important role in homeland defence, but this is also the responsibility of a variety of civil organizations, ranging from police and law enforcement agencies to fire departments, hospitals and health planners. The task of co-ordinating federal, state and local activities is immense. One of President Bush's most significant responses to the attacks of September 11th was the creation on October 8th of a new Office of Homeland Security under former Pennsylvania governor Tom Ridge. Governor Ridge moved into the West Wing of the White House and his job title – Assistant to the President for Homeland Security – gives him analogous powers to those of the National Security Advisor, Condoleezza Rice. But the new homeland security chief has already been widely criticized by legislators and commentators for having too few powers. His job is essentially to co-ordinate the domestic security activities of more than 40 government agencies. It is a daunting task even for a cabinet-level appointee, supposedly with access to the President. Critics say he has the symbols of power without the ability to demand that disparate agencies follow his wishes. Encouraging the FBI and the CIA to work better together is a major job in itself; add into the mix the Immigration and Naturalization Service, the Customs Service, the Federal Aviation Administration, let alone the Pentagon, and the magnitude of the task facing Governor Ridge becomes all too clear. But combating terrorism may not be just a question of budgetary or organizational reform; it may require new styles of thinking as well. And one influential academic, Joseph Nye, Dean of the Kennedy School of Government at Harvard

University, has urged the establishment of new research bodies, independent of government, along the lines of the RAND Corporation, to study terrorism and confront the conventional wisdom.

The need for a new approach was clearly shown by the way various agencies responded early on to the anthrax threat. There were different operating procedures, a confusion of messages, and an extraordinary delay in screening postal workers who might have come into contact with the contaminated mail. This episode demonstrated the panic and disruption that could be caused by even a relatively small attack with biological agents. Think of how much worse it might have been if an international terrorist group had released airborne spores into the World Trade Center's air-conditioning system – there could have been even more deaths than were caused by the impact of the two airliners, and the problems would multiply if a contagious disease-causing agent were employed. Governor Ridge and his new office are on a rapid and necessarily steep learning curve.

The threat of cyber-terrorism has also been discussed for a number of years. Multitudes of reports and position papers have been written but here, too, progress has been slow. The vulnerability of computer systems is exacerbated by the dominance that one company has over the market for operating software. Computer security is certainly an issue for government and the military, but it is even more of an issue for private businesses and corporations. Most of the critical infrastructure that must be defended, such as power supply companies or the signalling and control system on the railroads, is in private hands. President Bush has appointed a new special adviser for cyberspace security. But the problems of co-ordination here are even greater than those that must be overcome to provide defence against bio-terrorism. Long-standing complacency needs to be overcome, and as with so much of the new anti-terrorism effort, vigilance must go hand-in-hand with the maintenance of a liberal society. Otherwise, as a *New York Times* editorial writer put it, there is a danger that the information highway will be turned into a series of 'private information cul-de-sacs'.

Information in many ways is the key to the problem. Information systems may be a potential target, but information itself, in the very widest sense, is the key to waging this war on terrorism and probably to winning it. Terms here have to be redefined; victory may no longer be absolute, but rather a dynamic or relative concept. Vigilance, determination and disruption will seek to reduce terrorist incidents to a minimum with the hope that diplomacy will, along the way, reduce some of the reasons why people support such groups.

Intelligence is a central issue. The system failed to provide sufficient warning of the events of September 11th, and the United States is going to have to take a long, hard look at the way its vast intelligence-gathering community, as it likes to be called, operates. Better co-ordination is needed; more human intelligence (good old-fashioned agents on the ground); better linguistic and analytical skills and so on. A reformed intelligence system can then provide the cues for the initiation of military action – either covert missions by special forces or the use of elite police anti-terrorist squads, depending upon where the target is located.

However, the way that information is marshalled and disseminated in the wider government machine is also critical. It is far from clear that the current way in which the governmental institutions of many Western democracies are linked together is sufficient to counter this new terrorism with a global reach. It is not just a question of establishing new agencies or new co-ordination posts. While the citizen wants to be defended, he or she also wants to see the maintenance of the values that make our societies worth defending. There is going to be an understandable reluctance to dilute hard-won freedoms. In the realms of biological or chemical terrorism, the authorities are dealing with areas of science and public policy in which they have a poor track record; and people are understandably sceptical about what governments can deliver. Look at the way the foot-and-mouth outbreak was handled in the UK – would, say, an anthrax outbreak necessarily be dealt with any more efficiently? Take another area: the failure of the asylum and immigration system, which seems to deny safety to many worthy applicants while allowing entry to a small number of highly dubious characters. Surely such a system is both unfair and unacceptable, especially in an era when computers can facilitate all of the necessary record-keeping. September 11th was a tragedy, but it was also a wake-up call that few can ignore about the way in which we organize our affairs.

There are military lessons from this campaign and there are clearly military aspects to the wider struggle against terrorism. But if terms like 'victory' and maybe even 'war' itself need redefining, then so too does our understanding of what we mean by the security debate or the security agenda. Ever since the Cold War ended, the international system has been in turmoil with the break-up of countries, bitter ethnic struggles and the rise of organized crime. A whole new range of issues has been imported onto the defence agenda: the threat of large and uncontrolled population movements; the fight for scarce natural resources like water; the very issue of poverty itself, which, it could be argued, underpins more of the world's problems than anything else. The solutions to most of these issues go way beyond the purely military. But success in this 'first war of the twenty-first century', as President Bush dubbed it, is going to depend both on integrating the old and the new security agendas, and on finding ways of using both old and novel tools to confront the dilemmas of what threatens to be a new age of global disorder.

CHAPTER FIFTEEN

A NEW WORLD ORDER?

ALLAN LITTLE

Allan Little is a London-based World Affairs Correspondent, and a presenter on the Today *programme. He recently returned from successive postings as Southern Africa and Moscow Correspondent after several years reporting and writing on the break-up of former Yugoslavia. In 1989 he reported for the BBC on the end of communist rule in Eastern Europe. Here he gives his view on whether the tectonic plates of history have now shifted again, and what 'new world order' may emerge.*

There have been two moments in my life when I have understood in an instant that the world has changed in some fundamental and irreversible way. These two moments have acquired, in my mind, an intimate connection with each other.

The first was in a snow-flecked Wenceslas Square in the Czech capital Prague in November 1989. Four hundred thousand people had packed the square and we stood crammed together waiting to hear the famous dissident playwright Vaclav Havel when, unannounced, a tall, slightly stooped grey-haired old man emerged to take his place on the balcony. The young woman beside me audibly gasped. 'My God,' she said. 'It's *him*. It's Dubcek.'

The man who had led the Prague Spring, 21 years earlier, had spent two decades in internal exile. No one in Prague had seen his face or heard his voice in all that time. His photograph was banned from the newspapers. Television and radio were not allowed to mention his name. He had been air-brushed from history. Until this moment.

Now he stood before us. And when he approached the microphone, the first word he spoke – its five syllables washing over us like a sonorous tidal wave – was not some abstract concept like 'liberty' or 'democracy' but something much more visceral. He said the name of the country. 'Ceskoslovensko!' And the crowd roared in incredulity and an almost religious rapture because they knew, in that moment, with the speaking of that word that they were, indeed, liberated. And it hit me with the force of revelation that I had witnessed the world change.

The second of these moments came on September 11th 2001, at the moment the second plane crashed into the World Trade Center and we knew instantly that it had been no accident.

These two moments book-end a changing world. They represent polar opposites. In the first, entire peoples sought liberation from a system of oppression and absolute state control by pursuing an idea that the Western world had taken for granted: Civil Society. Czech steel workers marched out of their factories carrying placards calling not for higher wages or greater equality but for 'Plurality not Brutality'. They wanted what they could see the citizens of Western Europe and North America enjoyed: democracy, the rule of law, liberty under the law, plurality, the separation of church and state, free political and philosophical discourse. The political movement that overthrew communism in Czechoslovakia was called 'Civic Forum'.

The revolutions of 1989 and the almost-complete collapse of communism throughout the world led some to believe that Civil Society – the Western way – was in some sense the universal destination of all mankind. For a while, the popular imagination was seized by Francis Fukuyama's thesis that the human race had reached the 'end of history'. The veteran theorist of nationalism, the late Ernest Gellner, was sceptical and sounded an important warning. The Fukuyama view, he wrote, was dangerously complacent. 'In this manner, Civil Society is simply presupposed as some kind of inherent attribute of the human condition! It is the corollary of a certain vision of man. It is a naive universalization of one rather fortunate kind of man – the inhabitant of Civil Society... It is only the rediscovery of this ideal in Eastern Europe...that has reminded the inhabitants of the liberal states on either shore of the north Atlantic of just what it is that they possess and ought to hold dear.'

Since September 11th much public attention has rightly focused on the extent to which particular aspects of United States foreign policy have, over the decades, alienated and enraged Muslim opinion. These are well documented elsewhere in this book. But it seems equally important and valid to make a more fundamental point. The United States is unique; it is the wealthiest and most powerful nation, the only remaining superpower. It is also the nation that pioneered secular modernity, that enshrined in law the values of the eighteenth-century Enlightenment which turned 'liberty' – that seditious aspiration for which Britons were publicly executed or transported to Botany Bay – into a constitutional reality. Do not presuppose that Civil Society is 'some kind of inherent attribute of the human condition'. It seems to me that, along with the free condemnation of American foreign policy, the Western world should remember and, yes, acknowledge where the freedom so to express ourselves comes from.

* * * * * *

The prominent London-based Saudi dissident Saad al-Fagih gives this account of how news of the attack on the World Trade Center was greeted in Saudi Arabia. A trickle of text messages and e-mails – which quickly became a flood – started to crisscross the country's mobile phone networks and internet connections, from the offices of multi-billion dollar oil corporations to banks and finance houses and import-export companies. They were messages of jubilation and congratulations. When the news had begun to sink in, the messages became more specific. Groups of men made arrangements to meet at each other's homes to slaughter a sheep and share a celebratory barbecue.

Saad al-Fagih has his own reasons for so characterizing Saudi public opinion. His organization does not condone or take part in acts of violence, but he will not condemn even the events of September 11th. So closed is Saudi society that it is impossible to know whether his account is fair or exaggerated. But there is no disguising the fact that some in the Muslim world took real pleasure in the humbling of the United States. Many others – and not only Muslims – who condemned the attacks nonetheless argued that the United States had brought the tragedy on itself and in some sense 'deserved' it.

'The government is wrong to forbid us to show our joy. This is our religious and national obligation to rejoice at the killing of these Americans,' the editor of one government-owned newspaper in Egypt wrote. Another commented, 'I danced on the graves of all those Americans.' Osama bin Laden, in successfully wounding and humiliating America, and as a direct result of being identified by America as the 'evil master-mind' behind the attacks, is now revered as a folk hero in much of the Islamic world. Has that, as the leaders of the Western world insist, really got nothing to do with Islam?

'Many Muslims seem to be in deep denial about what has happened,' the American Islamic scholar Hamza Yusuf told the *Guardian* newspaper. 'Islam has been hijacked by a discourse of anger and a rhetoric of rage.' The *Guardian*'s own commentator Hugo Young added: 'It has bred terrorists with a cause endorsed by misbegotten theology, quite different, for example, from the Irish or the Basques. To pretend that this is mere criminality is deception on a grand scale.'

In 1993, the US political scientist Samuel P Huntington outraged liberal opinion in the English-speaking world with his essay 'Clash of Civilizations'. Far from reaching the 'end of history', he argued, the world was entering a new and dangerous epoch. 'With the end of the Cold War, international politics moves out of its Western phase,' Huntington wrote, 'and its centrepiece becomes the interaction between the West and non-Western civilizations, and *among* non-Western civilizations. In the politics of civilizations, the people and governments of non-Western civilizations no longer remain the objects of history as targets of Western colonialism, but join the West as movers and shapers of history.'

Until the French Revolution, the Huntington theory runs,

conflicts were largely between princes. In the nineteenth century they were between peoples, or nation states. That phase lasted till the end of the First World War. Then the Russian Revolution propelled the world into a new kind of conflict – the clash of ideologies. The epic battles between communism, fascism and liberal democracy scarred the twentieth century. 'These conflicts were conflicts within Western civilization', with the colonized non-Western world harnessed to the Western world's needs.

September 11th looked, on the face of it, to vindicate Huntington's apocalyptic prognosis – so much so that many liberal commentators rushed to denounce him. 'The quickest road to fame and riches for an intellectual,' wrote one respected commentator, 'is to come up with a seriously bad idea... Samuel P Huntington's "Clash of Civilizations" – enjoying fresh popularity since September 11th – is by a long chalk the most successful bad idea of our time.'

Huntington's idea is attacked on the grounds that he is imprecise about what constitutes a 'civilization'. The word is in any case hopelessly loaded. Perhaps the most serious criticism levelled at him is that his argument ignores tensions within each civilizational bloc. The West is not uniformly an empire of secular modernity. It includes within it many challenges to that way of living. The rise of the Christian right in the US, and the hold it now exercises over the political leadership of the country, owe nothing to secular modernity or rational thought and are in many ways profoundly hostile to them. And in the Islamic world there is a constant and dynamic discourse between tradition and modernity. Many Islamic states are struggling to embrace a modernity of their own making – not one imported wholesale from the West, but one that is fashioned from within an authentic Islamic identity. Iran, Egypt and Pakistan are all case studies in this unresolved struggle. What is more, the faultlines that Huntingdon identifies as the locus of the coming conflicts do not match the real experience of conflict across the globe. Why, for example, did America intervene in Bosnia and Kosovo to try to save hundreds of thousands of Muslims from ethnic cleansing? This seems to break Huntington's law.

But is there not an element of wishful thinking in this denunciation of Huntington? Defenders of liberal democracy do not want a clash between civilizations. They want the world to be made up of those who have attained peace, prosperity and freedom, and those who have yet to achieve it but remain for now oppressed by dictatorships – some foreign-imposed, some homegrown, some hostile to the West, some allied to it. The events of 1989 fit this world-view: entire peoples emerging from the shadow of repression to embrace Civil Society.

But that is why 1989 – that moment in Wenceslas Square, the fall of the Berlin Wall – is profoundly different from 2001. History will identify both as pivotal years, but for opposite reasons. The first marked the end of an old order and the apparent triumph of Civil Society – or at least its endorsement by millions who felt its absence. 2001 marks the beginning of something new, and a hostile rebuke to Civil Society from within a major world civilization.

Ernest Gellner argued that Islam is the only major world religion to have experienced no effective secularizing reformation. Islam has no formal clergy in the Christian sense because it does not recognize that there is a separation of church and state, or indeed a separation between church and society. In a pure Islamic society there is no need for a legislature to make laws because the law already exists. It is the word of God as dictated to the Prophet in the Koran, and all that is required of human beings is to interpret and apply that law. Political authority, such as it is, is 'accountable to God for implementation of religious–legal rules, but not to man for the practice of some civil ideal'. Secularism is 'morally suspect as a deviation from the divine will'. Writing before the rise of the Taliban in Afghanistan, Gellner identified the 'dictatorship of the scholar' as a principal characteristic of a worldwide Islamic resurgence.

There are of course many Muslims active in the Islamic world who aspire to the conditions of liberty, and who see in this no contradiction with their adherence to Islamic faith. But the long-term trend seems to be the gradual Islamicization of the state and its codes of law. The historian Hazhir Teimourian believes the world is now, indeed, separated into mutually hostile 'civilizational' blocks. 'The Muslim world sees itself as a rival to the Western world and yet sees no hope of ever catching up with it really. Therefore hit at them wherever you can. It takes me back to the old rivalry of Muslims and Christians in the eleventh century at the time of the first crusade and for several centuries after that. I think this has not died at all in the minds of Muslims, whereas, in fact, Christians have forgotten all about it... I have been horrified by the reaction of the Islamic world to this tragedy.'

There is an important qualification to this: the governments of the Islamic world, almost without exception, condemned the attacks of September 11th and agreed, rhetorically at least, to support the fight against terrorism. Translating that into specific action is another matter – the same governments condemn the bombing of Afghanistan with the same vigour with which they condemned the atrocity that triggered it. The American-led coalition tacitly acknowledges this by being careful not to press Islamic countries for the kind of assistance that would inflame anti-Western sentiment.

If it is not the Clash of Civilizations, what is it? It seems, most starkly, to represent a dramatic polarization of aspiration. The values around which our societies seek to cohere are more sharply defined than they were before September 11th, and there is a striking divergence between the Western and Islamic worlds. In late October, Tony Blair redrafted a speech in which he had been expected to denounce anti-war voices in Britain as 'lacking moral fibre'. The speech was trailed two days in advance, to the fury of many in his own party who'd expressed doubts. They now angrily responded that they did not oppose the war because they were cowards but – on the contrary – for a variety of legitimate reasons ranging from principled opposition to the use of force, to scepticism about the military effectiveness of bombing a country like Afghanistan. Blair changed the speech before delivering it in Cardiff and instead said, 'They [the terrorists] have one hope: that we are decadent, that we lack the moral fibre or will or courage to take them on...that we will lose our nerve... They mistake our desire for a comfortable life, our desire to live in peace, benign towards different races and cultures, for decadence. It is not decadence. It is progress, and we will fight to maintain it.' Thus the British Prime Minister defines it not solely as a campaign to eradicate terror but as a battle between 'progress' and some other conception of the way human beings should live. If the Western world is cohering around the philosophical and political values that define Civil Society, the Muslim world is sometimes viewed – and is increasingly represented by some of its own believers – as standing for values not only different from this, but also, in effect, hostile to it.

The September 11th attacks were aimed not only at America but at the pro-Western Muslim states – Egypt and Saudi Arabia. Saudi Arabia's relationship with the West is particularly vulnerable. It is denounced by many Muslims as a sacrilegious betrayal – an oil-for-guns deal that defiles Islam and loots the natural resources of the country. A growing polarization of opinion, if it ultimately threatens the House of Saud, will produce a world in which two major sources of energy – the Caspian region and the Arabian peninsula – are, simultaneously and for the first time, put in jeopardy.

If Al-Qaida's strategy was to draw America into something that could easily be represented as a war against Islam and, in so doing, to destabilize and eventually topple those regimes that have struck unholy bargains with America, the Great Satan, then at least in the short term it did not work. When the Taliban authorities collapsed across Afghanistan in the second month of the allied bombing campaign, most Afghans greeted their demise with undisguised joy. It is a far cry from the picture painted by Muslim radicals across the Muslim world – that the dispossessed masses of the Islamic world are ready to rise up as one and overthrow those Arab regimes that have done deals with the infidel West. The tension that exists in Islamic societies between modernity and tradition is more complex and more dynamic than that.

Nonetheless, hostilities always polarize opinion and intensify passions. The Bush–Blair alliance insisted at the outset that we must all choose sides. We were to be with them in the fight against terrorism or we would most definitely be against them. This they share with bin Laden who has said it is also the sacred duty of Muslims to choose sides. We should not really be surprised to continue hearing an Islamic-inspired extreme alternative to Civil Society articulated with growing confidence by some factions in the Muslim world. The question of whether that vision will ever achieve majority support remains unanswerable.

We knew well the shape of the world that came to an end in 1989. We understood its rules. The shape of the world that now replaces it – with its new set of rules – is forming before our eyes. In global terrorism, the West has an enemy again. It must learn how to fight that enemy without creating a new Cold War, a new bi-polar division of the world into two antagonistic blocs – the West versus Islam. It is not a war against Islam, but the perpetrators of the September 11th atrocities would like it to become one. The task before America and its allies is now to defeat terrorism without letting that happen.